Our Fire Survives the Storm

INDIGENOUS AMERICAS

Robert Warrior and Jace Weaver, Series Editors

Our Fire Survives the Storm

A Cherokee Literary History

Daniel Heath Justice

Indigenous Americas Series

University of Minnesota Press
Minneapolis • London

All royalties earned from the sale of this book will be donated to the Cherokee Nation Education Corporation, a nonprofit corporation chartered under tribal code of the Cherokee Nation. Its purpose is to provide educational assistance and preserve the language, culture, and history of the Cherokee people.

"Out of Ashes Peace Will Rise," "Where Mountain and Atom Meet," "When Earth Becomes an 'It,'" and "Conservation" are from Marilou Awiakta, *Selu: Seeking the Corn-Mother's Wisdom* (Golden, Colo.: Fulcrum Publishing, 1993). Copyright 1993 Fulcrum Publishing, Inc. All rights reserved. Reprinted with permission.

The two maps in the book were created by the author.

Published by the University of Minnesota Press
111 Third Avenue South, Suite 290
Minneapolis, MN 55401-2520
http://www.upress.umn.edu

Library of Congress Cataloging-in-Publication Data

Justice, Daniel Heath.
   Our fire survives the storm : a Cherokee literary history / Daniel Heath Justice.
      p.   cm. — (Indigenous Americas series)
   Includes bibliographical references (p.) and index.
   ISBN-13: 978-0-8166-4638-8 (acid-free paper)
   ISBN-10: 0-8166-4638-4 (acid-free paper)
   ISBN-13: 978-0-8166-4639-5 (pbk. : acid-free paper)
   ISBN-10: 0-8166-4639-2 (pbk. : acid-free paper)
   1. Cherokee literature—History and criticism.   2. American literature—Indian authors.   I. Title.   II. Indigenous Americas.
   PM783.5.J87 2006
   897'.55709—dc22

                                                                      2006004734

Printed in the United States of America on acid-free paper

The University of Minnesota is an equal-opportunity educator and employer.

12 11 10 09 08 07 06   10 9 8 7 6 5 4 3 2 1

Out of Ashes Peace Will Rise

Our courage
is our memory.

Out of ashes
peace will rise,
if the people
are resolute.
If we are not
resolute,
we will vanish.
And out of ashes
peace will rise.

In the Four Directions . . .
Out of ashes peace will rise.
Out of ashes peace will rise.
Out of ashes peace will rise.
Out of ashes peace will rise.

Our courage is our memory.

—Marilou Awiakta
(Cherokee/Appalachian)

Contents

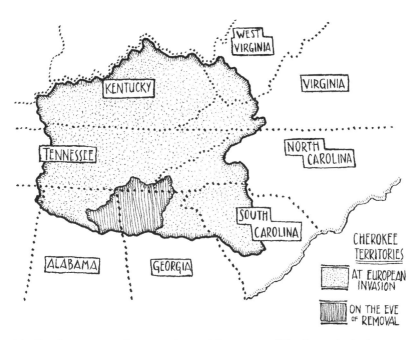

The Cherokee Nation, pre-Invasion to Removal. Designation of Cherokee territories from Mooney, Myths of the Cherokee.

Acknowledgments

*W*ords can't express my deep gratitude to the many people whose generosity during the research, writing, and revision of this book has helped to give it meaningful shape and substance. For such a gift, I thank you all.

I hope that this book is respectful to the teachings and guidance of my family, friends, mentors, elders, and correspondents, even though my opinions and theirs might have sometimes differed. Whatever life this book has beyond the printed page comes from their thoughtful engagement. Any errors, omissions, or misrepresentations in the text are my own.

Special appreciation goes to the administration and staff of the Department of English and the Aboriginal Studies Program at the University of Toronto for encouraging me and my work in so many ways. My colleagues at U of T are a joy, and they demonstrate daily all the finer qualities of scholarship. The ABS faculty and First Nations House staff have made me feel very much at home in Toronto, and I'm honored to call them my friends.

My graduate committee at the University of Nebraska gave me a strong intellectual and ethical foundation for this work: Frances W. Kaye, John R. Wunder, Malea Powell, Domino R. Perez, Venetria Patton, and Paul A. Olson. The members of UNITE, the faculty and staff of the UNL English department and the Center for Great Plains Studies, and my SIPS students (especially Natalia Torres) deserve a particular note of thanks.

Funding agencies that offered essential support, travel, research, and presentation funds include the University of Nebraska–Lincoln Department of English and Center for Great Plains Studies, the University of Toronto Department of English, the University of Toronto Connaught Committee, and the Social Sciences and Humanities Research Council of Canada. The staff at various archives in the United States provided helpful guidance, especially Chad A. Williams and Lillie Kerr at the Oklahoma Historical Society and Victoria Sheffler of Northeast State University in Tahlequah, Oklahoma.

I am indebted to many Native scholars for their counsel and support over the years, but three merit particular mention for their formal involvement with this book. Fellow Cherokee Jace Weaver has guided me with both kindness and careful rigor through the revision process, and the book is much stronger as a result of his patient shepherding. Robert Warrior (Osage) has been enthusiastic and unfailing in his support for my own growth as a Native scholar and for the project itself. I couldn't have asked for a better reader than the incomparable Craig Womack (Muskogee Creek/Cherokee), who pushed me far beyond my comfort zone to make this book so much more than even I dreamed it could be. I'd also like to thank Ginny Carney (Cherokee), Domino Perez (Chicana), Malea Powell (Eastern Miami/Shawnee), and Barbara Tracy (Melungeon/Cherokee) for their thoughtful comments on various parts of this manuscript, as well as for their friendship. *Wado!*

Thanks to Carrie Mullen, Jason Weidemann, and the rest of the University of Minnesota Press team for their enthusiasm for this project, as well as for their patience and professionalism.

I'd like to give a special thanks to Marilou Awiakta, Robert J. Conley, the late Talmadge Davis, Diane Glancy, Geary Hobson, Thomas King, Wilma Mankiller, Dean Palmer, and Charlie Soap for their response to my query for photographs and other materials to include in this book. Deep gratitude also goes to Principal Chief Chad Smith of the Cherokee Nation, who put together a committee to review the book in manuscript, and to committee members Dan Agent, Wyman Kirk, and especially Richard Allen for giving me such thoughtful responses. Chief Michell Hicks, Joyce Dugan, and especially Lynn Harlan of the Eastern Band deserve special mention for their generous reading of the manuscript. My cousin, Jim Warnell, gave me his copy of Emmet Starr's *History of the Cherokee Indians,* complete with genealogical commentary, and that gift has been a welcome guide.

Jim Cox, a brother in spirit and a friend of unwavering intellectual and ethical integrity, has walked through this project with me from the very beginning. He and my colleague Sarah Wilson provided detailed revision suggestions that helped bring these ideas to life and enhance their finer qualities. Energetic but good-natured debates with Sara Salih about identity, essentialism, and the nature of nationhood helped to clarify some of my thinking on these issues.

My students at the University of Toronto, especially those in the Aboriginal Studies Program and ABS300, give me much hope for the future of Indigenous continuity and decolonization. I'm grateful to them all for helping me to better understand these complicated issues and their human dimensions. These students are so smart, so courageous, and so very cool!

I've saved until last the three people most responsible for the best qualities of both the book and its author. The first is my friend, Jeremy Patrick, who has read every single draft of the manuscript and provided keen editorial insight throughout this lengthy process. His enthusiasm and generosity of spirit have been essential to the realization of this dream.

Most of all, my gratitude goes to my parents, Kathy and Jim Justice, to whom this book is lovingly dedicated. I learned to fight for what's right by their example. They have given unwavering support to my goals, stood beside me through my disappointments, guided me patiently home when I lost my way, and celebrated my triumphs with unrestrained joy. Life in Victor is tough: it's a place of many broken dreams and heartaches. But my folks have never become bitter or jaded; they have never once belittled my dreams or given me any reason to doubt that I could do or become anything in the world. They have taught me what true wisdom really is, and their good mountain sense guides my way in all things. Such unselfish love is a rare thing, and I've had it in plenty. Thanks, Mom and Dad.

A Note on Terminology

Certain terms throughout this book, such as *fullblood, mixedblood, traditional, progressive, assimilation,* and *acculturation,* are quite a bit more unstable than they might initially seem by popular usage, especially when referring to Cherokees. Their presence in this study reflects their complexity and contextualization in American Indian studies, as well as the specific meanings that some of these terms find among Cherokees.

The terms *fullblood, mixedblood, traditional,* and *progressive* are often used as absolute terms, in that fullbloods are seen as being traditional and mixedbloods are viewed as assimilated or acculturated. Such absolutes are rarely accurate. People of all quanta (a concept descended primarily from the intersections of political and scientific racism of the nineteenth century) have stood on all points of the cultural spectrum. For the purposes of this discussion, *fullblood* refers to those whose ancestry is predominantly or exclusively Cherokee, whereas *mixedblood* refers to those whose heritage reflects both Cherokee and non-Cherokee ancestry. Degree of blood quantum should not be read as a measure of commitment to Cherokee nationhood or identification *as* Cherokee.

Similarly, *traditional* and *progressive* can be tricky, but here the former might best be read as those cultural expressions and values most closely understood as having their origin outside non-Cherokee influence and within a more conservative Cherokee-centered context, often (though not exclusively) linked to aboriginal lifeways and philosophies predating European

Invasion. *Progressive* leans toward an embrace of many Eurowestern values, especially regarding social, political, and religious mores.

Assimilation and *acculturation,* although often conflated, are distinguished in this study. *Assimilation* here is the wholesale rejection of Indigenous values and their replacement with Eurowestern values, either through choice, coercion, or violence. *Acculturation* is both more proactive and amenable to Cherokee continuity, being the adaptation of certain Eurowestern ways into a larger Cherokee context, thus changing some cultural expressions while maintaining the centrality of Cherokee identity and values.

Outland Cherokees are those who are raised outside the geopolitical and cultural boundaries of the established Cherokee communities of northeastern Oklahoma, western Arkansas, or western North Carolina. The term *Eurowestern* is, to my mind, both more accurate and more inclusive than *Euroamerican,* as it acknowledges a number of shared cultural and political values held by colonizers of those European nation-states that are widely understood as "Western." I rarely refer to the citizenry of the United States as "Americans," as such terminology seems to me to be another appropriation by the colonizers of Indigenous presence. *Yoneg* is the Cherokee word for White Eurowesterners. Although "the Five Civilized Tribes" is the most common collective name for the Cherokees, Creeks, Chickasaws, Choctaws, and Seminoles, I prefer the less condescending "Five Tribes" to designate these communities and the sociopolitical history they share.[1]

For broader terms, I generally use *American Indian, Native,* or *Indian* interchangeably to refer to those tribal peoples descended from the original human inhabitants of North America and within the present geopolitical boundaries of the United States. *Aboriginal* (and occasionally *Native*) as a proper noun describes the Indigenous peoples of what is now known as Canada, whereas *aboriginal* as an adjective speaks generally to a subject's pre-European presence in this hemisphere. *Indigenous* as a proper noun is a more inclusive term referring to tribal peoples worldwide who maintain their kinship connections to a particular land and its inhabitants, and it includes American Indians and Aboriginal peoples, among others; as an adjective, *indigenous* is similar in usage to *aboriginal,* but refers more to the relational dimensions of that presence than simply the presence itself.

These are each admittedly imperfect terms, with much movement between the partial definitions I have provided here. At all times, please read the terms through the specific contexts in which they are discussed.

Part I

DEEP ROOTS

• Part I •

Deep Roots

*T*here are two types of Indians in the Eurowestern imagination, and they vary remarkably little by region and historical era. These two Indians have featured prominently in the popular culture of North America since the onset of Invasion, from early explorers' tracts to sepia photographs and dime-novel Westerns, all the way to Saturday morning cartoons, big-budget Hollywood epics, and prime-time television dramas. Eurowestern ideas of fierce and noble Native men culminate in the wild, handsome Lakota Warrior riding his pinto stallion across the golden prairie, his long black hair streaming with feathers, his voice raised in an eerie battle cry against his White oppressors. He is the epitome of savage sensuality, the personification in hot flesh and stoic charisma of the untamed frontier. White men fear and envy his freedom; White women long for his fierce embrace.

The second Indian of the pair is less dramatic but every bit as pervasive. She's the Cherokee Princess, everybody's great-great-great-grandmother: noble and beautiful, with high cheekbones and brown eyes as deep as still mountain pools. Her words are pure poetry. She seeks peace between Indians and their oppressors, always leaning toward the preordained civilized supremacy of White culture. She's the lover of White men, the Noble Savage savior of Eurowestern civilization whose body becomes the repository of White dreams of Indigenousness. While the Lakota Warrior fights against Manifest Destiny with a fury that transcends his supposedly inevitable death, the Cherokee Princess surrenders to the American dream, with resignation if not enthusiasm. She seems to be every family's variation on Pocahontas.

My paternal grandmother was no princess. I never knew her; she died of pulmonary tuberculosis in a Colorado Springs sanatorium on 7 November 1945, almost thirty years before I was born. She was a thirty-nine-year-old, hard-smoking Oklahoma Cherokee woman, twice divorced (although devoutly Catholic), with three children (two from her first marriage, one born out of wedlock), a sharp tongue that was balanced by a streak of mischief, and a raunchy sense of humor. Those who got on her bad side made an enemy for life. Those who treated her with respect received the same in turn.

Pearl (Spears) Justice Bowers died before the end of legal segregation in the United States; before the rise of the Red Power movement of the 1960s and 1970s; before the resurgence of Cherokee political autonomy and the 1975 Indian Self-Determination and Education Assistance Act; before N. Scott Momaday, Simon Ortiz, and Leslie Marmon Silko gave literary voice to Indian experiences in America; before Wounded Knee '73 and the U.S. government's undeclared war on Indian activism; before hippies and New Agers sought myopic enlightenment through appropriation of Indian traditions and spiritual beliefs. Grandma Pearl lived during a time when being an Indian was largely seen as a liability—even among many Indians—in a WASP-dominated America dedicated to obsessive consumerism and unrelenting capitalist individualism. She was born the year before Indian Territory became the state of Oklahoma, and she lived through the U.S. allotment policy, dying shortly before the similar devastations of termination and relocation. Life on the eastern plains of Colorado brought other threats, not the least of which was the Ku Klux Klan, which had no use for Indians, Catholics, "immoral" women, "race mixing," or the disabled. Her life was woven from threads of shame, pain, and fear as much as from pride and strength.

My grandmother was a strong Cherokee woman, but her life in no way reflected the vapid and melodramatic Cherokee Princess of the Euro-western imaginary—that artificial image speaks to the desires of colonialist America, not the realities of historical and contemporary Cherokees. It should come as no surprise, then, that although Cherokees are among the most widely studied Indigenous peoples in North America, we remain

Wedding photograph of Jesse J. Justice and Pearl Clara Spears, 1924.

one of the most misunderstood. Cherokee identity is often seen as conveniently porous and easily appropriated, diluted from an ideal Indigenous purity. Blood quantum jibes are endemic to discussions about Cherokees, no matter what your phenotype might be; you quickly learn all the variations of the more popular "Generikee" jokes. Many Cherokees are marked by both Whites and American Indians as being too White (or Black) while not being quite Indian enough, while those who are phenotypically Indian still have to deal with the jokes and insults. Even as thoughtful and incisive a writer as Sherman Alexie (Coeur d'Alene/Spokane) finds it hard to resist regularly linking any mention of Cherokees in his works with ethnic fraud. Civilized savages or washed-out wannabes—these are the iconic descendants of the Cherokee Princess.

Cherokee realities are far more complicated than these simplistic and simple-minded stereotypes. Indeed, there is little that is simple about Cherokees. During the first three centuries of European Invasion, we were the most powerful Indigenous nation in what is now the southeastern United States, and generations of non-Cherokees—Native and European alike—lived in admiration and no small fear of the proud *Ani-Yunwiya*, the Real People. U.S. Indian jurisprudence was shaped in large part by Cherokees who fought with courageous eloquence for their aboriginal land rights all the way to the Supreme Court. The Cherokee syllabary exploded into use in the early nineteenth century and became an incredibly effective tool for resisting Removal; it subsequently helped to rebuild educational and cultural institutions after the Trail of Tears. Our governments today are vibrant and engaged models of tribal democracy. Our long history of intermarriage, adaptation, and innovative accommodation has brought a wide range of physical features, cultural practices, languages, and ideas into our varied understandings of what it is to be Cherokee, and we thrive as a result. Our history as a people is one marked by cycles of change, trauma, regeneration, and growth. Cherokees have always met geopolitical and social challenges squarely with whatever tools and strategies were available at the time—from conservative separatism to enthusiastic accommodation, from discourses of kinship to those of blood and nationhood—and although there has always been internal debate and conflict about those choices, we still endure and thrive as a people.

Much has changed since my grandmother's death in 1945, not the least being Pearl's descendants, for whom being Cherokee is no longer seen as a liability—if anything, our status as citizens of the Cherokee Nation stands as the center of our political and personal identities. But the forces that drove my grandmother to despair before her death haven't disappeared. They still seek to uproot Indigenous peoples from traditional homelands; to contain, transform, displace, or otherwise erase ceremonial traditions and languages; to replace the Native presence in the Americas with the ahistorical mythology of Eurowestern cultural supremacy.

This book is an inquiry into the idea of "Cherokeeness" within the Cherokee literary tradition. Drawing from this rich and ever-expanding canon, I examine three primary features of historical and contemporary Cherokee life—nationhood, removal, and regeneration—through literary expressions of cultural continuity. Our literature is the textual testament to our endurance; just as our oral traditions reflect the living realities and concerns of those who share them, so too do our literary traditions. This study is a focused exploration of a few key historical moments, texts, writers, and issues that compellingly illustrate the transformative and dynamic discourses of what it is to be Cherokee in various times and places. In short, it asks a simple question: how does a historically rooted and culturally informed reading of the Cherokee literary tradition help us to better understand Cherokee social history, and vice versa?

The interpretive links between the social, political, historical, and cultural are of central concern to this study. It attends more to the experiences and conditions of western, outland, and Indian Territory/Oklahoma Cherokees than to those of the Eastern Band, largely for reasons of brevity, distinctions in historical experience, and my own research and familial connections. Given these parameters, this book is assuredly *not* intended to be the authoritative end of analysis; it's presented as a contribution to the ongoing scholarship that more accurately reflects Cherokee intellectual expression while challenging simplistic stereotypes and anti-Cherokee bigotry.

More than a restoration of Cherokee voices to narratives of national identity and history, this study is also an expression of family pride and cultural recovery. Nationhood is woven in large part from the lives, dreams, and challenges of the people who compose the body politic; as such, examining the interplay of broader social issues with lived human realities can immeasurably strengthen our understandings of the complicated discourses of community. To write about family and history is to try to give voice to silenced ghosts as much as to give strength to the living.

Toward that end, this project provides a Cherokee-centered intellectual and ethical challenge to those narratives of erasure. It's an open assertion of the liberating potential of our Indigenous histories and experiences, not a blanket rejection of Eurowestern ideas and traditions. We're not a doomed race that sacrificed Indigenousness for White civilization; such antiquated progressivism has impoverished outsider perceptions for centuries. Rather, we are a diverse, ever-changing people with rich histories fully rooted in the Indigenous heart of this hemisphere. Like the fabled Phoenix that has been an inspirational reflection of Cherokee endurance since the early nineteenth century, we have been burned and emerged again, renewed, from the ashes. We have survived the threatened apocalypse of European colonization through our ability to adapt and realign ourselves to the cosmos without abandoning ourselves in the process.

Through catastrophe, chaos, and change, our fire survives the storm.

Speaking the Truth for Ourselves

By examining a diverse range of texts through the multilayered weave of experience, history, and culture, I seek to provide provocative readings within the range of Cherokee literatures that fully engage with our distinct traditions and histories. We are a people of many shades and perspectives, many bloods mingled into shared senses of nationhood. Accordingly, this is a work of tribal nationalism—following the powerful example set forth by Craig S. Womack (Muskogee Creek/Cherokee) in his Creek literary history, *Red on Red: Native American Literary Separatism* (1999)—and takes for granted the primacy and centrality of Cherokee and other Native voices to the analysis. Part of my aim here is to realign reader expectations of nationhood and what it means in Indigenous contexts, which differ significantly from discussions about the coercive nationalism of industrialized nation-states. Indigenous nations vigorously protect their nationhood in defense of their treaties and government-to-government relationships, all of which work to preserve a sociopolitical boundary by which the sacred is protected.

My approach is explicitly activist and to some degree polemical: it is grounded in the firm belief that Indigenous nationhood is a necessary ethical response to the assimilationist directive of imperialist nation-states, and that Native people are well qualified to speak on these matters without need of non-Native translation or interpretation. It might thus be considered, in this regard, an essentialist text, one that offers no apologies for placing Cherokees at the center. I would argue, however, that such a move is not about policing the boundaries of "authentic" Cherokeeness but about exploring some of the varied understandings of what it is to be Cherokee—a significant distinction rooted in careful attention to the diversity of Cherokee social history. The most strident critics of essentialism assert the importance of cultural context; this study demands nothing less.

Of all the terms I engage throughout this inquiry, none is perhaps more important than "intellectual sovereignty," one of the philosophical underpinnings of the project. Robert Allen Warrior (Osage) provides the watershed example of this philosophy in *Tribal Secrets: Recovering American Indian Intellectual Traditions* (1995). He asserts in this book the significance of scholarship centered in the intellectual traditions of Indigenous communities, traditions which have largely been dismissed, erased, or appropriated by established Eurowestern academics. Such work is intimately tied *to* the continuance and growth of Native communities as much as it is drawn *from* them. Thus, intellectual sovereignty is a moral decision as much as a philosophical orientation, one that insists that the work not only *serve* its home community in some way, but that it also emerge, to varying degrees, from the cultural, intellectual, and spiritual realities and ideals of that community:

> In developing American Indian critical studies, we need to practice the same sort of intellectual sovereignty that many Native poets practice. As many of the poets find their work continuous with, but not circumscribed by, Native traditions of storytelling or ceremonial chanting, we can find the work of criticism continuous with Native traditions of deliberation and decision making. Holding these various factors (sovereignty traditions, community, process, and so on) in tension while attempting to understand the role of critics in an American Indian future is of critical importance.[1]

Applying Warrior's understanding of intellectual sovereignty to this book, then, is an expression of what Mary C. Churchill (Cherokee) calls a "Cherokee-centric hermeneutic," an interpretive model that is explicitly located within the body of Cherokee literature.[2] Similarly, it draws inspiration from the ethic of communitism—"community" and "activism"— that Cherokee religious studies scholar and literary theorist Jace Weaver has proposed in his own groundbreaking study of Native literature, *That the People Might Live: Native American Literatures and Native American Community* (1997).[3]

To ground one's work within Indigenous ways of knowing is not a necessarily exclusivist act that seeks an idealized cultural purity. Rather, it is, at its core, a deeply realistic and life-affirming act, as Womack notes:

> I would like to think . . . that I have not written *Red on Red* in a rejectionist mode but that, to the contrary, I seek to examine these histories to search for those ideas, articulated by Indian people, that best serve a contemporary critical framework. More specifically, in terms of a Creek national literature, the process has been based on the assumption that it is valuable to look toward Creek authors and their works to understand Creek writing. My argument is not that this is the *only* way to understand Creek writing but an important one given that literatures bear some kind of relationship to communities, both writing communities and the community of the primary culture, from which they originate.[4]

Intellectual sovereignty doesn't presume an insistence on tribal-centered scholarship as the *exclusive* model of sensitive or insightful analysis. It does, however, privilege an understanding of community as being important to a nuanced reading of the text. This notion is something rarely questioned in other areas of inquiry—after all, historical and cultural context is generally seen as essential to any substantive understanding of Shakespeare's plays—but the reactionary howl of "essentialism" rises up when we try to apply similar methods to minority literatures.

Intellectual sovereignty is the Native extension of this contextualizing philosophy, one that centers itself within the wisdom of Indian communities instead of merely concerning itself with the intellectual traditions of the Invader cultures. Intellectual sovereignty provides us motivation and a philosophical/political foundation from which to define the terms and conditions of analysis for ourselves.

THE CHEROKEE LITERARY TRADITION

In their book *Reflections on Cherokee Literary Expression* (2003), Cherokee scholars Mary Ellen Meredith and Howard Meredith propose that the "tradition of Cherokee literature is a constellation of literary texts, each of which bears in its content and style an indication of the works and classes of works which have left a deposit to the imagination and style of each author." Their study places at the center of its analysis "the use and understanding of the Cherokee language, which is the single most important element of that literary expression since the creation of the Sequoyah syllabary in 1821."[5] As a result, the Cherokee language is, in their detailed reading, the absolute foundation of any discussion of Cherokee literature:

> Certainly, Native American literature in English does not speak the same vocabulary as Cherokee literary understanding. English language approaches with Latin grammar, Greek logic, and Anglo-American critical thinking obliquely approach Cherokee literature. But without Cherokee language usage with its own inclusive grammar and logic, understanding is limited to one that is about a subject, without perception of the living essence of the literature itself.[6]

The Merediths devote their analysis to the ways in which the Cherokee language (and, as a result, a specific Cherokee worldview) shapes Cherokee literature, even within a number of texts that are written in English, such as the poetry of Diane Glancy and the novels of John Milton Oskison and Robert J. Conley.

The Cherokee language is certainly central to a large number of Cherokee texts, from hymns and translations of biblical scriptures to Cherokee medicine books, newspapers, legal codes, children's books, letters, and various other materials published and unpublished. The Merediths' project is a thoughtful literary extension of the unsurpassed work of Jack, Anna, and Alan Kilpatrick, whose studies of the worldviews, stories, and medicine texts of the traditionalist communities of Oklahoma are rooted in their own understanding of the Cherokee language, and that have resulted in a vast archive of Cherokee-language texts, many of which have yet to be examined on any substantive scale. Alan Kilpatrick quotes his father relating to this substantial body of Indigenous knowledge: "Recently I read in the *Encyclopedia Britannica* that no [N]ative American society north of Mexico has produced a literature: yet during the past five years alone I have collected from attics, barns, caves, and jars buried in the ground some ten thousand poetical texts, many of which would excite the envy of a Hafiz or a Li Tai Po."[7]

My own study addresses Cherokee literature through a different but hopefully complementary approach, by focusing on the body of Cherokee literature in English. Just as the Cherokee language is important to understanding the Cherokee literary tradition and cultural continuity, particularly in regard to the literature recovered by the Kilpatricks, so too is the English language, and I draw primarily upon this other significant body of texts in this analysis. Most widely published written works by Cherokees in the nineteenth, twentieth, and twenty-first centuries are in English. Although the English language was often imposed on Native peoples, many Cherokees eagerly embraced it as another tool for decolonization and access to social, political, and economic resources.

Rather than presenting English as an inherently alien and oppressive language, I find helpful here the principle of "reinventing the enemy's language" proposed by Joy Harjo (Muskogee Creek/Cherokee) and Gloria Bird (Spokane). In their anthology of the same title, Harjo and Bird discuss the power of the colonizers' language. Harjo writes:

> We have much in common, particularly that we have come to live in an age in which we are aware of ourselves as native women (in all the various constructs) in a language that we have chosen to name our own. When our lands were colonized the language of the colonizer was forced on us. We had to use it for commerce in the new world, a world that evolved through the creation and use of language. It was when we began to create with this new language that we named it ours, made it usefully tough and beautiful.[8]

This "usefully tough and beautiful" language is a primary means of meaningful expression for many Cherokees; rather than viewing this linguistic reality as a disability that inevitably separates us from any understanding of what it is to be Cherokee, this study presumes that there are different expressive ways of being Cherokee that don't require a rejection of one or the other. This isn't to deny the active and often brutal language oppression faced by many Cherokees, nor is it to claim that Cherokee language preservation isn't of vital significance to Cherokee continuity, because language revitalization efforts are firmly supported by both Cherokee governments and populations as a form of cultural recovery and survival. It is to say, however, that although some of the understandings and experiences of each language are different, *difference* isn't necessarily synonymous with *deficiency*.[9]

Besides, the English language has changed since Cherokees first encountered British colonists in the seventeenth century—it has been shaped by the experience, too, becoming indigenized when Cherokees and other Indians have taken firm control of their own linguistic economy. Womack's words are important here:

> When cultural contact between Native Americans and Europeans has occurred throughout history, I am assuming that it is just as likely that things European are Indianized rather than the anthropological assumption that things Indian are always swallowed up by European culture. I reject, in other words, the supremacist notion that assimilation can only go in one direction, that white culture always overpowers Indian culture, that white is inherently more powerful than red, that Indian resistance has never occurred in such a fashion that things European have been radically subverted by Indians.[10]

I would assert that Cherokee literature in English is deeply rooted in Indigenousness, by the sheer act of Cherokees asserting their nationhood and cultural continuity through whatever means have been available at the time. This body of literature is thus more than just a concession to the linguistic violence of an oppressive invader culture; instead, it—like the Cherokee language itself—is a powerful reflection of self-determination and agency by people who are deeply invested in the historical, genealogical, geographic, and cosmological significance of all that it is to be Cherokee.

Beyond the issue of language, there are two fundamental questions of concern to this study, one of origin and one of form: who do I define as Cherokee, and what exactly do I define as literature? The question of identity in Indian Country is highly vexed and controversial, especially for Cherokees, given the pervasive desire of non-Natives to claim affiliation through an obscure great-great-grandmother/Cherokee Princess.[11] Some of these identity issues are important—due to the complicated relationship between truth, representation, responsibility, and access to an ever-shrinking resource base—while others are more problematic and often either blindly racist or arrogantly appropriative. Two recent books by Native scholars, Choctaw and Cherokee respectively—Circe Sturm's *Blood Politics: Race, Culture, and Identity in the Cherokee Nation of Oklahoma* (2002) and Eva Marie Garroutte's *Real Indians: Identity and Survival of Native America* (2003)—are remarkably astute and provocative analyses of this issue, and both texts provide extended commentary on Cherokee identity concerns. Rather than try to demarcate the boundaries of "true"

Cherokeeness—a line which I would likely fall short of myself according to some definitions, being an English-speaking, light-skinned Cherokee citizen born and raised outside of the geographical boundaries of the Nation—I am interested here in examining the ways that Cherokees, in many forms and identities, have asserted cultural, historical, political, genealogical, and literary distinctiveness through the ages.

Still, I did have to make some decisions, for although I believe Cherokee nationhood to be necessarily adaptive, I don't believe that it's amorphous to the point of absolute inclusiveness. My working definition was to include those writers whose work is recognized by members of the expanded Cherokee community as being Cherokee—either through community affirmation or tribal enrollment. Those writers who are given particular attention in this study are, to varying degrees, recognized informally by other Cherokees and/or formally by their respective nations as Cherokee. I've talked to many other Cherokees while researching and writing this book, and the writers I've included have consistently been among those most often cited as compelling representatives of Cherokee experience. Enrollment, while important, isn't to my mind the only significant factor in determining Cherokee identity—kinship and being *good* Cherokees seem to me to also be important. I'm fully responsible for the choice of authors here; not all readers, Cherokee or otherwise, will agree with my inclusions or exclusions. The absence of any particular writer from this study shouldn't necessarily be read as a statement about their cultural authenticity, but there certainly are some writers about whom I think it's more useful to say nothing than to try to engage with their shifting or self-aggrandizing identity claims.

On the matter of literary definition, I've tried to keep with a rather consistent principle of openness, in viewing Cherokee literature as anything that Cherokees write or speak with the intention of meaningful endurance or, as Weaver proposes in *That the People Might Live,* "the total written output of a people" that includes any literary attempt "to impress form on the relative formlessness of a life or a culture, to exercise selectivity over what is to be included and what excluded, [which] is an act of literary creation."[12] I make few distinctions between the "literary" and the "nonliterary," preferring instead to examine a diverse range of texts that each speak to the processes of Cherokee nationhood. Creative aesthetics aren't a significant focus of my attention, although I do address them from time to time when they intersect with larger themes, issues, and discussions.

Reading the Homeward Fire

Cherokee social history—both the large-scale and the intimate—and its relationship to the Cherokee literary tradition is the central concern of this particular study. The texts examined in this study will include those that are distanced from my family's experiences as well as those to which I am quite intimately connected. Experiential contexts—personal, familial, community-wide—are often explicitly absent from Eurowestern scholarship, but they are inextricably a part of much Native writing and scholarship, as Beth Brant (Bay of Quinte Mohawk) asserts about Native women's poetry:

> We write poems of pain and power, of ancient beliefs, of sexual love, of broken treaties, of despoiled beauty. We write with our human souls and voices. We write songs that honour those who came before us and those in our present lives, and those who will carry on the work of our Nations. We write songs that honour the every-day, we write songs to food; we even incorporate recipes into our work.[13]

This book doesn't seek a distanced, "objective" perspective removed from human experience and contexts. Its Cherokee subjectivity is its strength. It embraces what Weaver understands as "a reading that is deeply experiential and narrative rather than simply theoretical," as well as "profoundly cultural," a reading that emerges from lived histories of kin, self, and community.[14] Chickasaw historian Amanda J. Cobb expands on this idea, connecting it explicitly to Indian survival when she writes, "If I had to discuss the ideas and name them, I would call them *continuance*—the remembrance of times, places, and people; the knowing of those times, places, and people through imaginative acts; and finally, the going on, the telling of the stories."[15] This book is dedicated to both the spirit and service of continuance.

The book is separated into three main parts spanning four chapters and an afterword. The first part, *Deep Roots,* grounds the analysis within Cherokee history and teachings. Chapter 1, "Beyond the Civilized Savage," explores some of the unifying social principles of Cherokee expression and their relationship to the interwoven sociopolitical concepts of Cherokee nationhood and sovereignty. Following that analysis is an inquiry into the histories of Tsiyu Gansini (Dragging Canoe) and Nanye'hi (Nancy Ward), whose respective duties as Chickamauga war chief and Beloved Woman exemplified the white/peace and red/war spheres that defined eighteenth-century Cherokee politics. These complementary philosophies, informed by the earlier examination of Cherokee nationhood, become the foundational methodology for my readings of subsequent texts, through the two principles that thread their way through Cherokee literary and cultural expressions: the "Beloved Path" of accommodation and cooperation, and the "Chickamauga consciousness" of physical and/or rhetorical defiance.

The second part—*Geographies of Removal*—draws from this foundational methodology to examine what are perhaps the two most traumatic geopolitical events in Cherokee history: the Trail of Tears of 1838–39, and the allotment of Cherokee lands of the Indian Territory in the early years of the twentieth century. Chapter 2, "The Trail Where We Cried," begins with responses to the events surrounding the Cherokee death march through the writings of John Ross and ends with an analysis of the Cherokee content and contexts of the notorious Treaty of New Echota. Chapter 3, "Unruly Cherokees in the Indian Territory," centers its attention on four Cherokee writers—Lynn Riggs, John Milton Oskison, Will Rogers, and Emmet Starr—and their negotiations of Cherokee identity during the hyperassimilative post-allotment years following the Dawes and Curtis Acts.

The third part of the book—*Regeneration*—shifts the focus of analysis to contemporary Cherokee literature, thus emphasizing the continuing vitality of our cultural traditions and ever-expanding intellectual and artistic canon. In chapter 4, "Readings in Contemporary Cherokee Literature," I examine the red and white spheres of influence on various texts, from the white reading of Marilou Awiakta's *Selu: Seeking the Corn-Mother's Wisdom* (1993) and Thomas King's *Truth and Bright Water* (1999) to a red reading of Wilma Mankiller's 1993 autobiography and Geary Hobson's novella *The Last of the Ofos* (2000). The final section of this chapter approaches texts by Robert Conley and Diane Glancy with an eye toward these authors' distinctive explorations of historical and contemporary Cherokee nationhood.

This study ends with an afterword, "The Stories That Matter," which looks to the future of Indigenous literary criticism and the place of Cherokee nationhood and nation-specific literary studies within that developing tradition. To be certain, today's body of Cherokee literature is as vibrant and expansive as at any other time in our history. Many contemporary Cherokee writers and scholars have expanded the range and quality of the

Cherokee literary tradition, thus reflecting and, in many ways, leading the development of Cherokee aesthetics and intellectualism in this new era.

I hope that readers—both Cherokee and non-Cherokee, scholars and those outside the walls of academe—will expand, challenge, develop, and otherwise engage with the ideas within this book and in other Cherokee-centered studies, always toward the goal of enriching our knowledge of Cherokee literatures and cultural expressions. The book is explicitly not *the* Cherokee perspective on the relevant issues and shouldn't be perceived as such. Although these readings are enriched by and often drawn from the histories and teachings of my family, elders, friends, teachers, colleagues, and forebears, the subjectivity remains distinctly my own. While this inquiry isn't intended to speak *for* all Cherokees, it does speak *from* Cherokee experiences and is thus a beneficiary and contributor to the continuing discourses of Cherokee nationhood, removal, and regeneration.

One voice among many voices joined. It's a ripple in conversations that existed long before my birth and that will continue long after I pass to the Nightland. I write this book in the service of cultural recovery and endurance. It's for my ancestors, my grandmother, my parents, my family—my people.

Beyond the Civilized Savage

Each generation has created and re-created the Cherokee in the
image of that age. . . . Ironically, this mythical Cherokee looms
so large today that the real one is in danger of being forgotten
by many Indians and by much of white society that has come to
believe many of these often-contradictory myths.

—Rennard Strickland (Cherokee/Osage),
"In Search of Cherokee History"

It had to do with what was right and what was wrong. It had to do
with things like jurisdiction and sovereignty, and it had to do with
the schemes of the United States government regarding the future
of the Cherokee Nation. It was about *duyukduh,* the Truth, the
great spiritual laws of the universe, the immutable and irrefutable
laws of God and man and decent behavior.

—Robert J. Conley (Keetoowah Cherokee),
Ned Christie's War

$\mathcal{M}$uch of the established scholarship in Cherokee studies is marked
by a preoccupation with contrasting and conflicting binaries: fullblood
vs. mixedblood, progressive vs. conservative, assimilated vs. indigenous,
Christian vs. traditionalist, savage vs. civilized. These categories are often
perceived as being rigidly fixed along the conceptual model described by
Roy Harvey Pearce's seminal 1953 study, *Savagism and Civilization,* with
little movement across the spectrum of cultural, philosophical, and experiential expression: much of the focus is placed on the perceived eclipse

of apparently naive "savage" fullblood traditionalism by the assimilated values and economic policies of the "civilized" Christianized mixed-bloods. As a result, Cherokee nationhood has been streamlined into the assumptions of Eurowestern progressivism, wherein Indigenous primitivism fades away before the inevitable cultural superiority of the White American empire. Cherokee nationhood thus becomes nothing more than quaint ethnic pride assimilated into the body politic of the United States, remarked upon only as an interesting bit of tribal color to the American character.

Characteristic of such cultural chauvinism is Hugh T. Cunningham's 1930 "History of the Cherokee Indians," printed in the *Chronicles of Oklahoma,* where he ends his lengthy treatise by asserting the death of Cherokee sovereignty in Oklahoma:

> Will there be any future for the Cherokee Nation? As a nation, no, for long since have the Cherokees sacrificed their nationality to make a more perfect whole of the great American people. But as Americans, yes—the Cherokees have a future, and a future not to be limited by the vain imaginings of finite minds.[1]

Those "finite minds," we can assume, would be those Cherokees who resist this assimilative sacrifice into "the great American people." Yet even as Cunningham wrote these words, a coalition of Oklahoma Cherokee groups was forming the Cherokee Executive Council to better serve the people's needs in the wake of decades of catastrophic U.S. Indian policy.[2] This council would provide the foundations of the reconstituted Cherokee Nation and United Keetoowah Band tribal governments by the mid-1970s, thus defying the assimilative American insistence that Cherokee nationhood was merely a vestige of the romantic aboriginal past.[3] Although forcibly eclipsed in the first seven decades of the twentieth century, the rekindled strength of Cherokee nationhood burns brightly today.

This chapter provides a conceptual map to the terrain of Cherokee nationhood, with particular attention to the influences of the relational peoplehood—the system of relationships between the People and the rest of Creation—and the complementary war/peace political spheres on the Cherokee literary tradition. By examining these key cultural principles, historical moments, and social movements, I propose a methodological foundation for reading Cherokee texts that is rooted in a range of Cherokee cultural expressions and understandings. This approach extends the strengths of historical and thematic analysis toward an explication of the dynamic interplay between Cherokee literature and Cherokee social history. Such a methodology is necessarily exploratory; the diversity of Cherokee experience is reflective of this varied literature's diverse interpretive possibilities. As a result, this is an analytical beginning, not an end point of discussion.

BEING AND BECOMING A NATION: PEOPLEHOOD, NATIONHOOD, AND THE REAL HUMAN BEINGS

In 1997, the Cherokee Nation faced its greatest governmental crisis since the allotment campaign of 1893–1907, when the U.S. government shattered the commonly held tribal lands of Indian Territory into individual allotments for the benefit of exploitative robber barons and their ruthless railroad interests and non-Indian settlers, most of whom were little more than lawless border trash. During the allotment era, the Cherokees faced not only the alienation and erasure of their land holdings, but also the forcible termination of their representative government.[4] The U.S. government declared the dissolution of the Cherokee Nation in 1906 as a necessary precondition of Oklahoma statehood, but defiant Nighthawk Keetoowahs, led by the grassroots efforts of the political and ceremonial traditionalist Redbird Smith (and with support by traditionalists of other nations, including the Creek Snakes under the leadership of Chitto Harjo), established a representative government to vigilantly protect "the rights and prerogatives of self determination in the National governmental affairs."[5]

The 1997 crisis, in contrast, focused on a constitutional struggle between the executive, judicial, and legislative branches of the Cherokee government itself, and erupted into open conflict when Principal Chief Joe Byrd fired tribal marshals who were, on behalf of the Cherokee judiciary, investigating rumors of financial mismanagement. During that year the clash between government branches escalated as three justices from the Judicial Appeals Tribunal were removed from office by the tribal council; the FBI and representatives from the U.S. Bureau of Indian Affairs investigated the Nation's internal affairs; a group of council members boycotted meetings and prevented business due to a lack of a quorum; and Byrd fired the staff of the nation's newspaper, *The Cherokee Advocate,* in response to what he believed to be biased coverage of the crisis. On June 20, a large group of Cherokees rose up to liberate the national courthouse, a public building that Byrd had ordered locked against the protesters. One of the demonstrators who was formally charged with inciting a riot—Chad "Corntassel" Smith, a lawyer, legal scholar, and descendant of Redbird Smith—would go on to successfully challenge Joe Byrd for the position of Principal Chief in the 1999 election, winning a second term in 2003 on a strong record of revitalized democratic process within the Nation and a firm reaffirmation of the constitutional structure of Cherokee government.[6]

In both cases, it was the sense of the Cherokees as a tribal *nation* that was under assault, and it was to protect that understanding of cultural and political distinctiveness that Cherokees rose up in protest. Whether from pressures imposed from outside or from within, Cherokees zealously protected their representative governments and the principles of sovereignty and self-determination implied by the maintenance of those governments. And as a result, in both cases that sense of nationhood endured. The 1997 constitutional crisis of the Cherokee Nation resulted in numerous reforms under Chief Smith's first administration, including a stronger emphasis on the Cherokee constitution and citizen rights, the formal editorial independence of the national newspaper (which had been rechristened with its original name, *The Cherokee Phoenix*), and a greater transparency of governmental affairs for the public.

The 1970 passage of Public Law 91-495 reestablished the U.S. recognition of representative Cherokee governments, along with those of the other Five Tribes, after the imposed dissolution of tribal governments during the allotment era. However, the sovereignty of the Cherokees in Oklahoma was not created with that law. Rather, Cherokee sovereignty had *always* been embedded within the tribal nations; the inalienable status of those respective sovereignties was simply reacknowledged in 1970 by the U.S. government. That act of acknowledgment—more often referred to in U.S. Indian policy as "recognition"—is an essential part of the government-to-government relationship that defines Indigenous nationhood in North America. The U.S. government didn't *create* Cherokee nationhood or sovereignty, but by recognizing the existence of such, the U.S. has acknowledged the fundamental right of Cherokees (and other Indigenous nations) to negotiate in the political arena as more than scattered ethnic or social constituencies, but as national bodies: peoples defined as much by their political relationship to one another as by their kinship ties and genealogies. Not all Cherokees are enrolled tribal citizens, but the number of those whose citizenship is acknowledged by their respective nations is considerable, and that formal relationship carries with it significant political and cultural weight. Today there are three federally recognized Cherokee governments—the Cherokee Nation and the United Keetoowah Band of Cherokee Indians in Oklahoma, and the Eastern Band of Cherokee Indians in North Carolina—with a combined citizenry of over 250,000.[7]

Whether on a daily level of governance, on the broader stage of international relations, or in the arena of literary and artistic expression, the exercise of nationhood continues to be a dominant social ethic among Cherokees. As with other Indigenous nations, community and its web of social relationships are the structural foundation of Cherokee life; they define the transmitted orature, the traditional ceremonial life and customs of syncretic Christianity, the sovereignty, constitutions, treaties, and legal systems, the language and its written expression in the syllabary, and the rich literary tradition in English. It is in relationship with the tribal nation that the individual Cherokee is defined, whether one is fullblood or mixedblood, raised as an outlander or rooted in the soil of the ancestors, conservative or accommodationist or on any point of the spectrum between. Within the principles of Indigenous nationhood and sovereignty, to be Cherokee is to be in relationship with the People; even those who are to varying degrees detribalized assert a relationship through perceived absence, and retribalization depends upon reestablishing those bonds of kinship.[8]

Assertions of Indigenous nationhood should not, however, be necessarily conflated with the nationalism that has given birth to industrialized nation-states, for the distinctions are significant. Nation-state nationalism is often dependent upon the erasure of kinship bonds in favor of a code of patriotism that places loyalty to the state above kinship obligations, and emphasizes the assimilative militant history of the nation (generally along a progressivist mythological arc) above the specific geographic, genealogical, and spiritual histories of peoples. Its primary function is to justify the existing economic, military, and political structure—largely through the assimilation of all subject constituencies into the culture of a monolithic and coercive state. Although there are notable examples of nation-states emerging from a revolutionary desire to overturn an oppressive status quo—such as the early French Revolution and the brief flowering of

Russian democracy before the rise of Lenin—most Eurowestern modern nation-states, even those that officially trumpet multiculturalism, such as Canada, demand allegiance to the economic and political authority of the state.

By contrast, Indigenous nationhood is a concept rooted in community values, histories, and traditions that, at the same time, asserts a sense of active sociopolitical agency, not simply static separatism from the world and its peoples. This idea is compatible with that of an autonomous ethno-nationalism drawn from the exercise of community self-determination, as proposed by Kahnawake Mohawk political theorist Gerald/Taiaiake Alfred. Indigenous nationhood, in this case, challenges the assimilative foundations of state nationalism by its assertion of an inherent distinctiveness based on tradition, culture, language, and relationship to the world and its various peoples. Fundamental to this distinction is the ability of Indigenous nationalism to extend recognition to other sovereignties without that recognition implying a necessary need to consume, displace, or become absorbed by those nations.[9]

Indigenous nationhood is more than simple political independence or the exercise of a distinctive cultural identity; it is also an understanding of a common social interdependence within the community, the tribal web of kinship rights *and* responsibilities that link the People, the land, and the cosmos together in an ongoing and dynamic system of mutually affecting relationships.[10] At its best, it extends beyond the human to encompass other peoples, from the plants and animals to the sun, moon, thunder, and other elemental forces. As Patrick N. Minges points out, such "[m]utually dependent relationships are partnerships of equality; the respect given to each creature's contribution imbues a profound recognition of the dignity of even the smallest of creations."[11] Tribal nationhood is, in this way, distinguished from state-focused nationalism by its central focus on *peoplehood,* the relational system that keeps the people in balance with one another, with other peoples and realities, and with the world.[12] Nationhood, then, is the political extension of the social rights and responsibilities of peoplehood. It is the underpinning of what Jace Weaver calls "communitism," which is something "more than merely 'community.' It involves a particular way of attempting to live in community as Natives."[13] In reference to Cherokees, this "particular way" has been defined as the Kituwah (or Keetoowah) spirit, a way of being that includes "loyalty to each other, concern for the spiritual power in their way of life, and their insistence upon the fundamental importance of tribal unity and harmony."[14]

The work of the late Cherokee anthropologist Robert K. Thomas is particularly useful in understanding this dynamic structural theory of peoplehood within Indigenous nationhood, especially as so many of its foundational concepts emerged from Thomas's longtime work among Oklahoma Cherokees. As explicated after Thomas's death in 1991 by Tom Holm (Cherokee), Ben Chavis (Lumbee), and J. Diane Pearson, peoplehood is the communitistic worldview within which the nation's understanding of itself and its place in the cosmos is embedded. Applicable to most "enclave" communities, and perhaps universal to Indigenous peoples in North America and throughout the world, the "peoplehood matrix" is composed of four interdependent elements: language, sacred history, ceremonial cycle, and place/territory. No element is distinct; they exist only in relationship with one another. Anything that injures or compromises one will be detrimental to all. The understanding of this relatedness is vital to the full functioning of this concept, as "the factors of peoplehood make up a complete system that accounts for particular social, cultural, political, economic, and ecological behaviors exhibited by groups of people indigenous to particular territories."[15]

Peoplehood is thus the dynamic and active participation in the relational reality of the tribal nation. One does not have the right of affiliation without also sharing the responsibilities of participation in at least some of the relationships that define the community. As Thomas emphasizes, many traditional Cherokees see

> the universe as having a definite order, as a system which has balance and reciprocal obligations between its parts. The individual Cherokee is a part of this system, and membership entails certain obligations. When the Cherokee does not fulfill his obligations, the system gets out of balance and the Cherokee no longer have the "good life."[16]

This "good life" is the result of mindful and balanced participation in the responsibilities of peoplehood. It isn't something that exists in the ideal abstract, as a timeless and fixed state of being, as with the nation-state; it requires attentive, ongoing engagement and continual contextualization in order to endure and thrive.

This sense of active participation in the continual creation of the People and their nationhood is reflected in the Cherokee ceremonies that honor and care for the sacred fire, the "earthly representative and ally of the Sun" and "principal symbol of purity"[17] that has been with the People from time immemorial and continues to share its wisdom and strength:

> Every year the traditional Cherokees gather to dance in the bright flame and dark shadows of the eternal fire and to ask for the help of the fire and the spirits. This fire of the Cherokees is believed to be eternal. When the world was young, this sacred fire was stolen by a conjurer and transformed into small white crystals in which the future might be seen. When the thief held the stones in his hand, the flames of the sacred fire came forth and revealed the way for the Cherokees. The Cherokees sent a warrior to recover the fire. The boy tricked the conjurer by asking to see the future in the stones. As the flames burst forth, the boy threw tobacco onto the blaze, and the flames consumed the evil one.
>
> It is said that, as long as the flame of the sacred fire burns, the Cherokee people will survive. Evil has been imprisoned in the fire, and the fire burns for the Cherokee people. The story of the Cherokees is told by the eternal fire.[18]

The survival of the People—of the nation itself—is thus directly linked to their thoughtful attention to their responsibilities as keepers of the sacred fire. Indeed, this relationship may be reflected in the very name "Cherokee" itself; while generally considered to be a derivation of the Choctaw word for "people who live in caves," as Weaver points out the name "may derive from *cheera tahge,* the term for wise ones, meaning 'possessors of the divine fire.'"[19] It should be little surprise, then, that the Phoenix, a spirit-bird of living and continually renewing flame, has been such an enduring symbol of Cherokee nationhood since the early nineteenth century. The spirit of the fire is also the spirit of the nation. According to Thomas, the "six great ceremonies of the Cherokee . . . have these elements in common: the ceremonial lighting of the sacred fire, the sacrifice of tobacco or wild meat to that fire, the purification of participants in the ceremonies, and a series of all-night dances"; each element is clearly linked back to the fire.[20] There are numerous accounts of the dangers of neglecting this spirit—which is, after all, interwoven with the health and well-being of the People—whereas returning to the fire is a significant assertion of relatedness for those who have reconnected to the traditional ceremonial grounds.[21] Thomas relates his conversation with an eastern

Cherokee man on this matter: "Sometime next winter we may want you to ask some of those Oklahoma chiefs to come down here and teach us all about the fire."[22]

Cherokee nationhood is, like the sacred fire, the embodied and dynamic peoplehood principle in which Cherokee continuity is rooted, shaped by political concerns as well as spiritual, physical, and intellectual ones. Nourished by the attention of the People or weakened by their neglect, this relational reality provides the philosophical and ethical heart of Cherokee nationhood, sovereignty, and self-determination. To examine Cherokee national literature and the discourses of Cherokee nationhood from within this understanding, then, is not to assert a frozen or static canon that mimics the assimilative directive of the U.S. nation-state. Instead, it is to become a participant in the continual processes of peoplehood, to return to the sacred fire of the Cherokees and add to its strength.

Methodologies of Literary Nationhood: Calling on the Ancestors

This broader study examines a wide and necessarily diverse range of Cherokee texts to better understand the ways that Cherokees self-define concepts of peoplehood. As noted at the beginning of the chapter, the established body of Cherokee scholarship has generally focused on a limiting dualism that is rooted in Eurowestern progressivist ideas of savagism and civilization. Yet the dualistic structure itself isn't inherently problematic, as various complementary pairings are deeply embedded in Cherokee culture and history, although not inevitably along the progressivist spectrum. This social and cosmological structure is a characteristic of many southeastern tribal nations, which generally hold in ceremonial contexts "that a balanced opposition existed between the great cosmic categories."[23]

For example, in the older wisdom traditions of Cherokees and other southeastern nations, the Upper World of order is the opposite of the Lower World of chaos; between them stands the Middle World, where humans try to find balance.[24] The four directions are two pairs of general opposites, as Cherokee scholar Mary C. Churchill points out: "east and west balance each other; that is, life opposes death, for instance. North and south balance each other as well, as in the case of trouble opposing peace. Thus, the concept of balance informs the meanings of the cardinal directions."[25] The animal people are opposed to the plant people in their relationships with humans, for when the animals cursed humans with diseases as a punishment for unbalanced hunting and cruelty, it was the plants who provided the healing medicines that are most honored by the Cherokees. Selu, the Corn-Mother and First Woman of the Cherokees, is balanced in her deep agricultural wisdom by her husband Kanati, Great Thunder and First Man, an unerring hunter and woodsman. Of their two sons—the Thunder Boys—one (Tame Boy) is born of their loving union within the structure of their ordered home, but the other, wilder son (Wild Boy) emerges undomesticated from the blood of Kanati's prey that Selu washes in a stream.

To acknowledge these dualistic pairings is not to presume an antago-nistic relationship of supremacy between them. The emphasis, rather, is balance and complementarity. The thresholds are strong but permeable. I am particularly indebted to the dialogical work of Mary C. Churchill, as her own observations on the manifestation of these principles in Cherokee women's literature provides an insightful and sensitive analysis of the re-lationship between Cherokee dualist concepts: "the dialogic is delineated by difference, separation, dynamism, and applied forms. It is only the dia-logical system . . . that allows for the coexistence of both within the same whole."[26] Whereas the progressivist interpretations of various Cherokee dualisms presume an inevitable eclipse or erasure of one of the pair, a more culturally rooted understanding looks to the *relationship* between them: Selu and Kanati balance each others' strengths and weaknesses, as do the animals and plants, the Upper World and the Lower World (or, in Churchill's work, the Above and Below worlds), and death in the west is balanced with life in the east. Again, as with the concept of nationhood, understanding Cherokee dualism is to understand its necessary comple-mentarity; it is a dynamic and relational perspective, not an assumption of unitary supremacy.

The interpretive methodology of this book draws from this principle as a challenge to the rigid progressivist binaries that affect such assort-ed Cherokee Studies works as Grace Steele Woodward's *The Cherokees* (1963), John Ehle's *Trail of Tears: The Rise and Fall of the Cherokee Nation* (1988), and Stanley W. Hoig's *The Cherokees and Their Chiefs: In the Wake of Empire* (1998). In particular, I extend the analysis beyond the cosmo-logical principles that Churchill addresses to the traditional Cherokee sociopolitical divisions of red/war and white/peace spheres of influence, where one group of community leaders guided the people during times of peace ("white"), and another group led during times of conflict ("red"):[27]

> During times of peace the white [peace] government was supreme in all respects except the making of war. . . . The two governmental structures were never in operation at the same time. The white government was essentially a stable theocracy of the older and wiser men of the tribe, who constituted a tribal gerontocracy. The red organization was, on the other hand, flexible, responsive to changing conditions and controlled by the younger warriors.[28]

Tom Holm draws on the teachings of Robert K. Thomas to expand on this concept:

> Each Cherokee town had peace (or civil) chiefs and war leaders. These leaders essentially constituted two separate priesthoods. The peace or "white" chiefs were usually elderly men who had gained respect over the years for their perspicacity, spiritual powers, and accumulated knowledge of tribal traditions. These "Beloved Men" conducted the traditional seasonal ceremonies and acted as councils that handled domestic affairs. Although the primary embodiments of Cherokee government, these councils did not serve as law-making or legislative institutions. Rather, they interpreted Cherokee law, sought consensus, and attempted, when internal problems arose, to restore harmony and order within the community. In times of war, they were essentially replaced as the embodiments of tribal government by a war chief or group of warriors with specialized war powers who presided over the rituals of going to war and led the warriors into battle. When the conflict was over, these "red" chiefs or priests conducted the ceremonies that restored the entire society to its normal functioning.[29]

Both descriptions highlight the responsibility of the leaders to the community they served, thus reflecting the Cherokee principle of authority as a characteristic developed by responsible fulfillment of one's obligations to the people, not the inherent possession of coercive power.

It's important to point out here, however, that the shared foundation of both the red and white spheres is war. Although popular ideas about the Cherokees as one of the "civilized" tribes minimizes the association, Cherokee culture, for all genders and ages, has long been shaped by the culture of war, even through the dedication of the People to trying to live in peace. Resistance is at the heart of many forms of Cherokee survival. For example, the Beloved Men and Women of the Nation were generally warriors in their younger years; it was only after their war service had ended that they became Beloved elders and diplomats for peace. Having shed blood themselves, they knew well the costs of conflict. Cherokees have served alongside other warriors in each major military exercise of the nineteenth, twentieth, and twenty-first centuries, from the U.S. Civil War onward. And even when a formal warrior culture lost its emphasis in the nineteenth century, Cherokee resistance—physical and rhetorical— continued on unabated. Red and white, war and peace: linked by the enduring Cherokee spirit of defiance.

I propose that this red/white structure, although officially discarded during the consolidation of the autonomous towns during the late eighteenth and early nineteenth centuries, has in fact persisted to the present day, albeit in altered forms. War chiefs and peace chiefs adopted different strategies in meeting their obligations, strategies that have remained firmly embedded in Cherokee national literature and relational principles of nationhood even today. The first response is what I call the red "Chickamauga consciousness," so named for the nationalist resistance movement of the late eighteenth and early nineteenth centuries that was devoted to armed response to U.S. violence and expansion into ancestral territories. Chickamauga consciousness, an extension of the red/war governmental division, is centered in Cherokee intellectual and artistic separatism, in a rhetorical rejection of literary, historical, or philosophical accommodation.[30] Coupled with the Chickamauga consciousness is a white "Beloved Path" reading that places peace and cultural continuity above potentially self-destructive rebellion. Neither exists independently; there is a necessary tension that brings the war and peace perspectives together into constant movement—again, the idea of nationhood as a dynamic concept. This interdependence and relationship provides an interpretive guidepost to much of the Cherokee literary tradition.

Yet what does it mean to articulate a literary theory rooted in the Chickamauga and Beloved methodologies? What, if anything, is achieved by the employment of these complementary political spheres? At the very least, such a methodology places the literature in relationship to some of its historical antecedents and its cultural contexts; at its best, it gives us a new vocabulary for expressing the depth and significance of Cherokee literature and intellectualism. War and peace in relation to one another, as read through their Cherokee cultural manifestations, can be understood as literary principles that help us to more accurately represent the complexities of Cherokee social history and politics. These principles argue for a realignment of our conversations about Cherokees from the civilized/savage binary to a more nuanced understanding of the many ways that Cherokees have asserted nationhood, sovereignty, and self-determination. Outside of such realignment, as Strickland reminds us in the epigraph to this chapter, Cherokees become little more than symbol or metaphor for the glories or excesses of the United States, and the dynamic fires of Cherokee continuity are again obscured. To focus on Cherokee social history through Cherokee literature, on Cherokee terms, returns the focus to where I believe it belongs: on those ideas and concerns that matter to Cherokees.

Before discussing specific examples of ways that the Chickamauga consciousness and Beloved Path inform Cherokee literature, it's necessary to examine the clearest manifestations of those philosophies: the political and social conflict between Nanye'hi (Nancy Ward), the famed Beloved (or War) Woman of Chota, and her cousin Tsiyu Gansini (Dragging Canoe), the war leader of the Chickamaugas.[31] This conflict—fundamentally a tension between the traditional positions of peace and war chief in an era dominated by the alien politics and policies of a predatory colonialist regime—starkly exemplifies the dual tensions present in the Cherokee literary tradition. The Chickamauga and Beloved Path distinctions represented by Tsiyu Gansini and Nanye'hi, as understood here, are distinctions in *degree,* not *kind*: they are historically rooted extensions of the shared red/white political structure that defined each Cherokee town before the governmental centralization (and which continue in various forms today), not just those of Chota. I will return at length to their stories later in this chapter, but first I will focus on the significance of these particular figures in this particular time to the methodological underpinnings of this project.

Nanye'hi was born into the politically powerful Wolf Clan around 1738 in the peace town of Chota (Echota), a community widely respected as one of the sacred mother-towns of the Nation.[32] She came from an eminent family; her uncle, Ada-gal'kala (known to the English as Leaning Wood or the Little Carpenter), was the most prestigious peace chief of the era, and likely the primary male influence on his niece. Nanye'hi came to prominence at seventeen in the Battle of Taliwa against the Muskogees. When her husband Kingfisher was brought down by a Muskogee bullet, Nanye'hi "took up his gun and . . . led [the Cherokee forces] in a rout of the enemy."[33] In honor of her bravery, Nanye'hi was awarded the title of "War Woman" and became a powerful voice in the women's council, in battle, and in national affairs. Later in life, in honor of her exceptional service to the People and in recognition of her wisdom and strength, she became known as a *Ghighau*, a "Most Honored" or Beloved Woman, joining the ranks of the most honored figures in Cherokee society—those women who interpreted the words of the spirits, spoke in council, pardoned the condemned, and worked toward the peaceful welfare of the People.[34] For the next sixty-seven years, until her death in 1822 at the age of eighty-four, Nanye'hi would demonstrate her integrity, skill, bravery, and wisdom as a Beloved Woman (and would in fact be one of the last Beloved Women until the mid-1980s, when Maggie Wachacha was honored as Beloved Woman by the Eastern Band). She was fully immersed in the life and duties of the Beloved Path, exemplifying the principles of peace and survival through adaptation. On this path, the tree that does not bend will break.

Nanye'hi's cousin, Tsiyu Gansini, was Ada-gal'kala's son. The influence of Ada-gal'kala on his son was likely very minimal, as the matrilineal Cherokee social structure saw the relationship of uncles to their sisters' children as the fundamental male–child connection, not that of fathers. As the fathers were of different clans from that of their children, they weren't related to them. Thus, Tsiyu Gansini's primary male model was likely his own uncle, whose name is not recorded. What is known is that the young warrior became a fierce opponent of British and U.S. intrusions into Cherokee territories, and as war chief of the Overhill town of Malaquo and later leader of the Chickamaugas, aimed both his rhetorical savvy and powerful war club against Eurowestern imperialism.

Nanye'hi, on the other hand, maintained close ties with her uncle Ada-gal'kala, working with him to guarantee peace between the People and the *yonegs* (Whites) who made unceasing and increasingly brutal demands for Cherokee land and resources. Both Nanye'hi and Tsiyu Gansini followed the traditions of their office—she fought for peace, using any available means, while he fought for freedom at any cost—and each found their efforts frustrated by those of the other. When Tsiyu Gansini and his warriors planned to drive White squatters from the Watauga and Holston valleys, Nanye'hi warned the Whites of the impending attacks. The negotiations arranged by peace chiefs and Beloved Women were only binding as far as other Cherokees would follow them; there were no coercive constraints on warriors who chose to take up the rifle and hatchet. In warning U.S. squatters of the Chickamauga plans, Nanye'hi was not betraying her people, but serving the functions of her office as Beloved Woman; similarly, Tsiyu Gansini was neither expected nor compelled to follow the guidance of the Beloved Woman if his conscience dictated otherwise.

Even a patronizing observer of Cherokee codes of law and justice, such as historian John Philip Reid, notices the absence of coercive authority:

> [E]very Cherokee was equal and every Cherokee had an equal right of participation. While this principle reveals much about Cherokee authority . . . it reveals but one facet of Cherokee equality, the right to be bound only by personal consent. In fact, equality was a constitutional concept of unlimited consequence, permeating every aspect of Cherokee life, a source of anarchy in leadership, and one reason why the primitive era of Cherokee government knew neither a Cherokee state nor a law of coercion.[35]

Reid's analysis continually expresses bafflement about the lack of authority to ensure social obedience; for him, order and law are best maintained by hierarchical power and structures. He discusses at length the difficulties Eurowesterners experienced when they assumed that treaties were binding to all members of the Nation, rather than to those who made the particular treaty. Eurowestern law held that the people were obligated to obey political authorities by the powers inherent in those particular positions; Cherokee law held that a leader received his or her authority from the consent of the people themselves, not from an abstract power, and as such the best leaders with the most influence were those who could best argue the case for a particular course of action. The most powerful Eurowestern leaders, by contrast, were those who were able to most efficiently and effectively wield the coercive powers of their office.

This fundamental difference in the definition of political authority frustrated Eurowestern leaders, who presumed and demanded that all Cherokees would be bound to a treaty that had been agreed to by a minority of the population. The Treaty of New Echota, which gave the United States the legitimizing excuse to drive most Cherokees onto the Trail of Tears, was such a document: less than five hundred Cherokees gathered to sign the document to sell the Nation's last remaining lands in the southeast, while nearly sixteen thousand protested the Treaty and refused to give their consent to it. The U.S. position, however, was rooted in self-serving hypocrisy: U.S. agents expected full and unanimous Native consent to treaties but refused to hold their own citizens responsible for breaking treaty protections of lands.

Chickamauga Consciousness

In comparison with nineteenth-century war leaders like Geronimo (Apache), Sitting Bull (Hunkpapa Lakota), Tecumseh (Shawnee), and Crazy Horse (Oglala Lakota), very little has been written about Tsiyu Gansini or his life, except as a footnote in the "precivilized" era of Cherokee history, which is generally not of the same interest to *yoneg* scholars as is the history of acculturated mixedbloods and the Trail. In his introductory note to *Cherokee Dragon* (2000), Robert Conley mourns this absence:

> One of the great figures in Cherokee history, Dragging Canoe (Tsiyu Gansini) has been sometimes maligned by historians and otherwise relegated to near obscurity in scholarly journals. One likely reason for that is that Dragging Canoe rose to prominence during the American Revolution and, because of the circumstances of the time, was set against the rebellious colonies during that turbulent period. Patriotism, it would seem, has demanded over the years that all enemies of the revolution be deemed—by historians of the United States—monsters, madmen, or at the least, villains. . . .
>
> Perhaps the fact that the Cherokees, in the minds of so many people, are regarded highly as a "civilized" Indian tribe has something to do with Americans' not wanting to acknowledge the greatness of Dragging Canoe. His cousin Nancy Ward is seen as a friend of the white Americans and a proponent of progress. Since Dragging Canoe and she did not agree, he must be seen, I suppose, as her opposite.[36]

Nanye'hi's role in this historical construction is as a handmaiden to American expansion, and she is thus redeemed in imperialist fantasy as another representation of the "Cherokee Princess"; Tsiyu Gansini, on the other hand, brought down as many Americans as possible, and is thus erased from the narrative of American exceptionalism and conquest. As Cherokee historian Brent Yanusdi Cox notes:

> Dragging Canoe was often labeled as a savage because of his attempt to thwart the god-sent advance of white civilization. . . . [H]e became the leader of Cherokee resistance toward imperialism and western expansion. American history only offers a biased interpretation of this warrior's life, and there [have] been few successful attempts to discover his actual identity.[37]

Tsiyu Gansini is an unpleasant reminder of the willingness of some people to kill and die in their defiance of U.S. imperialism; rather than such reminders prompting reflections on the rampages of a predatory nation-state, *yoneg* historians and writers have merely erased mention of such reminders, focusing instead on those figures more easily misrepresented (such as Nanye'hi) for the patriotic and guilt-free "American experience."

What little detailed information is available on Tsiyu Gansini generally agrees that he was born around 1730 at Running Water town.[38] He came to prominence in March 1775 during the treaty negotiations at Sycamore Shoals after his father, the Beloved Man Ada-gal'kala, and other headmen of the Nation signed away "all Cherokee lands between the Ohio River and the Cumberland divide, including central Kentucky and the portion of Tennessee north of the Cumberland River," in what would be known as the Henderson Purchase.[39] Tsiyu Gansini, already in his mid-forties and a well-respected war leader, refused to sign the agreement. As White settlers moved onto these lands, Tsiyu Gansini led warriors against them. His final words to the *yoneg* land speculators were an oath that he spent the next seventeen years fulfilling: "We have given you this, why do you ask for more? . . . [W]hen you have this you have all. There is no game left between the Watauga and the Cumberland. There is a cloud hanging over it. You will find its settlement dark and bloody."[40]

In the years to come, Tsiyu Gansini would lead his people, who came to be known as the Chickamaugas for their settlement at Chickamauga Creek, against U.S. settlement and expansion: they joined the British campaign to destabilize the embryonic settler-state, and even after the British withdrew from open warfare against the United States, the Chickamaugas defended their lands against the ever-growing wave of White invaders. Tsiyu Gansini was an early advocate of anti-imperial Native confederation and was, by some accounts, an early inspiration for Tecumseh's similar movement.

The U.S. military response to the Chickamauga defiance was terrorism in its most unsophisticated but brutally effective form: slaughter every-thing, from infant to elder, burn the crops, and raze the towns to the ground. In 1784, the main Chickamauga Lower Towns were destroyed; two years later, the rebuilt towns, located farther down the Tennessee River from old Chickamauga, were also obliterated by U.S. forces defend-ing the treaty-breaking "rights" of White squatters and land thieves.

In spite of the continued slaughters by the United States and its al-lies, the Chickamaugas battled on. In 1788, Tsiyu Gansini and other Chickamauga war chiefs drove back an invasion by John Sevier and his army, and three years later joined a confederacy under the leadership of the Miami war chief Little Turtle, subjecting General St. Clair and his U.S. troops to a decisive and humiliating defeat. The red chief continued leading his people in resistance and alliances with other defiant nations until his death from unknown causes at Lookout Town in 1792, following an all-night celebration in honor of recent Chickamauga successes.[41]

In death Tsiyu Gansini was as terrifying to the *yoneg* squatters as he had been in life. Cox relates a folk story regarding this fear:

> It has been said that White settlers and soldiers feared that Dragging Canoe had supernatural powers, and even possibly the ability to [resur-rect]. When Dragging Canoe was buried in 1792, it was said that white soldiers [confiscated] his body, and divided it into two halves. One half was left as his burial near Nickajack, and [the] other portion was taken away. This was done to prevent Dragging Canoe from coming back.[42]

Tsiyu Gansini's tenacity and brilliance were such that even death could not eclipse his influence. The truth of this story is less important than the fact that he inspired such fear among the land thieves; this demonstrates the power of the Chickamauga resistance movement.

For all his prowess as a military leader, strategist, and freedom fighter, Tsiyu Gansini was above all a traditionalist, a man who loved his people and who honored their ancient commitment to their homeland and the spirits that inhabited it, and he was as much a champion for Cherokee sur-vival as was his cousin Nanye'hi, the Beloved Woman of Chota. Cherokee historian E. Raymond Evans notes:

> At the beginning of the American Revolution it had seemed that the Cherokees might be completely exterminated, or at best survive only as a beaten and degenerate people like the Catawba. This disaster was avoided

by the firm holding action fought by Dragging Canoe. It was his determined resistance that made the Treaty of Tellico Blockhouse [2 October
1798] workable. Having felt the strength of the Cherokees, the whites
respected the treaty for more than a generation. This period of peace
made possible the brilliant flowering of Cherokee Culture during the
first quarter of the nineteenth century. . . .

Although Dragging Canoe did not live to see the end result of his long
years of fighting, his continued struggle was not in vain. The Cherokee
culture which Dragging Canoe and the Chickamauga Cherokees devoted
their lives to saving, is still very much alive. Today their descendants in
Oklahoma and in the mountains of North Carolina can still repeat with
pride Dragging Canoe's statement to the Shawnee delegation: "We are not
yet conquered."[43]

Tsiyu Gansini, and the other Chickamaugas—women, men, children, elders,
all dedicated to defying the extinction imperative of the U.S. government—
were well aware of the results of continued *yoneg* land hunger: "The
white men have almost surrounded us, leaving us only a little spot of
ground to stand upon, and it seems to be their intention to destroy us as
a Nation."[44]

It was not a fickle commitment that the Chickamaugas set themselves
toward, but an enduring struggle to remain the Real People in the face of
a ravenous fledgling empire. They would continue to fight, and to withdraw, throughout the nineteenth century, to join with the Cherokees who
followed Chief Bowles to Texas as well as the Cherokee Old Settlers who
traveled to "Indian Territory" in the decades before the Trail of Tears. And
they remain particularly strong today among the traditionalist communities of both the Cherokee Nation and the United Keetoowah Band, particularly among those who keep the fires at the Oklahoma stomp grounds.

Balance is primary; if anything can be said to be a feature of contemporary and past Cherokee traditions, it is the quest for balance in
all things. As the Beloved Path was and remains a negotiation that required strength, wisdom, and determination to effectively balance, so too
is the Chickamauga approach. Armed resistance, whether rhetorical or
physical, is by its very nature a dangerous commitment, as the colonizing
enemy is fully armed and will stop at nothing to eliminate opposition.
Thus, against those warriors who have embraced Chickamauga consciousness, the *yoneg* response has always been slash-and-burn warfare, utterly

without mercy and with full intention of erasing the opposition from the world. But Chickamaugas are survivors; it is through their defiance that so many of the old ways and traditions have been maintained. The balance Tsiyu Gansini maintained was between rebellion that preserved those ways and made substantive gains for the People and rebellion that was suicidal and self-destructive; during his long warrior's life, even with the loss of towns and family to the brutal reprisals of the Eurowesterners, that balance was kept. When the dangers grew too great, the Chickamaugas removed themselves from home and hearth to protect the most precious trust they honored: the spiritual and cultural life of the People.

THE BELOVED PATH

Nanye'hi was a strong advocate for peace and allegiance with the fledgling United States, in spite of the British Crown's attempts to limit colonialist expansion into Cherokee territory via the Royal Proclamation Line of 1763. Yet in spite of her wish for peace, U.S. troops attacked allied Cherokee settlements as readily as any others, though Nanye'hi was spared personal attack, even during the razing of Chota. The difficult nature of the Beloved Path is clear: when the opposition sees any maintenance of cultural identity as a threat, anything less than assimilation and erasure is unacceptable. When the focus centers on the survival and endurance of the People, peace itself can be as much an assertion of defiance as the Chickamauga consciousness of war.

Nanye'hi lived in times of extraordinary culture change and conflict. She rose to prominence due to her own intelligence, charisma, courage, and endurance, as well as a supportive tribal power structure that provided women a position and forum through which to exercise their abilities. She fought to maintain a balance, in whatever ways possible, between the world of her people and the encroaching influence of Europe and its North American colonies. She married a *yoneg* and learned to cross between cultures and their differing social mores; this skill served her children as well as her extended community. Nanye'hi's articulation of the Beloved Path throughout her life has helped give shape to an enduring consciousness among Cherokees today, as Cherokee scholar Virginia Carney points out: "Nanye'hi continues to be honored as a courageous mother and grandmother, a War Woman."[45] She is nothing like the palefaced Pocahontas that so many White writers have imagined her to be; she's a symbol of

strength and survival, with her spirit firmly committed to the survival of
the People.[46]

Her work as Beloved Woman was, by the early 1800s, far less accommodating to Eurowestern intrusions into Cherokee territory than it had
been in earlier years. Yet as her opposition became increasingly vocal, the
position of women in the leadership of the Cherokee Nation was swiftly
decreasing. The male leaders of the Nation worked hard to centralize political power on the model of the U.S. government; this centralization,
while preventing individuals from selling Cherokee territory without approval of the combined council, "had little room in it for Nancy Ward,
the War Woman of Chota, and other women."[47] The U.S. government's
"civilization" program had worked to shift the gender balance of power
to the males, and the introduction of patriarchal/patrilineal Christianity,
animal husbandry, slaveholding, and the movement of Cherokee men into
agriculture (the traditional domain of women), all combined to remove
women from political power.

Nanye'hi's life is less controversial than those of other Native women
who married and/or aided Whites in westward expansion—Tekonwatonti/
Molly Brant (Mohawk), Sacagawea (Shoshone), Pocahontas (Powhatan/
Tsenacommacah)—if only because of her rejection of further concession
to Eurowestern settlers in her later life. This rejection was the resurgence
of the implied War Woman within her Beloved status, the defiance inherent in Cherokee survival. Her behavior during the U.S. Revolutionary War
has been read outside a Beloved Path context as a betrayal of her people to
an enemy state, but Carney asserts that "[i]t was, in fact, a legal require-
ment among the Cherokees, as among many other Indian nations, that
warning be given of an impending attack."[48] Cynthia R. Kassee expands
on this point: "From these many accommodations to the 'Americans,' one
might get the idea that Nan'yehi [sic] was selling out the Cherokee people.
However, her political efforts proved to the contrary. She did not seek war,
but neither did she counsel peace when she felt compromise would hurt
her people."[49] And because coercion was antithetical to Cherokee political organization, which placed a strong emphasis on personal agency and
accountability, it was Nanye'hi's culturally defined duty to determine the
best course in following this path for herself and for her people.

As a Beloved Woman, the mother of a skilled warrior and two socially
and politically active daughters, a widow in her younger years, and a woman
of the Cherokee Nation, Nanye'hi was familiar with the consequences of

warfare with Whites, which included the likely loss of husbands, children, and other loved ones. The Beloved Path she followed was a difficult one that sought balance between concessions to a ravenous empire and defiance against being swallowed up completely. In the light of such a reading, Nanye'hi was anything but an accommodationist; she followed a different tradition that saw strength and survival in adaptation.

Nanye'hi sought peace and adaptation when she believed it to be in the best interests of her people. She also strongly opposed any sacrifice of land or sovereignty that threatened the Cherokees—an essential aspect of the Beloved Path, which centers itself within an enduring Cherokee presence. In 1781, she addressed the Cherokee Council and U.S. treaty commissioners, reminding everyone that some Cherokees had aided the United States and that peace was in the best interest of both the Cherokee Nation and the United States. Her speech demonstrates her keen understanding of the Eurowestern disdain for women as well as the Cherokee discomfort with such a philosophy (a discomfort that would sadly fade, at least among men, in the coming years): "You know that women are always looked upon as nothing; but we are your mothers; you are our sons. Our cry is all for peace; let it continue. This peace must last forever. Let your women's sons be ours; our sons be yours. Let your women hear our words."[50]

Later in her life, too ill to attend an 1817 meeting with U.S. treaty negotiators, she "sent her son, Five Killer, carrying her distinctive walking cane to represent her" in her stead, along with a written response—signed by twelve other powerful Cherokee women—to Eurowestern suggestions for voluntary removal:

> we do not wish to go to an unknown country which we have understood some of our children wish to go over the Mississippi but this act of our children would be like destroying your mothers. Your mothers and sisters ask and beg of you not to part with any more of our lands. . . . [Nanye'hi] to her children Warriors to take pity and listen to the talks of your sisters, although I am very old yet cannot but pity the situation in which you will hear of their minds, I have great many grandchildren which I wish them to do well on our land.[51]

Nanye'hi did not live to see her descendants driven onto the Trail of Tears, but she foresaw the possibility and, by appealing to the ancestral respect that Cherokee men gave to the women in their lives, sought to influence them away from negotiating too far with the land-hungry and predatory young nation. As Carney points out in her incisive analysis of Nanye'hi's rhetorical strategies, this final statement "emphasizes a number of traditions which continue to play a vital role in cultural persistence, and which help to explain the resistance of many contemporary Cherokees to assimilationist policies," including the association of the sacred homeland with their mothers and the reminder that, as a matrilineal people, "it is the women who should be deciding how their descendants will live."[52]

It is also important to note that Nanye'hi's "cry for peace" was anything but naive: the British had long been cruel, but the U.S. citizenry struck back against any attack on allied Whites with a merciless brutality far beyond anything practiced by the Cherokees. The aftermath of the American Revolution demonstrates well the threats of militancy:

> The effects upon the Cherokee of this irruption of more than six thousand armed enemies into their territory was well nigh paralyzing. More than fifty of their towns had been burned, their orchards cut down, their fields wasted, their cattle and horses killed or driven off, their stores of buckskin and other personal property plundered. Hundreds of their people had been killed or had died of starvation and exposure, others were prisoners in the hands of the Americans, and some had been sold into slavery. Those who had escaped were fugitives in the mountains, living upon acorns, chestnuts, and wild game, or were refugees with the British. From the Virginia line to the Chattahoochie the chain of destruction was complete. [53]

Cherokee demographer Russell Thornton points out that the U.S. response to Cherokee defiance was particularly fierce because of their intent to "dissuade the Creeks from joining the British."[54] Dislocation and land cessions might have been terrible, but the merciless carnage that followed the red path against this particularly violent enemy was much more immediately worse.

Cherokees today understand Nanye'hi's often contradictory approach toward preserving her cultural identity while adapting to the demands of the present: as one of the so-called Five Civilized Tribes, and as the U.S. tribal nation most widely perceived as assimilated into White ways and beliefs, most of the Cherokee people have long fought to survive on the Beloved Path by shaping Eurowestern cultural, religious, and political structures to serve the interests of Cherokee nationhood. It has been an ongoing battle, but the Cherokees remain among the most economically

Talmadge Davis, The Confrontation. *Courtesy of the artist. www.heritageartmarketing.com.*

independent, culturally conscious, and populous tribal nations in the Americas.

Red and white together. The Chickamauga consciousness and Beloved Path work toward the preservation of the spiritual commitments, physical bodies, and cultural lifeways of the Ani-Yunwiya, through the ever-fluid balance of strategic accommodation and tactical defiance. It is through the study of these contrasts that the dynamic strengths of Cherokee endurance are most starkly contrasted and illuminated: Tsiyu Gansini and Nanye'hi are the cultural forebears of the contemporary discourses of Cherokee nationhood. Together they are the clearest examples of the ancient manifestations of the red and white spheres of Cherokee political consciousness (though by no means the last, as I will demonstrate throughout this study). By recovering Tsiyu Gansini and returning him to his rightful place in the story, Nanye'hi is reinterpreted according to her duties and her concern with Cherokee continuity. In returning the missing half of the story, the other half changes as a result of this reinterpretation, and both are understood through their relationship with one another and the People. They dance together under the star-strewn sky—one bearing the swan-wing of peace, the other holding the rifle of war—as the voices of Cherokee men sing in time with the rattling rhythm of the women's turtle shell leggings. They dance around the sacred fire, and the Real Human Beings remain strong.

Part II

GEOGRAPHIES OF REMOVAL

• Part II •

Geographies of Removal

Tribal people have deep bonds with the earth, with sacred places
that bear the bones and stories that tell them who they are, where
they came from, and how to live in the world they see around
them. But of course almost all tribal people also have migration stories that say we came from someplace else before finding
home. The very fact that tribal nations from the Southeast were so
extraordinarily successful in making so-called Indian Territory a
much beloved home after the horrors of Removal and before the
horrors of the Civil War underscores the ability of indigenous
Americans to move and in doing so to carry with them whole
cultures within memory and story.

—Louis Owens (Choctaw/Cherokee),
Mixedblood Messages

What is home? Is it a place we're born and raised, where the stories
and lives of our families are woven into our own experiences so deeply
that it is impossible to tell where their memories end and our own begin?
Is it a sense of security, of comfort and fulfillment, or a place that aches
with the weight of history, conflict, and struggle? Can we belong to a place
we have never been, or a place we know only through our dreams and
imaginations? Can we pull ourselves free of a home that we no longer
want, or is it always a part of us, twisted and tangled inextricably into our
identities like strands of DNA? Does home stay in one place, or does it
travel with us, no matter how far we go?

Whatever home may be, its roots can draw both rich nourishment and withering poison from the stories we carry about who we are, about our relationships with the world, and about our imagined pasts and dreamed futures. Thomas King (Cherokee/Greek) puts the point most succinctly: "The truth about stories is that that's all we are."[1] Indigenous wisdom traditions throughout the world hold great reverence for the sacred power of words and stories; these stories can create the world or destroy it, and each person is called upon to treat words carefully. Stories make meaning of our world, and the quality of life we find in that world depends in large part on the ethical content and purpose of those stories. Some scholars, politicians, and spiritual leaders inspire us with stories that speak to relationship and the values of generosity, kindness, and understanding, while many others prefer to share the self-serving stories of fear, paranoia, and myopia that make the world a smaller, crueler place. What is "America," after all, but a construction of stories that have led people to acts of great courage and great brutality? "Civilization," "savagery," "socialism," "democracy," "freedom": each of these words bears its own storied burdens and possibilities.

Indigenous people know our ancestors and others when we know their stories, and we thus return to a meaningful place within the web of relationships and responsibilities; this is why Eurowestern assimilation policies have always targeted Indian stories, words, languages, and voices. A people who know their own stories are strong; this is why historical recovery work has been so important for Indigenous decolonization, and why the backlash has been so blindly vicious. It isn't just the old stories that are important, because the new stories speak to our continuity as well—we're not just museum displays locked in the past. When we question the stories that erase us and replace them with stories of both our past and current *presence,* we speak ourselves into an existence that reaches to the future.

Written words have particular resonance among Cherokees, as so much of our cultural expression explicitly invokes the generative powers of language, from the syllabary and bilingual *Cherokee Phoenix* to novels, poetry, political texts, and the written sacred formulae of Cherokee medicine-makers. In spite of the five-hundred-plus-year insistence of Eurowesterners that we're dying out or fading before the onslaught of White supremacy, our stories endure to give strength to each new generation, who add their own stories to the mix, sharing new knowledge with old. And often these stories are concerned with our ideas of *home.*

One story about the Cherokee relationship to the land is well known to many Eurowesterners, if only by the negative example of the ethnic cleansing now called the Trail of Tears. In this story, the Removal is most often represented by non-Natives as a regrettable but temporary blight on the innate virtue of the United States and its citizenry. For Cherokees, on the other hand, Removal is more than a metaphorical concept: it is a historical trauma that continues to reverberate in the memory and cultural expressions of Cherokees today. To understand nationhood in the Cherokee literary tradition, we must also examine the complicated relationship between the People, the land, and the forces of removal, as Cherokee stories have long been concerned with this relationship.

Chapter 2 extends the book's analysis to some of the texts that emerge from the Trail of Tears, in particular the Cherokee rhetorics of Chief John Ross and those embedded within the controversial Treaty of New Echota. Moving beyond this notorious period in Cherokee history, chapter 3 engages with both the history and the literature of the allotment era of 1887–1907, when the lands and tribal governments of Indian Territory were shattered by the General Allotment Act of 1887 and the 1907 creation of the state of Oklahoma.

Cherokees today are a diverse people of many perspectives and traditions, yet we are linked, at the very least, by shared histories of trauma that shape our understandings of history, community, continuity, and identity. Nationhood, far from being a unitary concept, is rooted in contradictions and conflicts, as well as forces that move toward balance. Neither Nanye'hi nor Tsiyu Gansini encompassed the whole of Cherokee experience through the cultural responsibilities they respectively embraced as Beloved Woman and war chief; it was only through their dynamic interaction with one another that a more representative story of Cherokee nationhood is revealed. Similarly, neither the Christian fullblood nor the mixedblood ceremonialist reflect the totality of "Cherokeeness" today; these categories are meaningful, but they're still just two points along a broad, complicated, and occasionally contradictory cultural spectrum.

EARLY REMOVALS

When asked by Cherokee literary scholar Sean Teuton if movement is an integral part to Cherokee identity, Robert Conley responds:

The history would seem to indicate that. On the other hand, in more recent Cherokee history, people from that core group of Cherokees in Cherokee communities here at home don't ever leave. But if you think of the total group, which includes all the mixed-blood population, we're all over the country; they move all the time. And the historical migrations; movements in the more recent history of the 1850s; mass movements to California, when some came back, some didn't. Yes, it's in the history.[2]

In a very real way, removals are at the heart of contemporary Cherokee nationhood, and their influence has been more significant than many commentators acknowledge. The links of the People to their homelands have shaped Cherokee worldviews and cultural expression; so, too, has the wounding of those links. Although the stories of the Trail of Tears and, to a lesser extent, the allotment era are some of the most famous removals to affect the Cherokees, there are other, older removals that influence historical and current Cherokee contexts.[3] Although Cherokee wisdom traditions include stories about the creation of the world in what is now southern Appalachia, they also include stories about migrations and movements from lands far removed from those mountain ridges. The specter of removal first begins to haunt the Cherokees in these stories.

Eurowestern anthropology frequently points to an extrahemispheric origin for the Cherokees, usually in the form of the Bering land bridge account, which posits that the ancestors of all Indigenous Americans were the inhabitants of what is now Siberia and northeast Asia tens of thousands of years ago.[4] As Louis Owens notes in the above epigraph, many Indigenous nations have ancient stories of migration within their ceremonial traditions; others hold that their people emerged from the earth or a hollow log or otherwise came into being in the land they call home. The peopling stories of the Ani-Yunwiya are of both traditions—rootedness and movement together—and give voice to multiple histories:

> In spite of that tribal sense of our genesis in the Southeast, others believe that our Cherokee ancestors migrated south from somewhere around the Great Lakes. . . . Still other students of America before the Europeans came make a case for our people having come from South America, tracing a long migration trail north, then east, then south, finally stopping in the Great Smoky Mountain region. There is even one legend from our Cherokee oral tradition that seems to support that particular theory. This

legend says the Cherokees originated on an island off the South American coast.[5]

Indigenousness doesn't always require an eternal presence in a particular
location: though not necessarily elastic, the relational principle of peoplehood is adaptable to multiple spirits and sacred landscapes. Again, the
emphasis is on the totality of relationships, not simply the participants;
this gives us room for the possibility of what Craig Womack calls "multiple homes" that are as much dependent upon our visionary imaginations as are our physical locations in the world.[6] A fully contextualized
understanding of the Cherokee literary tradition is only possible through
attention to these homeward relationships of rootedness and movement,
the geographic bonds of those who live in the lands of the ancestors as well
as those of outland Cherokees, whose relationships to home are figured in
different ways. To ignore these relationships to the land, in all their messy
variation, is to "divorce our narratives from the landscapes that should
give birth to them," thus impoverishing any attempt at an informed engagement with those narratives. "Geographic and cultural specificity,"
Womack asserts, "enriches narratives rather than limiting them."[7]

We find such enriching specificity in the Cherokee migration stories,
which explain that the People were once the inhabitants of a fertile land.
For various reasons, that landscape became uninhabitable, and they were
forced to flee to a new home, sometimes splitting apart into separate communities as a result. These removals are generally the result of natural
phenomena—floods, earthquakes, and other ecological upheavals—or
long-term human actions like overpopulation, and generally carry less
emotional and moral weight than do the later forced emigrations.

The analysis of these pre-Invasion removal narratives shouldn't be read
as a necessary rejection of the other origin traditions that are rooted in the
southeastern mountains, for both acknowledge that particular landscape
as the formative environment of aboriginal Cherokee tradition. Unlike the
creation accounts in the biblical book of Genesis, which assert an authoritative account at the exclusion of others, Native spiritual and intellectual
traditions have a long history of inclusive flexibility. A world that's imbued
with innumerable spirits has room for the different entities and worldviews of other peoples. This flexibility is marked by an attention to relationships, which require sensitivity and engagement to stay healthy. The
history of monotheism, on the other hand, is one of a myopic insistence on

a single "Truth" that leaves no room for alternative understandings of the world. It's either Truth, or it's not; a predetermined philosophical product, not an ongoing process of creation. Whether Cherokees came from another land or were created within those cloud-shrouded peaks—or both—the People have been shaped by their relationship with the spirits of that land for tens of thousands of years. Just as the Chickamauga consciousness and Beloved Path coexist in mutual association, so, too, do the varied Cherokee peopling stories, for they connect the multiple threads of tribal consciousness and experience to illuminate the complexities of Cherokee historical and cultural traditions.

Of the multiple versions of the migration story, two stand out as particularly evocative in this regard. The first is "How They Came on This Maine," which was recorded in 1725 by Alexander Longe, a British trader and diplomat.[8] The second account is the *Cherokee Vision of Elohi,* originally recounted in the *Vinita Indian Chieftain* by Nighthawk Keetoowah Sakiya Sanders in 1896, and reprinted as a bilingual book in 1997. The Longe version begins with the acknowledgment of a homeland "far distant from here," where "the people Increased and multiplied so fast that the land Could not hold Them so that they were forced to separate and travel To look out for another country."[9] Their travels took them to bitterly cold lands and "mountains of snow and Ice," where the sun disappeared and they lost "a vast quantity of our people by the unseasonable Cold and darkness." Yet under the guidance of their priests, the People "pursued the sun again" and "came to a country that could be inhabited."[10] This new land was so naturally bountiful that they "multiplied so much that [they] overspread all this maine," but without overwhelming their newfound home.

The account then shifts to explain a division among the People due to "the pride and ambition of some of Our leading men that caused a Civil war amongst the Tribes."[11] In the separation that followed, the single language changed—"[t]hey separated from one and the other and the language was Corrupted"—and no longer functioned as the unifying force it had been in their old homeland.[12] Similarly, an ancient form of writing ("not on paper . . . but on white deer skin and on the shoulder bones of buffalo") that predated Sequoyah's syllabary was lost due to the "proudness of the Young people" who "would not obey the priests nor learning but let their minds Run After hunting of wild Beasts," and thus "could not be Recovered again."[13]

In her analysis of this story, historian Sarah H. Hill points out that "this narrative of migration is also a story of separation," where some "stayed behind, while others began a long journey to the south and west to find a country closer to the sun *(nv-da),* to the place it rested in the west *(wudeligv-i).*"[14] The People are split apart first by the emigration, then by the pride of the "leading men," then again by the shortsightedness of the younger generation:

> Like most migration stories, this one told of the past and foretold a future. Portending the devastation occasioned by the deerskin trade, the tale reveals a divergence between tribal traditions and new ways, a rift between generations, dissension among leaders, and, finally, a tear that rent them all. Communication faltered, their common language diffused, many kinds of knowledge disappeared, and harmony disintegrated. Like a morality play, the migration story warned the people of the peril of tribal discord and affirmed the importance of tradition to their survival.[15]

The story is both a chart of primal Cherokee history and an exhortation toward proper relationships with the world and with one another, placing dedication and personal responsibility at the balancing center of those relationships.

Like Longe's account, the *Cherokee Vision of Elohi* begins with an assertion of a faraway homeland and a larger community—"When we lived beyond the great waters there were twelve clans belonging to the Cherokee tribe"—then moves immediately into the crisis that necessitates removal: "back in the old country in which we lived[,] the country was subject to great floods." After attempting to "build a store reaching to heaven" and being twice thwarted by spirits (or, in this account, gods) who destroy the food storage towers, "the tribe held another council and concluded to move out of the floody *[sic]* country and hunt one more dry and suitable to their liking." This movement "continued for many years," and the People were never aware "that they crossed the great waters." The way back was lost, however, "by the submergence of a portion of the land into the deep sea," a fact that didn't surprise the emigrants, "as they were used to the workings of the floods."[16] Only seven of the clans made the journey; the other five were lost to the old country.

Whatever the reason for emigration, the result in each narrative is fragmentation of the original tribal body into two main groups: those who fled or were forced away, and those who remained in the broken homeland.

Both accounts give hope for mending that fragmentation, particularly the prophetic *Elohi,* when all the people combine as one again: "the race will, . . . according to the oracle of the stone of truth, containing the image, be driven to the seashore, where they will cross the waters[;] . . . landing in the old country from whence they came[,] will find the five lost clans, become reunited into twelve clans, into one people again."[17]

While the Longe version limits its attention to the internal struggles of the People themselves, the *Elohi* continues on to include conflict with other communities, from hordes of "dark terrible warriors" to, much later, land-hungry "white beings of the white canoes" who "put on [their] white skin for the purpose of deceiving"—all of whom bring pain and suffering to the People.[18] Yet only the latter "white beings" endure to torment the People and drive them from their long-sought homes. This is perhaps partially reflective of the story's post–Trail of Tears context, which focuses much more attention on the influences of external human forces than does Longe's eighteenth-century transcribed account of internal power conflicts.

The wisdom-bearers in each account watch as the old ceremonial knowledge is lost, either to the inattention of the younger people or because "the original [sacred] fire, the eternal and primitive, has been allowed to become extinct by destroying the wise *oocatene [uk'ten'],* . . . the wise of the tribe. He can never be found again until the other clans be found and the tribe reunites."[19] Yet while much is lost in these movements from the ancient territory, each account provides a possibility for community healing through principles of peoplehood: an engaged relationship with their new homeland, a rededication to the ceremonial history of the People, the renewal of kinship and familial ties, and a healing of the fractured language.[20]

Another common account of early forced removals focuses on bitter conflicts between the Cherokees and their neighbors. Wilma Mankiller elaborates on the theory that the Cherokees migrated south from what is currently known as the Great Lakes region:

> This theory is based largely on linguistic evidence, because we speak an Iroquoian tongue related to the languages of the Mohawks, Oneidas, Onondagas, Senecas, and Cayugas—all tribes that formed the Iroquois League. Others point to the tribal history of the Delawares, which describes a long, protracted war in which the Cherokees were ultimately driven south.[21]

Cherokee historian Emmet Starr connects the tradition of a southern origination firmly to that of the Iroquois/Delaware conflict:

> The Cherokees most probably preceded by several hundred years the Muskogees in their exodus from Mexico and swung in a wider circle, crossing the Mississippi River many miles north of the mouth of the Missouri River. . . .
>
> . . . The Cherokees were forced back from the vicinity of the Great Lakes and Atlantic by assailants, led by the valorous Iroquois, until they reached the southern Appalachian mountains, where they held all enemies at bay and created a neutral strip extending north to [the] Ohio river, on which no tribe or warrior dared settle with impunity.[22]

Whether by overpopulation, geological catastrophe, or conflict with other peoples, these accounts all point to the removal of the Cherokees from lands recognized as home, and all echo hauntingly across the ages to the later experiences of the People. This search for home—for a relational connection between the People and the spirits of a particular place—is never free from the geographies of removal, yet it is never eclipsed by those shadows.

Although the shadows gain shape and strength over time, they are always balanced by the ability of Cherokees to survive and thrive: the sacred fire endures to drive back the shadow, and the People continue on. The endurance of removal in our stories provides a touchstone for later Cherokee responses; although each removal is different in its way, each hearkens back to those that came before, and it is through the balance of ancient wisdom and adaptive response that we look for the strength to weather the threatening storm.

• 2 •

The Trail Where We Cried

After every major upheaval, we have been able to gather together as a people and rebuild a community and a government. Individually and collectively, Cherokee people possess an extraordinary ability to face down adversity and continue moving forward. We are able to do that because our culture . . . has sustained us since time immemorial.

—Wilma Mankiller (Cherokee Nation),
Mankiller: A Chief and Her People

*D*uring the late hot summer and early bitter winter of 1838–39, troops of the U.S. government, assisted by Georgia militia and White squatters, drove nearly sixteen thousand Cherokees from their homes into ill-equipped concentration camps, then herded them onto cramped boats or wagons for a brutal, thousand-mile trek to the Darkening Lands of the West, where the spirits of the dead reside. The Cherokees were subjected to physical abuse, disease, malnutrition, and dislocation from the lands they had known as home for ages. When the survivors arrived in their new "home"—the dumping ground for Eastern nations known as "Indian Territory"—they found themselves in conflict with their kin who had made the westward journey earlier (the Old Settlers and the Treaty Party), and with the Osages and other Indian nations who already called that land home.

Native people have employed and continue to develop a wide range of strategies in the defiance of colonialism, including open warfare (as with

Tsiyu Gansini and the Chickamaugas), subterfuge, conciliation and cooperation (the method used by Nanye'hi), withdrawal (the Chickamaugas, Old Settlers, Texas and Mexico Cherokees), and rhetorical appeals for alliances and confederations with other tribal nations (as with the Shawnee leader Tecumseh) or to Whites beyond the borders of the particular nation. These strategies are put into effect by grassroots activists fighting for sovereignty and self-determination, and they provide valuable intellectual nourishment for Native scholars seeking tribal voices that have been erased or silenced through much non-Native scholarship. The success of each of these strategies varies according to historical circumstances, tribal support, and individual skill, and this is nowhere more true than in the case of the Cherokee Nation in the nineteenth century and its Principal Chief, Guwi Sguwi, better known to his people and to history as John Ross.

To fully understand the Cherokee texts that emerged from the removal crises of the nineteenth century, one must understand the political and cultural histories that influenced those writers. Thus, as this study draws from a wide range of literary forms, so too does it draw from Cherokee histories and the rhetorics of the Eurowesterners who sought to displace/ erase the Cherokees from their ancestral lands. This chapter begins with an analysis of the ways in which Eurowesterners—most notably Thomas Jefferson, Andrew Jackson, and other *yoneg* politicians—constructed and justified their claims on the continent, particularly in response and reaction to the presence of Indigenous peoples.

From this contextualizing history, the chapter moves to the specifics of the Cherokee resistance. Most studies of the Cherokee voices of this period focus overwhelmingly on the writings of Elias Boudinot and John Ridge, who are generally depicted as tragic martyrs in a doomed battle for the survival of their people. Instead of contributing to a methodology that reinforces the notion of inevitable Indian erasure, this section examines the Removal through a red/white analysis, starting with the defiant Chickamauga rhetoric of John Ross, whose political centrality to the Cherokee struggle—and to subsequent narratives that reinterpret this chaotic era—has in many ways been overlooked or minimized in favor of attention to the Treaty Party of Boudinot and Ridge. Reading Ross within these Cherokee responses, rather than outside of them, gives us a better understanding of the more vexing issues of Georgia's campaign of ethnic cleansing and the Cherokee response.

John Ross, Principal Chief of the Cherokee Nation, ca. 1860s. Courtesy of the Research Division of the Oklahoma Historical Society.

Yet just as Ross's Chickamauga spirit is essential to such an understanding, so too is a Beloved reading of those who challenged his position by signing the controversial Removal treaty. Rather than focus on Boudinot, Ridge, and their allies exclusively, however, I look instead at the document that was at the center of the Cherokee controversy, the Treaty of New Echota itself. This document, though heavily influenced by the demands of U.S. treaty negotiators, is also deeply informed by the concerns of its Cherokee co-creators, and thus represents a remarkable (if troubling) complexity that places it firmly within the more difficult of Beloved Path texts. Though most often represented as nothing less than the physical embodiment of the Treaty Party's treachery, the Treaty itself is a much more complicated document of resistance, particularly in its concerns about the People's ultimate survival.

This chapter is not simply another study of this well-traveled history; it's a critical conversation between the individual and collective histories, writings, and struggles that emerged from a troubled time, and the relationship of those people and texts to other texts in the Cherokee literary canon. But the story of the Trail isn't just one of tragedy, although it's unmistakably that, too. It's also a story about defiance, about enduring the unimaginable and still continuing on, living to rebuild and emerge from the ashes sadder but stronger than ever. We are those people, survivors in this postapocalyptic frontier.[1]

For a long time I've been a Ross man. It has never been easy for me to fully forgive or understand the motivations of the Treaty Party, those men who signed the 1835 Treaty of New Echota, the document that would be used to legitimize the Cherokee Removal against the will of most of the Nation. When I read, years ago, that I might be related to three of the men suspected of killing John Ridge for his part in the Treaty, my heart swelled with pride and Cherokee patriotism.[2]

That puffed-up pride was short lived, however, when I came across another name in the records of that time, a name to which I was clearly related. The name was Charles F. Foreman, one of the signers of the Treaty of New Echota.

I don't know much about Foreman, only that he was the cousin to my lineal ancestor Charles Spears and, if the records are correct and the three brothers who executed Ridge are indeed of this line, possibly a cousin to men who brought vengeance on the end of a knife to one of his compatriots. The lives of most of those who signed the Treaty of New Echota are largely unknown to written history; some are forgotten by all but their descendants, and some known by name only.

I'd like to know what prompted these men to act as they did; I can imagine many scenarios and wonder which is most accurate. Why did Charles sign that hated document, a treaty that even the supporters disliked but signed anyway? Maybe he struggled with the quill, his hands shaking as he slowly wrote his English name in sharp, narrow strokes, but did it to save the People, to give the Nation a fighting chance in lands far from the greedy hand of White predators. But I can also see him pledging his unwavering allegiance to the colonial powers and boldly writing his name with a careful certainty and deliberation. Maybe he had a premonition about the thousands who would cough up bloody pestilence in the stinking swelter of concentration camps, or die on that frozen trek to the Ghost Country, the children and elders who would struggle their way through the stinging sleet, perhaps lingering in ravenous delirium with nothing but moldy bread and rank strips of maggoty salt pork to stave off the hunger. What of those who struggled their way through the fierce winds, leaving trails of scarlet behind their brittle, bandaged feet, if they were able to walk at all? Perhaps Charles truly believed that this trek was the best way to ensure Cherokee survival, with the alternative being even more horrifying, given the unending rapes, beatings, and murders that were taking place on a daily basis in their traditional lands by White squatters encouraged in their predations by the state of Georgia. Maybe total oblivion was the only alternative he could see. Did he look around at the men standing with him and share Major Ridge's understanding that he'd signed his own death warrant? Or did he focus his attention on the document, certain of his righteousness, clear on the necessity and the inevitability of such an action?

And what of Archibald, Joseph, and John Spear/Spears? I wonder what went through their minds as they and twenty-two companions rode in the early morning hours through the scrubby oaks of Indian Territory toward the house where John Ridge and his family were sleeping. Were they coming to appease the spirits of those who had died along the death march from the old lands, or were they here for bloodlust, to bring pain upon a man who had signed away the Nation? Were they coming as resolved representatives of tribal law, or as bitter vigilantes? As three men dragged Ridge from his bed, maybe it was the voices of the dead and the survivors of the

Trail that filled the air, or maybe it was the sound of Ridge's wife Sarah and their children screaming in horror. And as Joseph Spear plunged his knife into Ridge's nightshirted body again and again, shifting the blade across the dying man's throat until burning wet crimson spattered starkly in the dull gray morning before dawn, did he move with a warrior's grim necessity or with a murderer's killing joy? He might have understood Ridge's abiding love of the People, but he might just as easily have seen only his own mingled pain and love. Did the men let loose shouts of victory as they thundered away from the carnage, or did they weep?

RHETORICS OF REMOVAL

The idea of Removal for Cherokees is more than a symbol of erasure, the exile of a community from homeland and hearth. It's the physical, brutal, bloody attempted elimination of a people. Indians were removed during the early nineteenth century because the White leaders of the U.S. government and states like Georgia believed themselves entitled to Native lands and resources. They also saw the self-determination and sovereignty of tribal nations as threats to their own assertions of authority and superiority; indeed, the very idea that these "savages" would have the temerity to assert equal status as political sovereignties challenged the very notion of White supremacy. The justifications for this particular removal—*the* Removal—were many and varied. The assumption of cultural superiority coupled with a fear of a sophisticated and "civilized" Other in the contested territories, greed for land and wealth, and a desire to prove beyond any doubt that Whites were indeed the God-ordained inheritors of North America combined in a ruthless and brutal terrorism campaign against the Cherokees and all other Indian nations in the East.[3]

Of all the Indigenous nations that experienced forced relocation by the U.S. government in the first half of the nineteenth century, the Cherokee case has become the most infamous in the annals of North American history, even while it is largely glossed over in U.S. history texts. Non-Native commentaries—both past and present—largely focus on the moral tragedy of the Removal in two ways: 1) it is tragic only because the Cherokees were "civilized," and the dispossession of a "civilized" nation is a moral outrage, and/or 2) it is tragic because it casts a shadow over the popular mythology of the United States as an unwavering defender of human rights. During debate over the Indian Removal Act in May 1830, Vermont Representative

Horace Everett stated to the Georgia delegates who advocated Cherokee expulsion: "The evil, Sir, is enormous; the violence is extreme; the breach of public faith deplorable; the inevitable suffering incalculable. Do not stain the fair name of the country: it has justly been said, it is in the keeping of Congress on the subject."[4] This concern with the "fair name of the country" is echoed by British commentator Frances Trollope:

> If the American character may be judged by their conduct in this matter, they are most lamentably deficient in every feeling of honour and integrity. It is among themselves, and from themselves, that I have heard the statements which represent them as treacherous and false almost beyond belief in their intercourse with the unhappy Indians. . . . You will see them one hour lecturing their mob on the indefeasible rights of man, and the next driving from their homes the children of the soil, whom they have bound themselves to protect by the most solemn treaties.[5]

Even Helen Hunt Jackson, the famed late nineteenth-century critic of U.S. Indian policy, writes: "In the whole history of our Government's dealings with the Indian tribes, there is no record so black as the record of its perfidy to [the Cherokees]. There will come a time in the remote future when, to the student of American history, it will seem well-nigh incredible."[6] Her introduction to *A Century of Dishonor* makes clear her primary aim: "What an opportunity for the Congress of 1880 to cover itself with a lustre of glory, as the first to cut short our nation's record of cruelties and perjuries! the first to attempt to redeem the name of the United States from the stain of a century of dishonor!"[7]

The issue becomes *America's* shame, *America's* crime. Even though these writers and politicians clearly have concern for the suffering of the Cherokee people and other Indian nations, the Cherokees are removed again, this time through rhetorical erasure as the emphasis shifts to the stain of the glory of the United States and its international and generational reputation.[8] While this may have been the most effective strategy in response to a racist government—after all, given the administration's callous disregard for Indians, direct appeals to their human suffering wasn't likely to elicit as positive a response as the possible threat to the United States' good name—it's still one that fundamentally erases Indians from the discussion. The full human devastation of the Removal has largely been ignored or obscured due to a focus on the stained honor of the United States.[9] Such a rhetorical shift allows for the most heinous actions to take place with little more than a sad shrug, as Maureen Konkle notes: "sympathy for Indians has been the U.S. intellectual's pose ever since the early nineteenth century, helping to explain away as inevitable something that was not inevitable at all."[10]

To fully engage with Cherokee responses to varied removals, we must first engage with the issues surrounding the Removal itself, namely that U.S. policy that led to the Trail of Tears. It is in this legislation that the complicated patterns of *yoneg* paternalism and greed weave together into the noose that would slowly tighten around the Nation and its homelands.

The 1830 Indian Removal Act is a curious document, a guarantee of Native suffering masked in benign patronage. It asserts a willing exchange, an equitable trade of one land for another:

> it shall and may be lawful for the President of the United States to cause
> so much of any territory belonging to the United States, west of the
> river Mississippi, not included in any state or organized territory, and to
> which the Indian title has been extinguished, to be divided into a suitable
> number of districts, for the reception of such tribes or nations of Indians
> as may choose to exchange the lands where they now reside, and remove
> there.[11]

It says little about forced relocation, although the contentious debate within the press and in the hallowed halls of the U.S. Congress made clear the intentions and anticipated results of the Removal: the Indians would lose their lands and homes, and Whites would take them.

The very word "removal" in the Act implies choice: "it shall and may be lawful for the President to cause such aid and assistance to be furnished to the emigrants as may be necessary and proper to enable them to remove to, and settle in, the country for which they may have exchanged"; "*And be it further enacted,* That it shall and may be lawful for the President to have the same superintendence and care over any tribe or nation in the country to which they may remove."[12] It's the language of avoidance used by famed Oklahoma historian Grant Foreman, and an indication of the reasons he was summarily dismissed as a "Two Gun Historian" by the Cherokee historian Emmet Starr.[13] The process is shrouded in kindness, fair dealing, and generosity: land is "exchanged," Eastern Indians "remove" themselves ("to be protected, at their new residence, against all interruption or disturbance from any other tribe or nation of Indians"), and "aid and assistance" are provided to these apparently willing travelers.[14] The most obvious way of demonstrating Native accord is through treaties, ostensibly sacred contracts between equals but more often used by the United States as tools of White expansion forced upon nations weakened by war and disease. Here, the treaty-making process becomes a sign of White munificence and Indian agreement: "nothing in this act contained shall be construed as authorizing or directing the violation of any existing treaty between the United States and any of the Indian tribes."[15] No mention is made of the planned complicity between U.S. agents and state authorities in ensuring Indian acquiescence, even at the end of a bayonet or drawn tight with starvation and despair.

There are rhetorical cracks in the Act, however, through which the full measure of "removal" is revealed:

> it shall and may be lawful for the President to exchange any or all of such districts . . . for the whole or part or portion of the territory claimed and occupied by such tribe or nation, within the bounds of any one or more of the states or territories, where the land claimed and occupied by the Indians, is owned by the United States, or the United States are bound to the state within which it lies to *extinguish the Indian claim thereto.*[16]

In Section 3 of the Act, the language becomes even clearer: "*Provided always,* That such lands shall revert to the United States, if the Indians *become extinct, or abandon the same.*"[17]

The end is clear: Indian title will be "extinguished," and the land will "revert to the United States," by the choosing of the Natives or through their extinction. Andrew Jackson and other proponents of the Indian Removal Act had no intention of Indian survival. To them it was just a matter of time: whatever word they chose, "removal" meant "extermination."

CULTURAL CHANGE AND CHEROKEE RESPONSE

Since the first European invaders arrived in Native America, the Cherokees have been one of the most prominent nations in the Indian policies of every foreign power on Native soil, from interactions with the Spanish expeditions of Hernando de Soto (1540) and Don Pardo (1566–67), to fluctuating alliances with the French from the early eighteenth century through the so-called French and Indian War (ending in 1763), into diplomatic relations with England and its sociopolitical successor, the United States of America. The English and Americans were unlike the other colonizers in many ways, as Wilma Mankiller explains: "Cherokee culture shock occurred . . . when we came face to face with the English.

Although not as overtly cruel as the Spanish, they were at best an imperi-
alistic people capable of destroying entire villages of Cherokees, including
women and children."[18] In discussing the same issue, historian Roger L.
Nichols writes:

> Clearly the ease with which the colonists shifted their priorities from
> incorporating the tribal people to excluding or even destroying them
> indicates that many of the English never seriously considered including
> large numbers of Indians within their Virginia society. Other and later
> English settlements had similar experiences and in general, along with
> the Dutch, seemed to be the most unwilling of European invading groups
> to consider any real degree of fusion between the two cultures. To a de-
> gree the Spanish, and even more so the French, proved to be more accom-
> modating with their native neighbors. English determination to exclude
> or at best acculturate and marginalize native peoples proved a distinct
> difference from the French and Spanish North American colonial ac-
> tivities for a time. In addition, it indicated clearly to the Indians that the
> English despised them and their culture[s].[19]

Following English political custom (which dated from before Henry VIII's
revolt against Rome and was based in part on the papal Inter Cetera Bull,
which sanctioned and encouraged the political overthrow and forced conversion of pagan nations) the fledgling United States brought treaty making as the primary form of diplomatic interaction with Native nations.
With the English treaty process came the assumption of the "Doctrine of
Discovery," an ideology that split the world between humans—those who
professed Judeo-Christianity and, on occasion, Islam—and nonhumans, a
category that included everyone else. Those Christians who "discovered"
a land presumed a right to claim it and its resources, with treaties working
to verify the transaction for posterity.

Historian Robert A. Williams Jr. elaborates on this paternalistic tradition of extending White influence and authority over tribal nations:

> That tradition, originating in the medieval Catholic Church–sponsored
> Crusades to the Holy Lands, provides the historical context for under-
> standing the development of Indian rights under the white man's Indian
> law. That tradition denies "infidel" and "savage" tribal peoples the same
> basic human rights of self-determination recognized as belonging to the
> peoples who colonized them centuries ago. According to this tradition,
> and the white man's Indian law, indigenous tribal peoples rightfully be-

long under the superior sovereignty of the Western colonizing nations—even in the postcolonial world of today.[20]

All subsequent political relations were influenced by the assumptions and prejudices accompanying the Doctrine of Discovery.

The Cherokees were quick to recognize that this fact defined the way the fledgling United States interacted with them. By the late eighteenth and early nineteenth centuries, many Cherokee children, usually of mixed ancestry, were sent to be educated in White missionary schools and to learn about Eurowestern cultural practices. Once adults, their bicultural knowledge and skills made them a powerful force in the political arena and formidable opponents to U.S. Indian policy. Yet the drawbacks of such cross-cultural consciousness were numerous and significant:

> Cherokee society began to erode as many of the mixed-blood youths,
> swayed by their fathers' religion, decided the old ways were heathen and
> bad. Mixed-bloods exerted tremendous influence on the tribe. Eventually
> they would ascend to the ruling class in Cherokee society, replacing the
> old form of government. The purebloods and traditionalists tried to hold
> on, aware that the balance of our world was going awry.[21]

By the dawn of the nineteenth century, bicultural Cherokees were the dominant political force. And as Cherokee culture became more threateningly "civilized" to Whites, as more Cherokees were physically indistinguishable from their White neighbors, became Christianized, were White educated, and became plantation and slave owners, political pressures by the U.S. government and individual states—namely Georgia—became almost overwhelming.

For the Cherokees, nineteenth-century politics were to be dominated by Cherokees who were deeply acculturated into Eurowestern values, even while they asserted their cultural distinctiveness as Cherokees. The lives and traditions of the ceremonialists did not die, but neither did they eclipse the political prominence of the syncretic culture of the acculturated Cherokees, who often believed that Christianity and "advancement" on White terms were the only way to survive as a people.

ARCHITECT OF REMOVAL: THOMAS JEFFERSON

While many of the problems experienced by Native peoples in the Americas have been the result of the willful malevolence of the Invaders, the ostensible kindness and good intentions of many Whites have often resulted in greater devastation. Such is the case with Thomas Jefferson, third president of the United States and foundational apologist for Indian Removal. While some historians have claimed that Jefferson "lionized Indians" and "considered Indians at least the equals of white men," he made no secret of his belief in the superiority of White culture to that of Indigenous nations.[22]

A product of Enlightenment humanist education, Jefferson saw Indians as representing a primitivism that was destined to fade before Eurowestern civilization. In 1787 he published *Notes on the State of Virginia,* largely to disprove the writings of the official naturalist of the French court, Georges de Buffon, who claimed that all the indigenous species of North America, including Indians, were inferior to their European counterparts intellectually, physically, and sexually. Jefferson's defense was vigorous, yet it couldn't escape his belief that while Indians represented some of the best qualities of the "New World," they also inescapably represented the primal state of humanity. Such a state could only surrender to the supposedly superior culture of those Whites who could best integrate European civilization with American energy and drive.

To Jefferson, the future of Native America was embedded solely in its contribution to the vitality of White Eurowesterners; like many Whites of his time, he believed that environment played a profoundly generative role in biology. The most significant value of Indians in this model was their innate heartiness and strength; add that to the ambition and civilization of Whites, and you have the best presumed qualities of both groups creating a stronger citizenry that would be assimilated into U.S. sociopolitical values. Jefferson supported this generational erasure of Indian nations as both a naturalist and as a politician. According to historian Anthony F. C. Wallace, Jefferson "painted a picture for the Indians as a people doomed to extinction—not to biological extinction, but to cultural extinction as 'a separate people'":

> [Jefferson wrote:] "The ultimate point of rest and happiness for them is to let our settlements and their[s] meet and blend together, to intermix, and become one people. Incorporating themselves with us as citizens of the United States" will be the best way "in which their history may terminate." But he also envisioned other futures if the tribes refused. . . . One was for them to "remove beyond the Mississippi"; if any tribe should

be so foolhardy as to take up the hatchet, he proposed, "seizing the whole country of that tribe, and driving them across the Mississippi, as the only condition of peace."[23]

The language Jefferson uses is telling. He advocates the *terminat[ion]* of Native history, and presence, the *remov[ing]* and *driving* of the people from their *seiz[ed]* lands, and the full assimilation of Native America into both the Eurowestern body and body politic. Whatever the Indians' nobility, the ultimate fulfillment of their fate to Jefferson is through erasure or elimination. While Jefferson's rhetoric asserts the justice of the U.S. rebellion against a brutal British regime, any similar defiance by Native peoples is cause for land seizure and removal, as it obstructs the vanishing/breeding out that Jefferson imagines.

Jefferson was either oblivious to or unconcerned with the clear hypocrisy of this construction; he accepted that his presumption of authority was enforced by printing press and, ultimately, by the enduring symbol of U.S. diplomacy: gunpoint. He saw these policies as necessary to the physical survival of the Indians, but they would be dark-skinned versions of his yeomen farmers, not independent political and cultural bodies. And since "the Indian by nature possessed the capacity for civilization, Jefferson admitted the responsibility of the whites to aid the natives in attaining that great goal."[24] Yet he also knew that "this view of the ultimate result of continuous cessions of land . . . would upset the Indians if known to them."[25] Secrecy, fraud, and deception became the means by which Native lands were taken. When those methods failed, the military muscle of the U.S. government finished the negotiations.[26]

In 1802, under Jefferson's guidance, the United States and Georgia state governments

> [n]egotiated an arrangement by which Georgia surrendered its colonial charter claims to the region that now includes the states of Alabama and Mississippi. In compensation Georgia received . . . a pledge that the United States government would acquire all the lands held by Indians within the new boundaries of the state as rapidly as it could be done "peaceably" and on "reasonable terms."[27]

By the mid-1810s, Georgian authorities had tired of waiting for the federal government to fulfill its part of the agreement, and they began a campaign of terrorism and oppression to force the Cherokees to "remove" themselves to the West, which expanded dramatically after the Cherokees ratified their 1827 Constitution and asserted an unyielding determination to remain in their ancient homelands. Federal administrators and Indian agents frequently appealed to the Cherokees to surrender their homes and territories, but with little to show for it, except for a few small emigrations of conservative Cherokees who, tired of the incessant White intrusions, would become known as the Old Settlers.

By the late eighteenth century, the Cherokees had adopted and adapted many of the ideas and beliefs of Eurowestern society, including animal husbandry, the separation of governmental powers into a three-tier institutional system that loosely reflected the U.S. model, a written Constitution, Christianity, and African slavery. Pre-Invasion Cherokee wisdom traditions represent a complex cosmology of celebration as well as a significant tension between all living creatures, a delicate balance between the four-footed tribes, the plant nations, and humanity, as well as the many spirit beings of this world and those beyond. These traditions also included tales of the West: Usunhiyi, the Darkening Land (or Nightland), which was home to Tsusginai, the Ghost Country. The West was the home of the dead, a place of fear and darkness. It would live up to its name in the years to come.

THE CHICKAMAUGA NATIONALISM OF JOHN ROSS

The Cherokee Nation of the early nineteenth century consisted of strong minds, women and men who represented all facets of the society: full-bloods, mixedbloods, acculturated Cherokees, traditional ceremonialists, Christians, and syncretic individuals who balanced the two spiritual paths. Among them were the delegates who frequently traveled to Washington, D.C., on the business of the Nation, including the young merchant John Ross, who was rising through the ranks of Cherokee politicians. His connections to the political life of the Nation were practically inborn: the grandson of Tsiyu Gansini's close friend John McDonald, Ross was raised in the shadow of Chickamauga strength that accompanied the 1794 Treaty of Tellico Blockhouse, which ended the military resistance to the U.S. revolutionaries. E. Raymond Evans's words from chapter 1 are relevant here: "[i]t was [Tsiyu Gansini's] determined resistance that made the [treaty] workable. Having felt the strength of the Cherokees, the whites respected the treaty for more than a generation." John Ross came of age in that "period of peace," and was familiar with the unwavering spirit of Cherokee resistance.[28]

Ross was, to many White observers, a contradiction: only one-eighth Cherokee by racist blood quantum standards of the day, a lukewarm Methodist, and a wealthy plantation and slave owner who had only rudimentary knowledge of the Cherokee language. Yet he was a passionate Chickamaugan defender of Cherokee land tenure and was strongly supported by the majority of the Nation during his nearly forty-year service as Principal Chief, including the mass of fullbloods and ceremonial traditionalists. He was a shrewd and able leader for some of the most traumatic times in Cherokee history.

Politics alone were only part of Ross's ability: he was also a prolific and intelligent writer whose many letters on the subject of the Removal were widely disseminated among both the People and *yonegs*. His letters, written alone or in collaboration with other Cherokee leaders, are remarkable and underappreciated documents that synthesize Cherokee beliefs, history, rhetorical traditions, Christian philosophical ideals and concepts, Eurowestern and U.S. history, political thought, and the rhetoric of the fledgling Indian reform movement to further the cause for Cherokee self-determination and sovereignty.[29] Ross was a prolific writer, and only a very small sampling of his work is addressed here, but even this limited number, when read through the red/white lens of the Beloved Path/ Chickamauga consciousness, shifts the discussion away from his frequent tokenization as a "civilized" Indian chief whose Scots ancestry was the predominant source of his intellectual acumen to an analysis of his fully Cherokee political and intellectual response to an overwhelming threat against his people.

Ross was heavily involved in Cherokee politics from an early age, becoming a delegate to the United States at the age of twenty-nine. After traveling to what was then known as Washington City in 1819, Ross and the other delegates sent a letter on November 2 to President James Monroe expressing their strong opposition to the continued U.S. insistence that the Cherokees remove to the West. The Cherokee rhetorical principles of the letter are clear, beginning with the honorific title given to the president: Monroe is referred to as "Beloved Father" at the opening of each paragraph, reflecting the Cherokee tradition of addressing honored peace leaders as "Beloved," thus both honoring the president and reminding him of his responsibilities to the Indian nations over which he claims authority. For

Eurowesterners, such paternalistic rhetoric represented the Great Father as "do[ing] the best for the Indians according to white norms, which translated into protection, subsistence of the destitute, punishment of the unruly, and eventually taking the Indians by the hand and leading them along the path to white civilization and Christianity";[30] for the Cherokees, however, the concept was more one of mutual respect and acceptance of a culturally prescribed set of responsibilities and familial duties. Such was the philosophical underpinning that accompanied Cherokee responses to White encroachments.

One sign of Eurowestern values seeping into these responses, however, is through the emphasis placed on fathers as the ultimate authorities over their children. In traditional Cherokee communities, fathers were, in a strict sense, unrelated to their children (due to their different clans) and thus had little authority or influence over them; it was the brothers of the wife, most often the eldest brother, who fulfilled the role of male authority in children's lives. Thus, while some measure of traditional Cherokee family bonds are evident in these letters, so too are distinctly Eurowestern understandings of the relationship between fathers and their children. This isn't an erasure of traditional Cherokee values; far from it. Reading the letter through a Chickamauga lens provides a better understanding of the skillful rhetorical construction of the document.

The delegates open the letter explaining their high respect for Monroe's predecessor, Thomas Jefferson, and their contentious yet respectful relationship with him, noting that "Ten years have nearly passed since our warriors visited Washington City when [he] occupied the beloved seat"—highlighting the wisdom and dedication to justice that they expected from the highest political office in the United States, an expectation they would have for their own Beloved leaders. They then express their concern about treaty negotiations which connect the Cherokees of the Nation to their recently emigrated kindred in the West (who were, at the time, considered by many eastern Cherokees as having surrendered their ties to the Nation through the surrender of their ties to the land): "Our Nation is much involved in debt, a large portion of which has been contracted by the Arkansas Cherokees which we conceive in justice they ought to be accountable for and would therefore beg your interference." At the end of the letter, they close with assertions of loyalty to the United States and an optimistic faith in the man they six times call "Beloved Father," again reminding Monroe of his responsibilities to the Cherokees over whom he claims authority.[31] Monroe may have fashioned himself in the role of a benevolent Eurowestern patriarch, but as a Beloved leader who claims to represent the best interests of the Cherokees, he is here held accountable to the Cherokee values embedded in the old red/white political division.

In a letter to David Brown, a White friend and ally from Connecticut, dated 13 July 1822, Ross writes:

> Yet I cannot believe, that the Indians are doomed to perish in wretched-ness, from generation to generation, as they are approached by the white population, until they shall be annihilated from the face of the earth. Surely there are motives and feelings daily engendering, in the minds and hearts of the citizens of the U. States, which have never been heretofore pursued, or even felt, by them towards the Aborigines of this vast conti-nent. The small experiment made by the exertions of benevolent societies, through their faithful missionaries, has awakened the American people to a sense of what might be done to better the conditions of the Indian race. Under such circumstances, when the Indians are themselves seen to manifest a thirst to reach after the blessings and happiness derivable from civilized life, I cannot believe that the United States Government will still continue to pursue the luke-warm system of policy . . . to effect the purpose of removing nation after nation of them from the lands of their fathers into the remote wilderness.[32]

Ross was well aware of the frequent assertions of White southerners that Indians, being "savage" and "uncivilized," had no valid claims to land title; the Cherokee civilization programs were one way by which the People sought to nullify opposition to their claims. Here Ross's Chickamauga defiance turns the standard missionary story on end, pointing out the impact of Christian missionaries on the attitudes of White Americans: the missionaries are clearly bringing Whites to a "civilized" standard of justice and mercy, rather than having any appreciable influence on those Indians who are already seeking "the blessings and happiness derivable from a civilized life" for themselves.

In 1822, Ross and sixty-two other members of the Nation sent a letter to the U.S. Secretary of War, John C. Calhoun, which placed "before [him] the sentiments of the Cherokee People on the subject of the contemplated Treaty for the extinguishment of their title to lands for the benefit of the

State of Georgia."[33] Following tradition in dealing with political correspondents, Calhoun is addressed by the honored familial title of "Brother,"
and his good sense and humanity are appealed to throughout the letter:

> More land, more land, the whole limits of our chartered limits. Yes
> Brother such are their avariciousness, that we despair of ever sattisfying
> [sic] their desires, If we had but one mile square left they would not be
> sattisfied [sic] unless they could get it. . . . But we hope that the United
> States will never forget her obligation [the 1798 Treaty of Tellico] to our
> nation of an older date than her promises to the State of Georgia. . . .
> We hope and trust that they will improve and enjoy all the blessings of
> Civilization & refinement on this our soil which contains the relics of
> our Fore Fathers.[34]

The appeal is made, yet again, to the "advancements making by our nation
toward attaining that happy state of condition" as a marker of value in
Eurowestern terms, as well as the tribal ancestral connection to the land
that holds the bodies and spirits of their ancestors. The letter goes on to
assert Cherokee faith in the U.S. government and its promises, in spite of
the fact that "we have repeatedly complained to your Government of the
injuries done to our nation by our white Brethren of the frontier States, in
direct violation of the good faith solemnly pledged by your Government
to our nation in our Treaties," and ends with another appeal to the paternal
relationship between the United States and the Cherokees: "We cannot but
believe it would mortify the feelings of our Father & Brother to see our
children sinking into . . . bad practices and laying aside the excellent qualities which they are receiving from a moral & religious education."[35] Terms
of familial relationship bind the letter's recipient to the responsibilities of
such roles within Cherokee society, especially those of the elder "Brother,"
and they remind Calhoun that the "excellent qualities" long sought among
Cherokees by Jefferson and other politicians was threatened by the failure
of the United States to fulfill its obligations. Even claims of assimilation
became a way of defying further exploitation.

As land pressures increased, the Cherokees decided against sending
further messages through the unresponsive Secretary of War, instead directing a letter on 19 January 1824 to President Monroe himself. It contains
the now-standard address to Monroe as "Father" and provides an appeal to
the prejudices underlying the civilization policy: the Cherokees, they point
out, "are now progressing as rapidly as can reasonably be expected. . . . [A]s

the old stubbles disappear, the new sprouts will flourish under cultivation." Yet the tone quickly moves from an appeal to an assertion:

> The Cherokee Nation have now come to a decisive and unalterable con-
> clusion not to cede away any more lands, the limits reserved by them
> under the treaty of 1819. . . . We would now beg your interposition with
> Congress in behalf of your red children the Cherokees, so that provision
> may be made by Law to authorize an adjustment between the United
> States and the State of Georgia, so that the former may be released from
> the existing compact [of 1802] so far as it respects the extinguishment of
> Cherokee title to lands within the chartered limits of Georgia.[36]

But even reminders of U.S. promises to the Cherokees that they would forever remain in their homelands and appeals to policies directed toward the Cherokees for their "advancement" were not enough to stop the gathering clouds.

After Monroe's term came that of John Quincy Adams, and the tone of the Cherokees' letter to Adams is far more desperate than assertive, claiming that "The crisis seems to be at hand, which must forever seal [our] doom. Civilization & preservation, or dispersion & extinction, awaits [us]—and this government is the tribunal which must pass the sentence." Again, Ross and his cosigners assert that a "removal of the Cherokees, can never be effected with their consent, consequently if removed at all, it must be effected by such means, as would engender irreconcilable prejudices, and their dispersion and ultimate extinction would inevitably follow."[37] They here challenge the paternalistic insistence of the U.S. government that Removal was in the best interests of the Indian nations; the writers knew exactly what the consequences of such actions would be, as they were familiar with the struggles of the Old Settlers and other communities in the new Indian Territory. Similarly, Cherokee leaders knew well that their cause was gaining support in Washington and White urban centers in the northeastern states, through Ross's own substantial private correspondence to influential White friends, the efforts of Elias Boudinot, the longtime editor of the Nation's newspaper, the *Cherokee Phoenix,* and the activism of various missionaries; the Cherokees were the symbol of the success of the "civilization policy," and any crime against the Nation was a crime against the underlying premises of White civilization.[38] Gone is the language of "Beloved Father"; although mention is made of the President being a father to whom Indians "look for protection and preservation," the letter opens with the salutation of "Respected sir" and ends with "Your unworthy but most Obt Hble Servts." It's sadly clear by this point that kinship obligations are of little concern to the political lives of U.S. leaders.

The Cherokees weren't naive enough to believe that Adams was an ally: while the President would, just a few years later, champion the African slaves who had risen up against their captors on the slave ship *Amistad,* Adams's approach to Indians was another matter entirely:

> [I]n appropriating to ourselves their hunting grounds we have brought upon ourselves the obligation of providing them with substinence *[sic]*; and when we have had the same good fortune of teaching them the arts of civilization and the doctrines of Christianity we have unexpectedly found them forming in the midst of ourselves communities claiming to be independent of ours and rivals of sovereignty within the territories of the members of our Union. The state of things requires that a remedy should be provided—a remedy which, while it shall do justice to those unfortunate children of nature, may secure to the members of our confederates their right of sovereignty and soil.[39]

Adams was unhesitant about the "remedy" that would be required. He followed Jefferson's model, which was to move the southeastern nations on the other side of the Mississippi River, thus "out of the way of the intended trajectory of white settlement and civilization." This proposal would be embraced as a "genocidal national policy by his successor, President Andrew Jackson, after the U.S. Congress passed the Indian Removal Act of 1830."[40]

The forces against the Cherokees were fierce and well armed, and they were soon encouraged by the discovery of gold deposits on Cherokee lands claimed by Georgia. Rich farmland and the sudden publicity surrounding the gold strike helped motivate Georgia's greed, and the success of the Cherokees in the White-dominated culture of the South was almost an insult to the *yonegs* of that state, as historians Theda Perdue and Michael D. Green point out:

> The strides the Cherokees had made toward "civilization" convinced many Georgians that the Indians were strengthening their hold on their land. Well-educated Cherokees not only were more difficult to trick or intimidate, they shared many of the economic and social values of the Georgians. They understood the productive worth of their land, and the

marketplace held many of the financial attractions. Furthermore, it was hard for Georgians to point to Cherokee planters and businessmen and claim that God intended "uncivilized" Indian hunters should give way to "civilized" white farmers.

The federal program to "civilize" the Cherokees made many Georgians nervous but the Cherokees' 1827 constitution outraged them.[41]

In her compelling analysis of the Cherokee resistance, Maureen Konkle notes that Ross, along with the other leading Cherokee political figures of the time, "claimed to form a modern Indian nation, one that could not be characterized as representing a timeless prepolitical state of nature, but one that existed in time, as European nations did."[42] Rather than being static museum pieces or artifacts of a primal prehistoric era, Ross and his contemporaries asserted the inherent political right of Cherokees to be an adaptive, changing, and self-determining people fully within the flow of time, while still remaining true to their ancestral values and the land that was their inheritance. Georgia's response was to extend its authority over Cherokee lands and political affairs, thus defying both U.S. claims of exclusive control over Indian affairs as well as Cherokee social and political sovereignty.

Indeed, the blind rage with which the leaders of Georgia responded to the 1827 Constitution seems to mirror some of the current hysteria in the United States about same-sex marriage. It seems that it's not the difference of race or sexuality in these cases that causes such outrage, but rather the unashamed and unflinching affirmation of the *legitimacy* of that difference. When people marked as inferior "others" refuse to view themselves as second-class citizens, as toxic outsiders to the body politic, or as flawed and marginal participants in the community, the response by those who depend on that negative definition for their own fragile sense of superiority is rarely well reasoned or dignified—rabid and bigoted fury in defense of privilege is, sadly, a far more common response.

While the "civilization" policies of the United States had made extraordinary changes in Cherokee society, they didn't define the mass of the People, "three-quarters [of whom] were full-bloods and traditionalists [whose] resistance to missionaries was as strong and persistent as that in any tribe."[43] Most Cherokees still followed the traditions and cultural practices of their ancestors, and while acculturated Cherokees dominated the political sphere, the ceremonialists maintained the social structure and stability within the Nation in the face of increasing outside pressures—a strategy more tactical than coincidental, as it was precisely that population that most persistently and unequivocally opposed removal, and they provided Ross with his mandate of defiance. That Ross consistently held the support of these traditionalists during his nearly forty years as Principal Chief demonstrates his ability to balance a personal life far different from that of most of his kin and yet still sensitively represent their interests.

In 1828, Ross was elected Principal Chief of the Nation, and the following year Andrew Jackson, Indian-killer and advocate of the Removal itself, was elected President of the United States, bringing the Cherokee crisis to new heights of tension. In his address to the Nation on 13 October 1828, printed in both Cherokee and English, Ross discusses the Georgian campaign of terror, which increased tenfold due to the transformations of the Cherokee governmental structure, and the Cherokees' tense but hopeful relationship with the U.S. government:

> The circumstance of our Government assuming a new character under a constitutional form, and on the principles of republicanism, has, in some degree, excited the sensations of the public characters of Georgia, and it is sincerely to be regretted that this excitement should have been manifested by such glaring expressions of hostility to our true interests. By the adoption of the Constitution, our relation to the United States, as recognized by existing Treaties, is not the least degree affected, but on the contrary, this improvement in our government, is strictly in accordance with the recommendations, views and wishes of the Great [George] Washington.[44]

He then moves on to dissect the "pretended claim of Georgia to a portion of our lands," analyzing and dismissing all three arguments: discovery, conquest, and compact. Ross asserts the treaties between the Nation and the United States as the supreme law by which all the participants, including Georgia, must abide, and in doing so places the Cherokee Nation, as a *nation,* on equally sovereign status with the United States. There is no attempt to mediate or negotiate with Georgia or the United States on this point: reason, justice, and common sense alike reveal the truth of Cherokee sovereignty, and Ross fearlessly sets forth the facts in the full spirit of red resistance.

Ross had many duties as Principal Chief: arranging diplomatic negotiations with other Indian communities; deciding government policy while

maintaining a delicate harmony between often-fractious Cherokee con-
stituents; overseeing the Nation's budget and finances; maintaining respectful relationships with the conservative traditionalists as well as with
their more progressivist-minded kin; hosting both domestic and international guests; and leading numerous political delegations to Washington. Between these various tasks, Ross corresponded with a wide variety of
people, from antagonistic politicians to evangelical missionaries, report-
ers, tribal leaders, and philanthropic U.S. citizens. Despite the differences
in audiences, Ross always made the same arguments: the Cherokees were
the rightful aboriginal possessors of their homelands; Eurowestern "civilization" had contributed greatly to Cherokee culture and had brought
them from ignorance (though not "savagery," the term of choice among
racist *yonegs* at the time) to an understanding of the value and purpose of
Christianity and democracy; and, no matter how fierce the opposition to
Cherokee land title might be, in the end goodness and justice would win,
and the Cherokees would be free to remain in their homelands.

The enormous pressures brought against the Cherokees resulted in
deep divisions between supporters of emigration and those who advocated remaining in their homelands. Before the Trail of Tears, from "1791
to 1820[,] thousands of dissidents and traditionalists withdrew in true
Cherokee fashion, crossed the Great River [Mississippi], and preserved
what remained of traditional lifeways in a new world," yet the majority
of the Nation remained in their ancestral lands until all but about a thousand were driven out onto the Trail of Tears.[45]

The strong support Ross enjoyed from the mass of Cherokees was, in
fact, a major source of debate between pro- and anti-Removal advocates.
Pro-removal crusaders, including the signers of the Treaty of New Echota
who came to be known as the Treaty Party, maintained that Ross, due to
his education and apparent cunning, had deceived supposedly ignorant
Cherokees into believing that there was any hope in remaining in their
traditional lands. Later Ross antagonists in the aftermath of the Trail, including White lawyers Samuel C. Stambaugh and Amos Kendall, would
put it in much sharper terms and draw on many Eurowestern construc-
tions of Indian authenticity in their anti-Ross rhetoric:

> John Ross is an extraordinary man. With scarcely enough Cherokee
> blood in his veins to mark him as of Indian descent, he has made a
> large majority of his deluded countrymen believe that he is true to the

aboriginal race, while his full-blooded rivals are traitors to their country and their kindred. His ruling passion is avarice. He has been able to gratify it to an extent almost unprecedented, by playing upon the ignorance and prejudices of the Cherokees, and obstinately opposing the policy of the United States. "Cherokee difficulties" are the elements of his power.[46]

Members of the Treaty Party, even one as genuinely concerned for the welfare of the Cherokees as John Ridge, consistently constructed their traditional kin as ignorant, illiterate, and unsophisticated in thought; his father, Major Ridge, even though of the old Chickamauga towns, asserted that "an intelligent minority had a moral right, indeed a moral duty, to save a blind and ignorant majority from inevitable ruin and destruction."[47]

Ross, while certainly a problematic figure in some regards, always asserted a respectful self-knowledge inherent in the People; unlike Major Ridge and other members of the Treaty Party, he saw his leadership as a mandate granted to him by the community, not as a position that was his by virtue of intelligence or moral virtue. As Perdue and Green note:

> While Ross's position may very well have enhanced his family's fortune, as principal chief he understood something about the nature of Cherokee politics that members of the Treaty Party failed to recognize. Despite major changes in the structure of Cherokee government since the days of town councils in which everyone participated, political ethics remained relatively unchanged. Cherokees still believed that leaders should represent a consensus. This is precisely what Ross did: the vast majority of Cherokees opposed removal and wanted to resist the United States and Georgia at any cost. If Ross had followed any other course, he would have lost his mandate to govern.[48]

He represented the ceremonialists not as backward and ignorant, but as people able to comprehend the world and the issues they faced. In his role as their elected representative, he fought for their wishes and worked to bring all Cherokees together in their stance of defiance. In addition, the majority of the People were literate in Cherokee following the widespread introduction of Sequoyah's syllabary throughout the Nation in the 1820s, and White missionaries had taught many to read and write in English. These two facts, plus the wide availability of the *Cherokee Phoenix* and the general inclusion of interested males in the debates and speeches before the council, put the lie to any idea that the traditional people were either ignorant of the full measure of issues under consideration or that they were duped, hoodwinked, or deluded.

Their refusal to surrender their homelands and emigrate to the Darkening Lands wasn't due to foolishness; it was the collective exercise of nationhood by a people well aware of the possible consequences of such resistance, but fully determined to fight for their ancestral homeland. Theirs was a fully integrated balance of defiant Chickamauga consciousness coupled with a largely peaceful Beloved Path approach that gave the U.S. representatives the opportunity to live up to the virtues of their rhetoric.

The Georgian methods of terrorism, which were ultimately successful in driving the Cherokees onto the Trail of Tears, would be used against other nations and the Cherokees again in the future, in spite of "lawful" Native opposition and entreaties to the U.S. federal government. The process is captured succinctly in the story "The Dispossession" by Cherokee writer Glenn J. Twist, in which Rachel, the White wife of a Cherokee man, confronts a Georgia sheriff and his minions as they take possession of her home: "You and your pack of thieves will spend the week stealing the Indian possessions, and driving them into the woods where it's against Georgia law for them to even kill small game. Then on Sundays you-ens will sit stiff-backed in church singing praises to the Almighty."[49] The Cherokees fought the hypocrisies of Georgia and its land thieves all the way to the Supreme Court of the United States, losing the landmark case of *Cherokee Nation v. Georgia* in 1831 but winning *Worcester v. Georgia* in 1832.[50] President Jackson, staunch ally of the Southern cause who believed that "treaties with the Indians [were] an absurdity not to be reconciled with the principles of government,"[51] is reputed to have said in response to the ruling of *Worcester,* "John Marshall has made his decision; now let him enforce it."[52]

In his 14 October 1829 annual message, Ross continues the same line of argument as in the 1828 message, stating:

> In the archives of the U. States are to be found public documents that afford abundant evidence to convince the world that this land is the soil of the Cherokees, that the boundary line between this and the Creek Nation has been definitively and satisfactorily established, and this agreement recognized and sanctioned by the treaties with the United States, and also acquiesced in and observed on the part of Georgia.[53]

In this short note he again displays his rhetorical savvy; as the message is carried in the *Phoenix,* which was read with great interest among Whites in the northeast, particularly by those sympathetic to the Cherokee cause, Ross is asserting both indigenous land tenure and the U.S. recognition of that inalienable relationship—both Cherokee and *yoneg* authorities are cited, thus connecting to both primary audiences, local and extended, of the *Phoenix.*

Ross continues his discussion by focusing on the conflict looming in the future as a result of Andrew Jackson's election to the U.S. presidency:

> A crisis seems to be fast approaching when the final destiny of our nation must be sealed. The preservation and happiness of the Cherokee people are at stake, and the United States must soon determine the issue. . . . Our treaties of relationship are based upon the principles of the federal constitution, and so long as peace and good faith are maintained, no power, save that of the Cherokee Nation and the United States jointly, can legally change them. Much, therefore, depends on our unity of sentiment and firmness of action.[54]

The message hints at growing divisions within the Nation, and of Ross's attempt to maintain a unified front in the face of Georgian aggressions and growing U.S. hostility under the Jackson administration.

By 1835, the political leadership of the Nation, and indeed the citizens themselves, were split into two very distinct groups: the majority of Cherokees, including most of the remaining traditionalists, led by Ross, and what would come to be known as the Treaty Party, the most public of whom were Major Ridge and his son John, and half-brothers Elias Boudinot (Buck Watie) and Stand Watie. This latter group, in violation of the will of the vast majority of Cherokees but with the assertion that their actions were in the People's best interests, was the one to which the U.S. government's ambitious agents, General William Carroll and Reverend John F. Schermerhorn, went to gain nominal Cherokee approval of the Removal. Although vastly outnumbered by anti-Removal Cherokees, the Ridges, Boudinot, and Watie were among the names signed to the Treaty of New Echota on 29 December 1835, and it would be this document that would be recognized by the U.S. Senate—not the petitions bearing the signatures of nearly fifteen thousand Cherokees who opposed the Treaty.[55]

THE TREATY OF NEW ECHOTA:
THE BELOVED PATH NARROWS

In December 1835, Georgians were robbing, brutalizing, and killing Cherokees in increasing numbers. When Georgia conducted a land lottery of the
Cherokee homelands, thousands were left homeless and impoverished.
Death, raiders, and disease were making their way across the land. It was
a grim time for the Real People.

The Treaty of New Echota is a lengthy and complex document that
reflects the contrasting aims of both the Treaty Party Cherokees and the
representatives of the U.S. government. Although often vilified for their
betrayal, the actions and motivations of the Treaty Party are far more
complicated than generally acknowledged. The process that led to the
signing of the Treaty was dogged by Jackson's threats and Schermerhorn's
deceit, as well as by sharp tensions and occasional violence between those
who opposed removal and those who reluctantly supported it. The Treaty
was signed in New Echota, the capital named for the ancient peace city,
Chota, as an attempt to impress upon the Nation that this was a legitimate
text. Yet the general sentiment against the Treaty was so strong that the
prelude to the articles is a multipage history of the document that works
toward numerous aims and audiences.

The prelude is, in fact, the part of the document most clearly emerging from the Cherokee representatives themselves, whereas the terms and
conditions that follow have none of the passion or desperate claims of legitimacy present in the prelude. The language is similar to that of Elias
Boudinot's own writings of the time, with the same assertions and appeals. In the prelude to the Treaty of New Echota, the overall emphasis is
on the Treaty Party's willingness to do that which Ross was unwilling to
do: guarantee the survival of the Nation by agreeing to the U.S. government's "liberal overtures."

The Treaty Party members, along with Schermerhorn and General
Carroll, had a number of problems to overcome in the drafting of this
document. The first was the emphatic and almost unanimous Cherokee
claim that the push for removal was unjust. This is countered by the opening paragraph of the document, in which they erase any mention of the
social context for the Treaty—the murders, threats, and land theft imposed on Cherokees by the *yoneg* squatters of Georgia—and instead assert
that the Cherokees are willingly removing themselves to the West:

and with a view to reuniting their people in one body and securing a per-
manent home for themselves and their posterity in the country selected
by their forefathers [the Old Settlers] without the territorial limits of the
State sovereignties, and where they can establish and enjoy a government
of their choice and perpetuate such a state of society as may be most con-
sonant with their views, habits and condition; and as may tend to their
individual comfort and their advancement in civilization.[56]

Their second difficulty was John Ross, and his position as Principal
Chief and representative of the Nation. To undermine his legitimacy, they
briefly assert his refusal to "submit propositions as to [the Senate's offer of
five million dollars for the removal process] to be arranged in a treaty."[57]
By placing themselves as the patient and reasonable negotiators, with Ross
and his allies characterized as obstinate, greedy, and irresponsible, the
Treaty Party and the U.S. commissioners obscure the unceasing and hostile coercion of the decade-long process and the growing threats of bloody
and brutal reprisals for Cherokee defiance.

This attempt to undermine Ross's position is followed immediately
after by an endorsement of the primary Treaty Party members, with the
names of John Ridge and Elias Boudinot first among them. The difficulty
here is to give the Treaty Party members the legitimacy that they seek to
strip from Ross. Their position, however, is visibly unstable in the document. Thus, in the fifth paragraph of the prelude, they note that they "represented that portion of the nation in favor of emigration to the Cherokee
country west of the Mississippi" and "entered into propositions for a
treaty." Following that dispassionate note, they then assert at length the
claims of *necessity* that drive the Treaty Party to negotiate with the United
States:

> And whereas the Cherokee people, at their last October council at Red
> Clay, fully authorized and empowered a delegation or committee of twen-
> ty persons of their nation to enter into and conclude a treaty with the
> United States commissioner then present [Schermerhorn], *at that place or
> elsewhere* and as the people had good reason to believe that a treaty would
> then and there be made or at a subsequent council at New Echota which
> the commissioners it was well known and understood, were authorized
> and instructed to convene for said purpose; and since the said delega-
> tion have gone on to Washington city, with a view to close negotiations

there, as stated by them notwithstanding they were officially informed
by the United States commissioner that they would not be received by the
President of the United States; and that the Government would transact
no business of this nature with them, and that if a treaty was made it
must be done here in the nation, where the delegation at Washington last
winter *urged it should be done for the purpose of promoting peace and harmony among the people*; and since these facts have also been corroborated
to us by a communication recently received by the commissioner for the
Government of the United States and read and explained to the people in
open council and therefore believing said delegation can effect nothing
and since our difficulties are daily increasing and our situation is rendered more and more precarious uncertain and insecure in consequence
of the legislation of the States; and seeing no effectual way of relief, but in
accepting the liberal overtures of the United States.[58]

The rhetorical claims made in this paragraph are complex but consistent.
First, they note that the Nation agreed to "authorize and empower a delegation or committee" to draft the terms of the Removal. This is the first
claim of legitimacy. This is followed by a point-by-point assertion that the
people of the Nation knew a treaty would be made, that it would be made
in the Nation, and that Ross himself had insisted that all negotiations take
place in the Nation itself. The chief's attempts to undermine the treaty negotiations in Washington City are thus presented as not only hopeless, but
as contradictory to his own long-held position. This is the second claim of
legitimacy, and from it emerges another attack on Ross's own credibility.
The final claim of legitimacy in the paragraph is an appeal to the good
sense and frustrations of the People.

It is in this passage—"since our difficulties are daily increasing and our
situation is rendered more and more precarious uncertain and insecure
in consequence of the legislation of the States"—that the document comes
closest to naming the veiled but unmistakable influence of the Indian
Removal Act and of hostile U.S. Indian policy. In that moment, the members of the Treaty Party most clearly reveal their own frustration, fear, and
helplessness.

They then move on, noting that Carroll and Schermerhorn "were appointed commissioners on the part of the United States, with full power
and authority to conclude a treaty with the Cherokees east and were

directed by the President to convene the people of the nation in general council at New Echota." Yet the document shifts tone again as they note that Schermerhorn and Carroll

> informed [the Treaty Party] that the commissioners would be prepared to make a treaty with the Cherokee people who should assemble there and those who did not come they should conclude gave their assent and sanction to whatever should be transacted at this council and the people having met in council according to said notice.[59]

The threats are now unmasked. The United States has tired of waiting for Cherokee consensus, and it will have its way. Those who bow to its will might be spared, but those who resist will be swept away. The Treaty Party has made the choice. They will try to negotiate the best terms possible within the limits they have been given. It is a bargain with the devil— damnation either way—and they know it.

The rest of the document is a general listing of terms for the Removal itself, but certain articles are noteworthy in a Beloved Path reading, as they quite clearly highlight the concerns the Treaty Party had for their people and the strange new world in the West. Article II outlines the new territories and the rights of the Cherokees for self-determination. This article, however, also acknowledges the presence of other Indian nations and hints to conflicts with their soon-to-be neighbors, with particular emphasis on the Osage boundaries. Conflicts between the Old Settlers and the Osages were already bloody, and the tensions would no doubt continue to be, as is hinted in article IV, which would be the source of much conflict between Osages and Cherokees, as it "extinguish[es] for the benefit of the Cherokees the titles to the reservations within their country made in the Osage treaty of 1825 to certain half-breeds."[60] As the Treaty was intended to secure Cherokee political autonomy, the document drafters included two articles—V and VII—to assert both the independence of the Cherokee Nation and a possible diplomatic delegate to the House of Representatives, "whenever Congress shall make provision of the same."[61]

The drafters' belief in the ultimate nobility of the United States (a quality that Ross himself shared) emerges with painful clarity upon reading some of the articles of the Treaty. They sought schools, "useful farmers mechanics and teachers for the instruction of Indians according to treaty stipulations,"[62] a fund of $50,000 "expended towards the support and education of such orphan children as are destitute of the means of subsistence,"[63] and even a disability annuity for those warriors wounded in the service of the United States against England. Their attention to the rightful repayment of all Cherokee losses is highlighted by the bulk of the text, which details the multiplicity of losses the Treaty Party saw looming for the Nation. They were clearly concerned about the growing poverty among Cherokees—largely as a result of increasing land incursions by White squatters—and they attempted to rectify this situation as much as possible in the terms of the Treaty.

The Treaty Party members walked a narrow path on 29 December 1835, when they signed this contested document. They saw few choices available to them, and they shared with Ross a certainty that, eventually, the United States and its citizens would honor the ideals of "civilization" and Christianity they had imposed on the Cherokees. The careful, detailed terms of the Treaty are clear indications of Native self-determination. Schermerhorn and Carroll were largely unconcerned with the problems of the Nation; their intent was simply to get the Cherokees to sign a removal treaty and abandon the territory claimed by Georgia. Given the growing crisis with increasingly brutal White land-grabbers, and the hopelessness they perceived in insisting on remaining in their homelands, the Treaty Party members sought to arrange as beneficial a deal as possible, something that would protect both wealthy Cherokees (thus the "spoliations" allocations) and those who were impoverished. The Beloved Path is a sometimes-treacherous balance of Cherokee autonomy and adaptation to White assimilative demands, and the story of the Treaty Party is an example of this delicate negotiation. Konkle points out that none of the "'elite' and 'acculturated' Cherokees . . . ever denied being Cherokee, abandoned the nation, or accepted subordination to whites."[64] Theirs was an attempt to remain strong *as Cherokees* in a land outside of the immediate influence of the United States, where the Nation could realize its greatest civilized strength.

Yet there is another side to the story as well, one that highlights the degree of self-interest within the Treaty Party:

> While the Treaty Party acted partly out of concern for the suffering of
> the Cherokee Nation, some members had less than pure motives for try-
> ing to subvert the Cherokee national government. . . . Since the Cherokee
> government controlled much of the economic activity in the Nation, some
> suspected Ross and others of using political power to further their own

economic interests. Furthermore, several Treaty Party members had been defeated in the 1830 elections, and John Ridge believed that only the subsequent ban on elections, caused by the extension of Georgia law over the Nation, prevented him from defeating Ross in a contest for principal chief. A willingness to negotiate also brought members of the Treaty Party some tangible rewards—the Georgia governor exempted the property of the Ridges and Boudinot from the land lottery. A fair share of jealousy, thwarted ambition, and self-interest, therefore, motivated the Treaty Party.[65]

The members of the Treaty Party moved to the western lands shortly after signing the contested document, taking with them much of their personal property (which was forfeited by those who remained to defy the United States and Georgia) and suffering comparatively little inconvenience during the journey—unlike those who were driven onto the Trail of Tears, who were tormented by disease, brutal weather, poor nutrition, fatigue, abuse, and other difficulties. Article XII names John Ridge and Elias Boudinot among the committee to determine "pre-emption rights" and "to select the missionaries who shall be removed with the Nation"; although Ross and a few of his supporters are named as well, the members of the Treaty Party have clearly asserted their own legitimacy as political leaders, and this claim is firmly embedded in the Treaty itself.[66]

The Treaty Party Cherokees knew their lives were in danger in the East, for it was a capital crime among Cherokees to sell the Nation's communally held lands without approval of the representative Cherokee government; in fact, Major Ridge had personally helped execute the Cherokee chief Doublehead in 1807 for precisely that crime, an irony that did not escape him when he signed the Treaty. As he placed his mark to the document, he is reported to have said, "I have signed my death warrant."[67]

THE CLOUDS BURST

John Ross had far more faith in the strength and endurance of the Cherokees than did the members of the Treaty Party, although he and his opponents shared a belief in the promise and possibilities of Eurowestern democracy and civilization for the Nation. In his 14 April 1831 address to the People, Ross wrote, "Our cause will ultimately triumph. It is the cause of humanity and justice. It involves a question of great magnitude &

one of the most extraordinary character that has ever been agitated in the United States."[68] With the Removal looming, Ross appealed to Jackson's presidential successor, Martin Van Buren, protesting the Treaty of New Echota as both a man dedicated to justice and a leader familiar with the concerns and welfare of his people:

> As the Principal Chief of the Cherokee nation, I say to the First Magistrate of the United States of North America, the interests of your people cannot be dearer to you, than those of mine are to me, of mine, whom I should be recreant were I to uphold less firmly now, when they are so feeble, so broken and so unfriended. I am told on all sides that if I will advise the Cherokee nation to remove forever from their homes during untold ages, within the lines at present encircling your comparatively new republic, they will remove and great and desolating troubles will be prevented.[69]

While at first glance it may appear that Ross is acquiescing to Removal, a closer look at the language defies that assumption. Ross notes that the Cherokees have been in this land for much longer than their Eurowestern counterparts—"during untold ages" versus the "comparatively new republic"—and that this land demand will clearly not be the last one, as evidenced by the "lines at present encircling" the United States. The rhetoric of Manifest Destiny is heavy in the air; the United States has slowly but quite clearly been extending its grasp over more and more territory. This will not be the last time the Cherokees will be forced to deal with this predator's unending hunger, and Ross clearly recognizes the threat. As already demonstrated numerous times, the promises of the United States are weak and transient, torn apart by political expediency and naked self-interest, but the love of Cherokees for their homeland is ancient and enduring. If they do not succeed in their stand now, here in the home place of their greatest strength and grounded memory, what will stop the land-hungry young settler-state from claiming their newly held lands to the west? Voluntary emigration is just a delay of the confrontation. For Ross, this is more than just a stubborn stand; this is the greatest chance the Cherokees have to fully thwart the U.S. theft machine, by appealing to the philosophies and creeds that stand as the ironic underpinning of the United States.

Under the false auspices of Cherokee solidarity, the delegations charged with creating the Treaty of New Echota returned to Washington, D.C., where the Treaty, though bitterly contested by the Cherokees, was ratified by

Congress in 1836. Fearing the wrath of their anti-Removal kin, most members of the Treaty Party traveled west shortly after signing the Treaty, while most Cherokees remained in the East, hopeful of a positive resolution.

Yet the clouds were dark on the horizon, and it was difficult for any to deny the stark significance of their situation: the Removal had begun.

• 3 •

Unruly Cherokees in the Indian Territory

But if, contrary to all expectation, the United States shall withdraw
their solemn pledges of protection, utterly disregard their plighted
faith, deprive us of the right of self government, and wrest from us
our land—then, in the deep anguish of our misfortunes, we may
justly say, there is no place of security for us, no confidence left
[that] the United States will be more just and faithful towards us
in the barren prairies of the West, than when we occupied the soil
inherited from the Great Author of our existence.

—Chief John Ross, Annual Message
to the Cherokee Nation, 1829

The white men had literally summoned the red men before them
to show cause, if any they had, why their name, as a people, should
not be expunged from its ancient place upon the annals of time;
why their national history, coming down through a constant series
of centuries and redolent with so many cherished traditions, should
not be brought, once and for all, abruptly to a close.

—DeWitt Clinton Duncan (Too-qua-stee) (Cherokee),
"A Momentous Occasion," 1897

*I*n the last years of the nineteenth century, the U.S. government sought
yet again to fully eliminate the so-called Indian Problem—and pave the
way for Oklahoma statehood—by imposing an allotment of the tribally
held lands of Indian Territory for the benefit of White settlers. Allotment—
like most U.S. policies relating to Indians—was ostensibly intended to

bring Indians to the level of civilization enjoyed by the U.S. citizenry. The irony was, of course, that the autonomous republics of the Five Civilized Tribes, especially the Cherokees, had long exceeded the "civilization" of their White neighbors:

> the Cherokee Nation, by the time of Oklahoma statehood, had produced more college graduates than did its neighboring states of Arkansas and Texas combined. It had created perhaps the world's first free, compulsory, public school system. It had built the first institutions of higher learning west of the Mississippi River, the Cherokee National Male and Female seminaries. The Nation continued to publish its own bilingual newspaper, which it had been doing since 1828. A Cherokee, Elias Boudinot, wrote the first novel ever penned by an American Indian. A Cherokee, E. D. Hicks, installed the first telephone line west of the Mississippi River.[1]

In spite of these accomplishments, the Five Tribes and their Indian neighbors were on land that was coveted by Whites, and that greed superseded any stated desire to help the Indians "civilize" themselves. The allotment policy would devastate the tribes of Indian Territory, and it would undermine decades of political, cultural, educational, and economic growth, forcing many to revisit the horrors of the Removal.

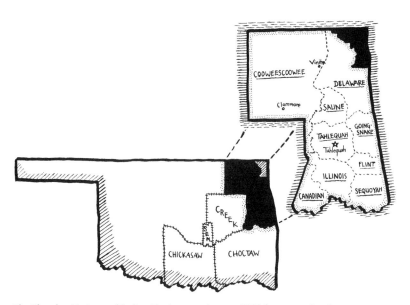

The Cherokee Nation and Indian Territory on the eve of Oklahoma statehood, 1906.

Put into force nearly sixty years after Chief Ross made the grimly pre-scient comment above, the General Allotment Act of 1887 stands as one of the most traumatic pieces of U.S. legislation ever imposed upon the Cherokees, second only to the Indian Removal Act of 1830. Most often called the Dawes (Severalty) Act for its sponsor and most vocal advocate, Senator Henry L. Dawes of Massachusetts, the Act's impact was sweeping and revolutionary, as Wilcomb Washburn notes:

> The act did not simply rearrange the landholding system of the Indians. It dealt, sometimes only in a tentative or partial way, with all aspects of the relationship between white men and red: it determined how much land the red man would retain and how much the white man would ac-quire; it determined whether past treaties would be honored or violated; it determined how much authority the tribe would retain and how much the Indian individual would acquire; it determined what type of law the Indian would be subjected to; and it determined whether or not he would become an American citizen or remain an alien in his own country.[2]

M. Annette Jaimes (Juaneño/Yaqui) reveals the effects of the allotment period and its aftermath even more starkly, noting that "between 1887 and 1934, the aggregate Indian land base within the U.S. was 'legally' re-duced from about 138 million acres to about 48 million."[3] Further, "the al-lotment process itself had been manipulated in such a way that the worst reservation acreage tended to be parceled out to Indians, while the best was opened to non-Indian homesteading and corporate use."[4] These are just a few of the debilitating effects of allotment on the Indian nations, and always with the assertion that the process was being done to "help the Indians"—an all-too-common claim by many Whites and assimilated Natives who would erase Indian agency and replace it with a paternalism that generally ends with White enrichment at Indian expense.

Although allotment was imposed on the tribes against their will, there were strong resistance movements. For the Cherokees, in the Chickamauga tradition, the old ceremonial Kituwah society emerged again as the Night-hawk Keetoowah Council under the leadership of Redbird Smith.[5] Chero-kee historian Emmet Starr writes:

> In 1895 when the question of the allotment of lands to the members of the Five Civilized Tribes was being agitated, the ancient Keetoowahs became very active in opposing the proposed change. In this, however, all the

Keetoowah element [ceremonialists and Christians alike] were united in their opposition to any speedy change. From this time to 1900 the following of Redbird Smith were designated universally as the "Nighthawk Keetoowahs" because of their vigilence [sic] in their activities.[6]

Among the Muskogee Creeks, another of the Five Tribes removed to Indian Territory by the U.S. government, the participants in the traditionalist movement were named the Snakes for their leader Chitto ("Snake") Harjo; their resistance was in many ways more interventionist than that of the Keetoowahs, as they "sent out their Light-horsemen to inflict corporal punishment—whippings—on those who accepted allotment deeds."[7] They, like the Keetoowahs, continued to gather and deliberate as tribal nations even when the treaty-recognized governments of their respective tribes had been "extinguished" by the U.S. government. As they didn't recognize the United States as the final arbiter of their identities or political and social structure, they continued life as best they could, and the fires of peoplehood—and nationhood—were never dampened.

Following allotment, many Indians, both traditionalist and acculturated, utilized a variety of strategies in resisting White cultural and political encroachments. With "official" tribal sovereignty abolished by U.S. federal decree, Native communities engaged in rhetorical practices, both subversive and overt, of maintaining cultural distinctiveness and sociopolitical sovereignty. Four of the most accomplished strategists in this rhetorical battle for nationhood were mixedblood citizens of the Cherokee Nation, and all lived at various times in the Cooweescoowee District in or around what is now Claremore and Vinita, Oklahoma, and all likely knew one another directly through family connections. This chapter will examine the work of these remarkable writers and examine the ways by which they asserted their varied understandings of what it was to be Cherokee in a time when the very notion of tribalism was heavily under siege.

The first of these writers, Rollie Lynn Riggs (1899–1954), was a Cherokee playwright and poet whose most famous work today, *Green Grow the Lilacs,* is best known in its musical form, Rogers and Hammerstein's *Oklahoma!* A popular and acclaimed contemporary of some of Broadway's greatest playwrights, including Eugene O'Neill and Tennessee Williams, Riggs sought to give a liberated voice to the marginalized throughout his brief but productive career. What is revealed through an analysis of his most personal work, *The Cherokee Night,* is a man struggling with the legacies of his people and his homeland, seeking to walk the Beloved Path but ultimately failing to find the balance the Path demands.

The second of these strategists was John Milton Oskison (1874–1947), an Ivy League–educated writer, journalist, and Native rights advocate whose literary output, like that of Riggs, focused heavily on the Indian Territory of his youth, while occasionally moving beyond Cherokee concerns to examine the struggles of other Indian peoples. Although mournful nostalgia and foreboding often haunt Oskison's imaginative landscapes and the Indians within them, both his published and unpublished work reveal a writer firmly committed to the Beloved Path in his invocation of the courageous spirit and enduring righteousness of Indian nationhood.

Will Rogers (1879–1935), comedian and social commentator who was arguably the most popular man of his era in spite of his often scathing criticism of oppressive American ideologies and practices, is the third figure in this study. He has often been portrayed by White scholars as the prototypical White American "everyman," yet a closer reading of his life and his writings reveal a Cherokee man who walked firmly on the Beloved Path (with more than a bit of Chickamauga fierceness) and skillfully negotiated the balance of accommodation and cultural pride in ways that evaded both Riggs and, to a lesser degree, Oskison.

The final subject of this chapter is Emmet Starr (1870–1930), the pioneering historian whose life work was dedicated to chronicling the history, cultural traditions, and kinship ties of his fellow Indian Territory Cherokees. He worked with the fervent hope that his histories would ensure the Nation's survival but, according to some scholars, Oklahoma statehood shattered his spirit, and he died alone in a St. Louis boarding house convinced of his failure. My reading of both his reasons for traveling to St. Louis and of his final years is significantly different from these earlier interpretations. He was anything but a broken man: he was a committed advocate for the People, the embodiment of modern Chickamauga consciousness.

Each of these men brought a geographic connectedness to their work, a consciousness and conscience rooted in the land of their birth. All spent their final days beyond the borders of the Cherokee Nation (Riggs, Rogers, and Oskison having lived the majority of their adult lives outside Oklahoma), but they saw themselves as the products of that distinctive land—Indian Territory of their births, Oklahoma in their adulthood. Each understood his mixed heritage differently, but all saw their Cherokee ancestry as central to their selves. It is through this knowledge that all came to express themselves as artists and social critics. As citizens of the Cherokee Nation and then inheritors of the statehood legacy of Oklahoma, Riggs, Oskison, Rogers, and Starr reflected on the injustices inflicted by White Americans on Indian communities, and all sought ways of effectively redefining and reimagining Indian lives, histories, and identities away from the self-serving distortions of dominant White political and social systems. Their success was varied, but all worked toward articulating Cherokee peoplehood in a historical period of great chaos and uncertainty.

RUNNING FROM HOME, FLEEING HOMEWARD: LYNN RIGGS'S *CHEROKEE NIGHT*

Not all Indians have been able to fully resist colonial intrusions and the dehumanizing social, political, and ideological policies of White supremacy, at least without experiencing substantial trauma. Displacement from one's family and community, land base, culture, spiritual ceremonies and worldview, language, history, and even one's place in the cosmos can often be overwhelming. This first section will focus on one such figure—the Cherokee playwright Lynn Riggs—and his battle for self-affirmation as an outland Cherokee far from the land base of the Nation, as a gay man in the first half of the twentieth century, and as an Oklahoman self-exiled to the artistic centers of the United States. By the end of his life, Riggs had experienced multiple levels of dispossession: from his homeland in Indian Territory/Oklahoma; from the Cherokee community and its traditions; and, ultimately, from himself.

Lynn Riggs, though always referring to himself as an Oklahoma Cherokee and spending his life seeking to understand the people of his home state and to "publish their humanity. . . . for them and for their descendants, falteringly, imperfectly, incompletely," lived nearly all that life far from Oklahoma.[8] He was often depressed, a complex and elusive man whose artistic ambitions were matched only by his insecurity. He was also a largely isolated gay man in the first part of the century, a time of brutal criminal and social sanctions against homosexuality, particularly during the height of his career in the 1930s and 1940s. According to historian John Loughery, it was a country at that time marked by a desperate desire "to limit or erase homosexual experience in the public sphere, render-

Lynn Riggs, 1922. Courtesy of the Joseph H. Benton Collection, Research Division of the Oklahoma Historical Society.

ing it unmentionable outside of specialized contexts and therefore almost unthinkable. It was a naïve, wasteful, and life-denying enterprise, but no less vigorously prosecuted for that."[9] Craig Womack extends this context to the complexities of Riggs's own life, noting that the playwright was "a closeted gay man dealing with an incredibly oppressive societal realm that sanctions what a gay man can say, sanctions what an Indian can say, and contributes to the silence and voicelessness that Riggs attributes to Oklahomans and to the Oklahoma artist trying to describe them."[10]

Most of Womack's insightful examination of Riggs's work focuses on the complexity of sexuality and racial identity in the latter's plays and poems; Jace Weaver, in both *That the People Might Live* and in his foreword for the reissue of *The Cherokee Night,* examines the Cherokee substance both of this play and of his most famous work, *Green Grow the Lilacs.*[11] For the purposes of this study, however, I would like to focus this Beloved reading primarily on Riggs's Cherokee identity and the ways in which removal, via the allotment policies of the U.S. government, contributed to his vexed relationship to the cultural traditions of his people, thereby adding to the despair he experienced as a closeted gay man who was, for most of his life, very much alone.

Riggs always sought, in both his life and work, a place of security, a sanctuary that was denied to him as much by the disenfranchisement of Indians and demonization of homosexuality as by the very real shattering of the collective land base and much of the sovereignty of the Cherokee Nation of that time. Unfortunately, as Womack explains, "a huge part of Riggs's life as an Indian man and as a gay man was either left unexplored, coded, or, worse, rejected in favor of endorsement of dominant white [and straight] history."[12] Such is the legacy of Lynn Riggs: a life half lived, dominated by fear and uncertainty, one in which isolation reigns supreme. It's a cautionary story, in some ways, about the corrosive impact that cultural and erotic dislocation can have on those with a sensitivity to the mysteries of the world. His story also strikes a note of warning about the dangers that such dislocation can have on the health of a people when any of its members are suffering.

Rollie Lynn Riggs was born in 1899, shortly after the passage of the Curtis Act, which extended the provisions of the Dawes Act over the previously excluded lands of the Cherokees, Chickasaws, Creeks, Choctaws, and Seminoles, and provided for the surveying and allotment of all Indian Territory lands of the Five Tribes.[13] When his mother Rose (Rosie) Ella Riggs died of typhoid fever in 1901, young Lynn, as an enrolled tribal member, shared an allotment inheritance in the Claremore area with his two siblings.[14] Though Riggs's stepmother, Juliette Chambers, was also Cherokee, "her relationship with [her stepchildren] ranged from indifference to total emotional rejection"; Lynn proudly acknowledged his Cherokee heritage and cultural connection through Rosie Riggs, the mother who died during his infancy, even though the most tangible physical connection he had to her was the allotment.[15] In later years, he "mortgaged the land and the mineral rights on it several times—a burden of debt he did not escape for many years. Eventually, he sold the land, which had served him well although he never lived on it as his own."[16]

Riggs's deep love of his home, and his sensitive understanding of the struggles and dreams of the people who inhabited that land, gave his plays an energy that audiences and critics responded to with general enthusiasm. After suffering a nervous breakdown at the University of Oklahoma when he was twenty-four, he traveled to Santa Fe, New Mexico, and became intimately connected with the avant-garde community of artists there. His own aesthetic leanings blossomed with the experience, and he began what would be a remarkable life of letters that would take him from Oklahoma to Santa Fe, Paris, Chicago, Hollywood (where he became a well-regarded script doctor and friend of some of the cinema's leading stars, including Joan Crawford and Bette Davis), and New York City. Although nearly all his works focus on Oklahoma or, often, Indian Territory just prior to Oklahoma statehood in 1907, and although most of the characters of the plays are the "Sooners," the White settlers who rushed to claim "surplus" Indian lands after allotment, Riggs maintained throughout his life that *The Cherokee Night* was his favorite.[17] Such a disparity in professional and personal emphases is initially puzzling: for a man who proudly claimed to be an Indian and asserted his Indian identity in personal correspondence and professional venues, he gave the bulk of attention in his work—thirty plays, two books of poems, and miscellaneous other writings—to the very invaders who dispossessed the Cherokees.[18]

Even *The Cherokee Night* is a problematic text in this regard, as it reflects what Riggs himself called "absorbed Indians" in a letter to theater critic Barrett H. Clark:

> The play will concern itself with that night, that darkness (with whatever flashes of light allowably splinter through) which has come to the Cherokees and their descendants. An absorbed race has its curiously irreconcilable inheritance. It seems to me the best grade of absorbed Indian might be an intellectual Hamlet, buffeted, harrassed *[sic],* victimized, split, baffled—with somewhere in him great fire and some granite. And a residual lump of stranger things than the white race may fathom.[19]

This passage could very well be an autobiographical statement, and it certainly reflects current readings of Riggs's life and works. Riggs was clearly "victimized, split, baffled" by life, but also possessed of that "fire and granite" that helped him fight for professional recognition and acceptance, while all the while assiduously avoiding too much examination by outsiders. The play seems to be Riggs's attempt to travel the Beloved Path of accommodating change while maintaining a coherent sense of Cherokee centrality, but it fails in that mission, ultimately giving way to despair and the doomed fading of Cherokees as deracinated shadows of a once great nation. Indeed, it is precisely because nationhood as such is almost absent from his work that despair and hopelessness about Indian continuity develop; the political agency and self-determination of the People are subsumed to a measurement of quantifiable and, ultimately, diminishing ethnicity. To Riggs, the continuity of the People is only possible in the comfort of nostalgia and fantasy, not the potentially painful realities of social and political sovereignty in action.

In *That the People Might Live,* Jace Weaver gives the following description of *The Cherokee Night*:

> The play is composed of seven loosely related vignettes spanning the years from 1895 to 1931. Forgoing straight-line narrative, events skip back and forth in time. The only consistent presence is the Claremore Mound . . . [which] Riggs turns . . . into a character that looms broodingly over the drama enacted before it, at once pointing to the Cherokee connection to the land and standing as a reminder of a time when the people were strong.[20]

The "connection to land" that Weaver describes moves beyond the Claremore Mound, as the effects of allotment are indelibly marked on every aspect of the narrative. The opening scene, "Sixty-seven Arrowheads," begins with Riggs's description of a gender-appropriate group of "[t]hree couples—boys and girls—[who] sit around [a fire at the base of the Mound], eating their picnic supper. They are all part Cherokee Indian, some a quarter, some a sixteenth or a thirty-second; one of them is a half-breed."[21]

This single passage illuminates what is perhaps the most fundamental concern of the play: the blood quantum theory of Native authority and authenticity. Womack untangles the complicated representations in the text, noting that "the character with the highest Cherokee blood quantum [Gar] . . . [is] the one most in tune with things Cherokee according to the play's endorsement of racial purity," and Gar "senses the haunted spirits [of the Mound] more than . . . the washed-out mixed-bloods in the play."[22] The higher one's degree of Indian ancestry, the higher one's supposedly inherent knowledge of one's culture and Indian identity. Some of the characters with high blood quantum (such as Gar and Old Man Talbert, who disturbs and frightens the picnickers) are unbalanced—indeed, it is Talbert's vision of fullblood, traditional warriors at the Mound that sends him into madness—but *all* the "absorbed" Cherokees battle with alienation and conflict, unsure of who they are or where they belong. Bee is a self-described whore; Art is a loathsome brute and wife-butcher; Viney is a social-climbing, sharp-tongued bitch. Whatever pride once existed in their Cherokee heritage has been diluted through the loss of the traditions and cultural legacies of that heritage. They are all "victimized, split, baffled," all the more so because the trauma is figured as being inescapably in the blood.

Such is the legacy of allotment, for the legislative successors to the Dawes Act and subsequent allotment guidelines determined Indian identity according to the identifiable Indian "blood" while erasing any consideration of kinship duties and obligations—those communitistic bonds that were more significant to Cherokee nationhood than the arbitrary designations of blood.[23] Those with higher amounts of Indian "blood" were accorded more legitimacy as Indians, but this often resulted in alternate U.S. discrimination via "competency" designations (thus relating "competent" mental ability to those with higher degrees of *White* blood).[24] Indians with lower blood quanta were often permitted full title to their allotments, while those with higher quanta were frequently marked as incompetent and subsequently forbidden to sell, lease, or manage their allotments without the authorization of an appointed personal trustee, often the local Indian agent or other, often-unscrupulous Whites eager to access the land or its resources. The allotment period was the testing ground for the full extension of the policy during the first two decades of the twentieth century.[25] Although Choctaw anthropologist Circe Sturm points out that "[c]ynical manipulation was not the only force at work in the adoption of blood quantum," adding that "blood quantum could just as easily have been introduced by naively well-meaning bureaucrats and liberal supporters who wanted to help 'deserving Indians' but had no effective way of identifying them except through the crude contours of genealogy," the actual implementation of blood quantum policies worked not to help build the tribal body politic or to ensure cultural survival, but to rid the continent of its Native inheritors through bureaucratic elimination.[26]

Blood trauma was Riggs's own cultural inheritance, and it's reflected in *The Cherokee Night*. Access to resources—alternately, the land and the culture—is indistinguishable from the characters' knowledge of themselves and their heritage. This knowledge is in turn dependent in the play upon the characters' degree of biological Indian ancestry, marked as "blood" in the play and in U.S. Indian policy. The more Cherokee blood they possess, the more connected they are to both their culture and the land around them; it's an innate link between the self, the soil, and the community. The one exception to this rule, Gar, is due to the inherent alienation of those to whom he turns for guidance—he reaches out for help from the community, but finds that the shattering of the Nation has undermined the very community values that might have saved him. (It should be noted that the deeper blood connection is not always a benevolent one, as in the case of Old Man Talbert, but it's nonetheless a connection that Riggs privileges over the unstable lives of those "washed-out mixed-bloods.")

Blood quantum and ethnicity, and the moral character that accompanies both in Riggs's Cherokee world, are consistently embedded within a concept of land that is central to the well-being of both individuals and cultures—concerns that were central to Riggs's own outland traumas. As Weaver notes, the play "reflects Riggs's inner struggle to live out his own Indianness and a firm stance against assimilation and annihilation," and that struggle is literally given center stage here—it's the doomed nature of the struggle *itself,* not any resolution of the struggle, that gives substantive shape to the narrative of *The Cherokee Night*.[27] In the third and perhaps most painful scene of the play, the mixedblood Cherokee sisters Viney and Sarah confront one another after ten years of estrangement: Viney is a cold, self-righteous woman who has abandoned all things Indian in her quest for social respectability and married wealth; Sarah, crippled by rheumatism and living in a bare shack with her daughter Maisie and son-in-law Roll Henley, has vigorously clung to her Cherokee identity, even in the face of overwhelming poverty. Their meeting is short and vicious, and it centers, once again, on land and identity:

> VINEY. *(Drawing her fur about her.)* You've used up your land allotment,
>   have you, Sarah?

SARAH. The mortgage took it.

. . .

VINEY. Your oldest boy must have got Indian land, too, didn't he? He
        was born in 1898 about. What'd he do with it?

SARAH. He sold it when he was twenty-one.[28]

"The land," Womack reminds us, "is an identity marker, literally an indicator of Cherokee national citizenship."[29] Just as removal from the old homelands radically alters many Cherokee understandings of community and identity, so too does allotment. As such, the sisters' conversation moves directly from land into identity in this richly textured scene, when Viney, reflecting on a former beau, lashes out: "That dumb Indian, that's all he was! You never could tell about him, couldn't get on to what he was up to! . . . He didn't have any *change* in him, he was stuck someway. He was broody and sullen, he couldn't seem to get hold of himself, like a lot of part Indians around here." When Sarah reminds Viney that she's "more Cherokee than Hutch," Viney replies "Well, I'm thankful to say it doesn't show."[30]

Viney's desire to hide her Indianness is, ultimately, a failure; whether being Cherokee "shows" or not, the legacy of blood can't be hidden. Sarah points this out in a moment of bitter insight: "You try too hard to deny what you are. It tells on you. . . . You say Hutch didn't have any *change* in him. They's nuthin' else in you but change. You've turned your back on what you ought to a-been proud of."[31] Later she remarks in a moment of particular pain, "We're both failures. But I tried, and you didn't. I wouldn't trade places with you."[32] Sarah, the representative of the old Cherokee ways, has been devastated by material poverty and its associated pain and deprivation; Viney, the representative of desperate assimilation, has so alienated herself from her heritage that all she can take comfort in is continual rejection of all things Indian and in the spirit-draining status of commodity culture: "And let me tell you something, Sarah. As long as I've got money and a good home, and am living right, I don't call myself a failure. And neither does anyone else, but you."[33] The Beloved Path here leads nowhere; a state of balance is impossible, for both defiance and submission bring about the destruction of the self. Whether Indian, White, Black, or somewhere in between, all is struggle and pain. There is no safe state of being for Riggs's Cherokees—the "vanishing Indian" is invoked again, this time by an Indian.

As Weaver notes, Oklahoma statehood and the loss of collective land holdings are in the background of the play, and consequently of Riggs's own conflicted understanding of his own Cherokee identity:

> Through all seven scenes, the Cherokee characters are depicted, since statehood, as seduced by materialism, rejecting the old ways, losing their connection to the land, desiring an assimilation into Amer-European society that never truly can be accomplished. They are depicted as a divided people—divided between progressives and pullbacks, between Christians and traditionals, separated from family, friends, even themselves. Only before statehood, before the loss of political, territorial sovereignty, was there any hope for wholeness. Now the only hope rests in memory, in not forgetting one's Indianness and in moving ahead along an uncertain path.[34]

It is clear throughout the play, including the battle between Sarah and Viney, that Riggs's sympathies rest with those Cherokees who have maintained as much of their tribal heritage as possible, even if crushing poverty is the tragic result. Riggs's romantic nostalgia allows only for a redemptive self-sacrifice outside of the cruel realities of this world, not a healing change in circumstance in *this* life. The sale of allotments is, to Sarah, a horror; to Viney, it is a positive sign of benevolent "change," but it's one that nonetheless strips her of any human connection to others. Given the emphasis on Indian lands in the other scenes of the play, could it be a surprise that Riggs waited so long to sell his own allotment, or that it was a pain so great as to be beyond description, one that reached to the very quick of his identity as a Cherokee, "absorbed" though he may have been?

Yet, as background, nationhood is subsumed before the pressures of ethnicity, privileging the mutable qualities of blood over the political manifestation of nationhood, a quality that Cherokee commentators from John Milton Oskison to Robert Thomas have noted as being a value that's been consistently privileged by Cherokees throughout history.[35] It's only in scenes 5 and 6 that the repercussions of Cherokee political suppression are overtly addressed, and then more as passing criticism. In the former, Gar—alienated and frantic, unable to succeed at college or anything else—flees to the compound of Jonas, the fanatical leader of a separatist religious congregation, on a bluff outside of Tahlequah. It's the only feverish hope Gar has for sanctuary from himself, as the Nation is gone: "No place for me anywhere! Come down to Tahlequah yesterday to see if—to see—I thought this bein' the head of—Listen, I'm half Cherokee. I thought they could help me out there, I thought they—Old men sittin' in the square! No Tribe to go to, no Council to help me out of the kind of trouble I'm in. Nothin' to count on—!"[36] Scene 6, Riggs's favorite of the play, is where he is most overtly critical of the political oppression of the Cherokee Nation, when the "tall, fair, righteous" White posse leader, Tinsley, kills the outlaw Edgar Spench in the home of the traditionalist fullblood, John Gray-Wolf, and remarks, "Let this be a lesson and a warnin'. Teach your grandson. Tell everybody what it means to oppose the law. You Indians must think you own things out here. This is God's country out here—and God's a white man. Don't forget that."[37] Yet the full measure of this indictment is eclipsed by the play's overwhelming focus on the tragedies that flow in the blood—a much more powerful threat to the Cherokees of this play than the legal and political struggles of the Nation.

In *The Cherokee Night,* Riggs explores the rippling repercussions of allotment on the Cherokees, and the overwhelming tone of the play is one of moderated despair: maintaining one's cultural heritage is paramount, but the quest is often all but impossible, as land loss and assimilation have taken a devastating toll on the people. Blood quantum is fixed, unchangeable, and as a result so too is one's fate. Assimilation is an option, but it's one that brings no peace. The fullblood and traditional Cherokees throughout the text, including Old Man Talbert and John Gray-Wolf and his mixed-blood but traditional grandson, represent the best option: cultural/identity wholeness, even at the cost of sanity and physical needs. Anything else is absolute destruction. Even fullbloods like the murderous bandit Spench can lose their Cherokeeness by "abandoning a Cherokee worldview toward balance and appropriate living that is not directly correlated to . . . degree of Indian blood."[38] Those whose blood quantum is numbered and known tend to be, according to Old Man Talbert, "Muck and scum! Who are you, anyway! Dribbles of men and women! What do you do to show yer birthright? Nuthin.' You're dead, you ain't no good! Night's come on you."[39]

Riggs echoes the position of many antiallotment activists: breaking the land holdings into individual parcels with the sole aim of transforming Indians into "civilized" yeomen farmers of the Jeffersonian tradition would devastate the community, largely by unraveling kinship ties through alienation and assimilation. As Wilcomb Washburn notes, nearly all the discussion about and drafting of the Dawes Act took place among Indian social reform groups composed mostly of middle- and upper-class Whites without any significant involvement by or consultation with the very communities that the reformers were claiming to assist.[40] (Indeed, most of the reformers never once met or spoke with an Indian.) First drafted at the exclusive vacation resort of Lake Mohonk by the so-called Friends of the Indian in 1885, then given political reality through its passage two years later, the sole purpose of the Act was to "civilize" the Indians at any cost: "nothing—even treaty obligations—should be allowed to stand in the way of the reformers' commitment to do good to the Indian."[41]

Some White observers of the time, such as Colonel William McMichael, saw the lie behind the promises:

> [The Indians] have schools, a representative government, an executive who rules over them. They have a system by which, as I understand, there is no pauper there. And what is it that they do *not* have? Why, they do not have the avarice and the selfishness which are necessary to the acquisition of private property.[42]

In spite of such observations, and in spite of the vociferous objections of most Indians through local newspapers, letter-writing campaigns, and political rallies, the Dawes Act was passed, and the ostensible quest to "civilize the Indian" by reducing the tribes to poverty, cultural chaos, and economic and political disenfranchisement was set in place. The policy would not be repudiated until Franklin Roosevelt's 1934 Wheeler-Howard Bill (the "Indian New Deal"), by which time so much had already been lost from Indian Country—and by that date, the political entity known as Indian Territory was gone.

Riggs wrote *The Cherokee Night* before the passage of the Wheeler-Howard Bill; this play thus depicts many of the conflicts of that threshold period.[43] To Riggs, the loss of land is clearly also a loss of cultural connection. Yet it shouldn't be assumed that Riggs was fully separated from his cultural roots, even if he lived most of his life far from Oklahoma and was ultimately quite pessimistic about the fate of the People. The Cherokee Nation was the place of his birth and childhood, the crucible in which his identities—and fears—were forged. In the first scene of the play, Old Man Talbert recounts a visitation he had from Cherokee spirits of the past, his words flashing out in poetic desperation:

> Not only in war—in quiet times—the way we lived:
> Have you forgot the smoky fire, the well-filled bowl?

Do you speak with the River God, the Long Person no more—no
more with the vast Horned-Snake, the giant Terrapin, with Nuta,
the Sun?

Are you a tree struck by lightnin'?
Are you a deer with a wounded side?
All of you—all our people—have come to the same place![44]

It's easy to imagine the studious and imaginative young Riggs sitting
around with his friends in Claremore, maybe even while working as a
cowpuncher at home with the other Cherokee folks employed by his father, listening to the old stories about *Uk'ten'*, the dangerous but powerful
antlered snake of Cherokee story lore, or of the Long Man, the Mississippi,
who wandered wide and ancient on the border of the old country. Maybe
he sought turtle shells in muddy red shallows, dropping them on anthills
until they were cleaned out and ready to be worked into stomp dance leggings or hand rattles. Perhaps he spoke with the Sun, *Nvda-egehi*, or feared
her wrath when drought cut the crops to parched stubble. Maybe he was
fascinated by the stories of the Thunder Boys, the sons of Selu and Kanati,
Mother Corn and the Great Thunderer, and the messages the Thunder
Boys sent to earth on the burning back of lightning. Did he know the
ceremonial power of lightning-struck wood? Did he respect *Awi Usdi*, the
Little Deer who inflicted rheumatism upon hunters who crippled and slew
deer without giving thanks or honor? Riggs's separation and feelings of
exile can't be necessarily conflated with an ignorance of the old ways; *The
Cherokee Night* clearly demonstrates his familiarity with some elements of
traditional Cherokee ceremonial life.

Riggs's alienation from land and community emerges early in his life,
but it's more a sense of exile and separation than a lack of any connection at all. This alienation is also seen in his expressions of sexuality: as
blood quantum (thus ethnicity) is, to Riggs, evidence of stronger cultural connection to both other people and to the land itself, *visible* difference thus implies the ultimate melding of self, community, and land. As
Womack points out in his discussion of the frequent objectification and
homoeroticism of dark-skinned men in *The Cherokee Night,* "Riggs was a
light-skinned mixed-blood, and throughout his life his lovers were often
Mexican and Hispanic men; he seemed to be attracted to darkness."[45]
Taking this argument further, I would assert that Riggs's erotic attraction
is deeply embedded in a desire to connect to something that he believes

rests in dark skin—namely, a *legitimized* cultural connection. Riggs spent some of the happiest years of his life around people of color, particularly among the Native peoples in and around his artist's colony in Santa Fe. In *The Cherokee Night* the brooding Claremore Mound becomes the site for explorations of forbidden sexuality, racial identity, and alienation from home and community; Riggs's own physical body—and those of his lovers—became the site(s) of his more intimate investigations.

Yet there is a cruel and violent side to Riggs's fascination with skin color, and it emerges in the disturbing scene 4, "The Place Where the Nigger Was Found." There is no evidence that Riggs's attraction to dark-skinned men ever extended toward physical intimacy with African Americans or Black Cherokees, even though Womack incisively notes that the scene includes "the most homoerotic passage in the play."[46] While the scene clearly reflects an erotic attraction to Blackness, it's an attraction inextricably interwoven with racism, violence, and denial. Three of the Cherokee youths—Gar, Hutch, and Art—are searching through the leaves for evidence of the murder of the previous evening:

> HUTCH. *(Kneeling, hunting in leaves.)* Somebody told me them old Creek
> Indians married niggers. Us Cherokees wouldn't do that. *(He has
> found nothing. He gets up.)*
> ART.   *(With contempt, facing him)* You ain't a Cherokee.
> HUTCH. I am! I'm a sixteenth. I got land, I guess.[47]

Art's comment is particularly intriguing: is he denying Hutch's claims to Cherokee affiliation, or is he denying Hutch's racist assumption about Cherokee and Black intermarriage? Although the latter is a hopeful possibility, the former is most likely, as this episode is preceded and followed by graphic details of the torture of Black male bodies. The boys even narrate their desire to use axes to cut apart those very Black bodies, their frenzied hatred exploding in a "savage cry": "[I]F *I* seen a nigger, I'd hack him! / 'F *I* seen a nigger, I'd hack him! / 'F *I* seen a nigger, I'd hack him! Hack him!"[48] The scene climaxes in a gruesome exoticization/eroticization of Black maleness when Art falls into the leaves and emerges with another man's blood on his hands. They flee the forest, and then a figure appears, the detailed stage directions evoking far more than simple theater scenery:

> *The trees move, swaying in the sunlight. A bird calls briefly. Then slowly,*
> *rising from the warmed and fertile earth, a giant* NEGRO, *naked to the*

waist, lifts himself into the sun from behind the thick underbrush. His
black body glistens. He stares off toward the fleeing boys, stretches him-
self, comes forward a step from sun into shadow, in a movement real and
ghostly, as if he were two presences: the murderer undismayed by his crime,
and the very emanation of the dead man himself. He stands a moment in
the gloom, his dark hulk tremendous against the sun. His eyes follow the
boys; one hand moves itself forward to a blackberry spray, in an uncalcu-
lated reflex, gathers two berries and lifts them idly to his mouth. Then he
yawns. Then the sun dies. All below becomes dark.[49]

Riggs, while aching for connection to a Cherokee purity evident in the "fullbloods" of the play, isn't free of a striking insecurity about that very desire. Light mixedbloodedness is a curse for some of his characters, but too much darkness brings with it racist fascination, terror, and physical torment as well. This brutal clash of desire and racism is inscribed on the bloodied bodies of Black men, and it reveals in sharp clarity the deep ambivalence that race in all its forms played in Riggs's own life.

Throughout his career Lynn Riggs furtively explored what it was to be a mixedblood Indian and a gay man in a society that had no use for either. The inner conflict that resulted was never fully reconciled, and his death of aggravated stomach cancer in 1954 brought any hope of successful resolution to a sad and lonely end. Though a brilliant and talented playwright, Riggs was also a deeply traumatized man who lived his life as best he could. The issue isn't how Riggs responded to oppression—his quest for wholeness on the Beloved Path was itself evidence that he didn't fully succumb to the despair that rests at the heart of *The Cherokee Night*—but how his struggles might better mark the trail for other Cherokees who followed.

A compassionate Beloved Path reading of Riggs's work acknowledges that "the enemy from whom Riggs is avoiding detection is not only others but himself, and the code functions as a deep denial, a way of writing about everything except what he really wanted to write about—being Indian and gay."[50] Sometimes the greater dangers are in the mindscape within, not the landscape without. By shifting his narrative attention so firmly away from the political to the intimate, giving little room for community self-determination or response, Riggs stripped the strength of nationhood from the Beloved Path, removing it from the balanced complementarity of both red and white concerns and instead directing the focus to a struggle of individuals seeking wholeness of self outside of rather than through community. In such a construction, hopeful Beloved alternatives collapse, and the only options are equally doomed: full assimilation or violent rebellion.

The allotment dispossession of the Cherokees of Indian Territory clearly shaped the course of Lynn Riggs's life, just as it continues to impact many Cherokees today and our relationships to our communities, tribal connections, and cultural responsibilities. We can honor Riggs for his artistic genius, his insight into the dreams, fears, and desires of the people of his homeland, and for his "coded" struggle against racism and homophobia. Yet we can honor his survival without embracing the pain and shame at its core. Sadly, a life of hopeful balance on the Beloved Path was, in the end, out of his reach.

JOHN MILTON OSKISON: SEEKING BALANCE IN THE "OLD I.T."

At the conclusion of his 1938 biography of the Shawnee leader Tecumseh, John Milton Oskison writes:

> What stirred Tecumseh to attempt the formation of an Indian confederation was a hope as old as the races of man: that it might be possible in a changing and turbulent world to find permanent peace and plenty. Because we understand that longing, and because in all of us burns some spark of resentment at the encroachment of our liberties, we know why Tecumseh has become, in the minds and memories of three peoples, a knightly symbol and an enduring legend.[51]

This statement is a compelling extension of the dedication to the book, in which the author states: "This book is dedicated to all Dreamers and Strivers for the integrity of the Indian race, some of whose blood flows in my veins; and especially to the Oklahoma Shawnee friends of my boyhood."[52]

Oskison's consistent concern with Indian continuity runs throughout these comments and the rest of the text, but so does the now-familiar tension of the Beloved Path: how can Indians remain strong when so much of what made them strong in the past is gone? How can Indians of the modern age accommodate some of the more acceptable Eurowestern values without sacrificing their Indigenous integrity? Is it an all or nothing proposition? It's the tension at the heart of these questions that allows Oskison to laud Tecumseh's accomplishments as a freedom fighter and political

John Milton Oskison. Courtesy of the Research Division of the Oklahoma Historical Society.

strategist while stating that he "was the dreamer of a hopeless dream which other Indian leaders . . . had fought to turn into reality." Oskison acknowledges the nobility of Tecumseh's martyrdom "for the right of his red brothers to live in freedom according to their own conception,"[53] while stating that it was ultimately "a hopeless fight. The white tide . . . could not be stayed; and its advance was merciless."[54] Connecting Tecumseh's story throughout the book with that of the Cherokees, Oskison makes the very same claim for his own people when he notes that the Shawnee leader's ambition of "saving . . . his race from contamination and eventual destruction" was largely "the same issue which motivated the long fight of a contemporary but very different chief, John Ross of the Cherokees." In spite of his "intelligence, sound sense, and unfaltering devotion to his tribe," Ross, according to Oskison, "failed as completely and tragically as did Tecumseh."[55]

Oskison's work, at first glance, resembles that of Riggs, particularly in its heavy emphasis on the Indian Territory, a world represented as a multicultural frontier where mixedbloods and fullbloods live, love, struggle, and coexist alongside the White masses whose numbers are daily increasing. (African Americans are notably underrepresented in all these texts.) Like Riggs, Oskison struggles with representing Indians as more than memories, but seems unable to fully realize a future of Indian possibility. And Oskison shares an uncertainty about his own relationship to a people whose past seems to shine so much brighter than their present.

Yet where Riggs forecloses on any hope for the Nation in his invocation of this tension, Oskison leaves the question open-ended. He acknowledges the importance of blood to his understanding of Cherokee identity, but emphasizes the primacy of Cherokee nationhood and political self-determination above the arbitrary distinctions of blood quantum. Kinship is a more distinctive value in Oskison's work than is racial purity; nationhood isn't a finite resource, but rather one that can be extended to encompass others into the body politic. Love and kindness hold more possibility in Oskison's world than in Riggs's, especially when they are devoted to a higher purpose. Oskison's Indian Territory is a wild and rough place where tradition often clashes with new fashions and values, but the aching despair of Riggs's world is largely absent; Oskison represents both the geographic location of the Territory and its political atmosphere primarily as a place where people are mostly just interested in getting along without undue interference from their neighbors.

There's no Indigenous, pre-White Eden in Oskison's writing; he generally concerns himself with the gritty observation of his boyhood home in all its diversity, conflict, and possibility. He emphasizes this point in his unpublished autobiography, *A Tale of the Old I.T.,* beginning the narrative with the following comment: "I have thought of myself sometimes as a replica in temperament of my restless, nervous, short-tempered father. I could not tell my own story without first sketching his nomadic life although I have little material, and no documentation whatever."[56] His father, John Oskison, was born on an English tenant farm in 1835 and orphaned in childhood. Brought to the United States by his brutal uncle, the boy was worked nearly to death on an Illinois farm before he fled at age seventeen on what would be the first of a lifetime of such moves. The elder John Oskison's wanderings as an oxen driver, farmer, prospector, and laborer eventually brought him to the Cherokee Nation and Indian Territory in 1870, where he met and married a widowed Cherokee woman named Rachel Crittenden. Young John Milton Oskison was born in 1874, the second of four boys who survived infancy.

That Oskison privileges his father in this narrative is hardly surprising, as his mother died when he was only four years old. Although Cherokees and other Indians surrounded the Oskisons throughout young John's childhood, it was his English father whose presence, authority, and temper were the most significant influences on his life. Throughout the autobiography, Oskison reflects on the often painful legacy of this relationship, and its ultimate value, for while the elder Oskison could be a fiery and unrelenting work-driver, he was also dedicated to education and used his farming and ranching resources to ensure that his second son could be educated in some of the finest universities in the country and with the freedom to pursue his own dreams.

After an early youth spent working for his father as a cowpuncher and farmhand, Oskison enrolled in Willie Halsell College, a Methodist preparatory school in Vinita, Indian Territory, and became a close friend of the "grinning, likeable son of a Verdigris river cattleman named Clem Rogers," a boy known in the college as "Rabbit" but who was more formally known as Will Rogers.[57] Among their adventures together was a railway journey with two other classmates to the 1893 World's Fair in Chicago, which included an overnight stay in St. Louis and a breathless study of a banned pornographic pamphlet with the ostensibly innocent title, "Only a Boy."[58] He continued working for his father during the summer breaks, and these months among the steers and ranch hands would add to a growing store of experiences from which he would draw in his later writing.

Upon graduation, Oskison traveled to Stanford, where he initially pursued studies in law, largely due to his father's influence. Young Oskison didn't resist the suggestion, for he saw a great need of trained lawyers in the Territory, as "there were many more whites than Indians in the Cherokee Nation, in the towns and on farms and ranches. Pressure on Washington to open Indian lands to purchase and lease by whites had borne fruit."[59] It was at Stanford that Oskison first encountered integration, expressing racist shock that Whites would heartily welcome and share the dining hall with a Black student; it was also where he began to encounter the expansive intellectual and ethical liberalism of Stanford's early days, and where he lost interest in law and began his published writing career for the student newspaper, the *Sequoia*—a fitting name for the first site of a Cherokee student's work. His "vignettes of range and farm life" in the Indian Territory, which he "had outlined vaguely . . . as [he] rode the range," were so different from the *Sequoia*'s standard fare, and so well written, that he was soon named associate editor of the paper.[60] From Stanford Oskison went to graduate school at Harvard and continued his writing, finding some success in such journals as *Century Magazine* (for which he won the 1899 prize for best short story by a college graduate) and *McClure's*. Writing was his love, but fiction soon gave way to a career in journalism as both writer and editor, with occasional forays into fiction and biography.

By the time of his death in New York City in 1947, Oskison had spent most of his life outside of what was by then Oklahoma, but the bulk of his fiction oeuvre focuses on the state's territorial predecessor and its peoples. Some of his works—such as his first two published novels, *Wild Harvest: A Novel of Transition Days in Oklahoma* (1925) and *Black Jack Davy* (1926), and short stories like "Young Henry and the Old Man" (1908)—have as their narrative focus the struggles of White immigrants in Indian Territory who, like his own father and the many homesteaders and ranch hands of his youth, work to make a life for themselves and their often mixed-heritage families.

Yet the political dimensions of nationhood are never far from these texts, and it's in this affirmation of a real social and political presence that Oskison's invocation of the Beloved Path is more hopeful of Cherokee continuity than Lynn Riggs's tales of the Territory. Indians and the political jurisdiction of the Five Tribes are fundamental to Oskison's fiction and biographies, as is his clear concern with the gradual erosion of Indian sovereignty due to the demographic changes brought by White desire for Native lands; his nonfiction essays are more complicated and inconsistent, ranging in tone and perspective from defiant to dramatically accommodationist. Mixedbloods and fullbloods alike are at the heart of his 1935 novel, *Brothers Three,* as well as his stories, from the crippled "half-breed" cowboy Hanner who sacrifices himself to a posse to save his best friend in "Only the Master Shall Praise" (1900), to the pragmatic and sensitive Lizzie Squirrel, who fights her abusive White husband but finds her escape thwarted by the local do-gooder newspaper editor in "The Man Who Interfered" (1915), to a young Cherokee socialite on the frontier who finds herself in an unexpected love triangle with a local outlaw and a justice-loving newspaperman in "'The Quality of Mercy': A Story of the Indian Territory" (1904). Other stories add a touch of humor to tales that are otherwise rather sad, such as "The Problem of Old Harjo" (1907), the touching story of an old Creek man who finds his new devotion to Jesus Christ thwarted by his equally passionate love of his two wives, much to the chagrin of the young White missionary trying to bring Old Harjo into the fold.

The struggle between frontier chaos and the legal jurisdiction of the Indian nations sets the dramatic stage for these stories; this is no generic Wild West, but a country in the growing pains of settlement and conflict. This centrality of Indians to the Territory, and particularly Oskison's own Cherokee specificity, is at its most evocative in the unpublished novel manuscript, *The Singing Bird*. Seen through the wide eyes of young Paul Wear, the story is, on the surface, the rather melodramatic account of a group of White missionaries—Paul and his uncle Dan Wear, Dan's wife Ellen, and the dedicated Miss Eula Benson—who come to the lands of the Old Settlers before the Removal to convert the Cherokees and stay on after the Trail to help the People rebuild in the midst of internal conflict and increasing external pressures. The most involved subplot is the clash between Ellen, the adulterous "singing bird" of the title—a spoiled society debutante who resents the sacrifices of missionary life and abandons her marital vows in her scheming for her husband's affections—and Dan, whose devotion to the cause of Cherokee self-determination is matched only by his sterling strength of character and his unwillingness to sacrifice his vows for Ellen's petty need for personal attention.

As might be expected, the tale is often punctuated with affirmations of the need for Cherokees to be "civilized" along Eurowestern standards, and the uncritical claim that

> like it or not, the Indians must learn our language and adjust themselves
> to what we called Christian civilization. English-teaching schools must
> be opened to them, and shops and mills provided. The white man's knowl-
> edge of farming must be theirs. [Dan] had added, with fervor: "However

men twist, travesty, or ignore the teachings of Christ, they will prevail.
Always remember, Paul, that upon no other foundation can a people live
securely."[61]

Although there are corrupt missionaries—later in the novel, the hypocrite
and money-grubbing schemer Otis Janes threatens Dan's position at the
mission—this is the exception that proves the rule of good and generous
White missionaries (Paul, Dan, and Miss Eula) giving of themselves and
their Christian virtue to the People. The negative dimensions of Christian
proselytizing are erased, and these noble heroes—true to melodrama
form—are the standard of human decency and righteous struggle.

Yet, in firm Beloved fashion, there's more to this narrative than a super-
ficial celebration of conversion; indeed, it's far more a story about Cherokee
sovereignty and survival than about Christianity or Eurowestern "civilization," in spite of the fact that the four central characters are White missionaries. Here Oskison tells a very Cherokee story by following the experiences of Whites within a Cherokee context, thus providing a striking
narrative double-consciousness; Paul, Dan, Ellen, and Eula might be non-
Indian, but they're wrapped in the world of Cherokee social and political
struggle, and their own White specificity, while never entirely absent, is
subsumed within the Cherokee communitism at the novel's center. Had
Oskison focused explicitly on Indians as the protagonists—Indians who
were generally not of the stereotypical mold of guttural savage or tragic
forest nobility—his primarily White audience may well have turned a deaf
ear to the significance of his story. But by firmly embedding romanticized
White protagonists in a Cherokee context, Oskison makes them part of
the Cherokee story, rather than making their Whiteness the primary narrative concern.

Much of this underlying emphasis comes from the text's structure,
which is ostensibly a fictional remembrance of the time told in Paul's
voice, but is much more a historical and ethnographic account of life in
the Territory in the years before and after the Removal. Oskison's greatest strength as a writer is his ability to bring the daily lives and political realities of Indian Territory to vivid life with a journalist's passion for
truth, eye for detail, and ear for language. These aspects of the novel are
so strong, in fact, that the significant weaknesses of the fiction plot become glaringly obvious in comparison. Oskison is a fine journalist and
historian, but a weak novelist, relying on mawkish sentiment, stock char-

acter types, and exaggerated and often absurd plot devices rather than
trusting his more restrained instincts about human behavior. Women in
particular seem to suffer from this narrative sentimentality, particularly through martyrdom, either to God (as with the death of the virginal
Cherokee convert Catherine Swan, and the dutiful Christian sacrifice of
Miss Eula, who gives up her love of both Dan and Paul for many years
while engaged in her mission work until suddenly deciding toward the
end to marry Paul) or to defiance against oppression (as with Ellen, who is
shot for stabbing the villainous Confederate Cherokee raider, Wah-ti-ka,
after he orders the mission settlement destroyed in the novel's dramatic
conclusion). The characters and their motivations are too often uncon-
vincing, marked as they are by histrionic monologues and gushing prose
that stand unsteadily next to the more restrained descriptions of the land
and its people and were, even in his own time, out of favor among a more
realist-oriented readership.

    While his characters and plots leave much to be desired—most scenes
with Ellen are cringeworthy in their forced drama and didacticism—the
actual *world* Oskison creates in *The Singing Bird* is the most fully realized
of any of his fictions, and the most devoted to representing the Cherokee
context of Indian Territory with as much honesty, detail, and sensitivity
as he brings to his biographies of the adopted Cherokee and politician
Sam Houston and the Shawnee statesman Tecumseh. Readers follow the
missionaries in their difficult travels through Cherokee lands in the old
country to those in the new, from eastern Removal pressures to the Western Cherokees' struggles to make a secure society in their new homeland in
the West, to the internecine conflicts between the Old Settlers, the Treaty
Party, and the Trail of Tears exiles after the Removal as well as the bloody
destruction of the U.S. Civil War and the years of peace between these
events. Cherokees famous, infamous, and obscure step through the text—
John Jolly, Sequoyah and his wife Sally, John Ross, John Ridge, and Elias
Boudinot—as do scores of Cherokee fullbloods and mixedbloods (ranging
from fully traditional to enthusiastically acculturated), Indians from other
tribes (generally less given to speaking anything but broken English),
Whites (ranging from deviant and filthy border-dwellers to noble and
principled travelers), and Black slaves both dutiful and depraved (and
who appear only incidentally in the book).[62] Oskison's Indian Territory
is imperfect and selective, but it's a Beloved gathering grounds at heart;
as a result, it's a place uniquely suited as much to the rich possibilities

of intercultural understanding as to the devastation of xenophobia and conflict. The mission at Oak Hill, the protagonists' second and most successful settlement, becomes a center of political activism and a site of narrative observation from which the narrators watch the Cherokee Nation struggle to survive the events of history.

The first meeting between Paul, Dan, and John Jolly—the civil (peace) chief of the Old Settlers—early in the novel provides a powerful illustration of this Beloved consciousness and its centrality to both this narrative and, I believe, to the bulk of the Oskison corpus. Jolly gives a short account of the political situation of the Old Settlers, criticizing the U.S. government's policy of forcing the Cherokees to fight against the Osages for Osage land, while bending to pressure by White settlers for the removal of both tribes from the Arkansas lands. When Paul asks why the United States is doing this, Dan replies:

> "Paul, the explanation is as simple as A B C. The Government at Washington is a government of the people, and the people are hungry for more and more land. They, or their land-hungry fathers, came from England, and other countries across the water, where land is hard to come by and is man's most valued possession. Their hunger has grown keener as it has been fed with one enormous gobbling of Indian lands after another. It will not be satisfied, even when every tribe has yielded its last acre, for then the land-hungry will fight one another until they are destroyed, or until the envy and scheming in their hearts are resolved by the power of Christ's teaching. You and I will never know that peace, but we can hope and pray for it honestly, work for it with all our heart and strength. Here is our field of labor, and I thank God that it is a promising one."[63]

A few points are of note here. First is the critical reflection on the "land-hungry fathers" who "came from England," a comment clearly applicable to the life of John Oskison Senior as well as the many European immigrants that young John befriended as a child, poor men from England, Ireland, Germany, and other countries, each seeking the class status and personal worth that came from being landed men. There is a call for accountability here, but one touched by a gentle understanding; in large part, the ravenous appetite of these hungry people—themselves dispossessed and despised in their original homelands—is beyond their control, a need and compulsion that only God can heal.

This passage gives a window, too, into the challenges that the Cherokees and other Indians face, for although their fight to save their homes is a righteous one, and although they demonstrate again and again their virtues as a strong, intelligent, and determined people, theirs is still ultimately a human battle, and humans are fundamentally flawed by "the envy and scheming in their hearts." Oskison touches on this concern throughout his writing, as in the essay "Friends of the Indian," where he issues a bitter warning against expecting justice from the United States in its relationships with Native peoples: "The moral of Indian litigation against the invading settler could have been read as plainly in 1886 as in 1876 or in 1905: The Indian, 'not taxed, not voting,' has no real standing in the courts organized by and for the American people." Furthermore, "The attitude of the settler, at whose request every Indian removal has been made and every tribal reservation extinguished, has been plain and consistent from the beginning. It has been equally plain that the settler, with a sympathetic and industrious representative in Congress, would decide the attitude of the Indian Department."[64] Oskison is quite clear on this point: to put faith in human justice is to put faith in weakness.

Throughout the novel, this message is driven home again and again, as all signs of terrestrial success and happiness are thrown down, from the destruction of the first mission when the Cherokees are driven from Arkansas Territory to Indian Territory, through the disintegration of Dan and Ellen's physical love, to the upheaval of the Cherokee Nation's economic recovery during the U.S. Civil War, and finally, to the destruction of Oak Hill mission and Ellen's murder. Armed rebellion isn't the way: Tecumseh's armed rebellion fails in spite of its righteousness. The only successes are those of higher purpose, like education of self and community, commitment to a cause beyond personal success, a love rooted in spirit above flesh, courage in the face of overwhelming injustice, and the full practice of those highest ideals of Christian virtue that show a merciful understanding of human frailty. The latter doesn't necessarily require conversion for those who are strong of mind and spirit: Dan gradually comes to believe that the traditionalists who are humbly committed to the betterment of the People, like Sequoyah, will attain salvation, even without accepting Jesus Christ. A good life is, in the end, more reflective of Christ's purpose than a declaration of conversion or a quest for personal salvation.

In short, it is some of the higher principles of communitism in action that gives hope for the future. Accountability, personal responsibility, and a selfless life of service to the People give the only kind of strength that will endure the storm. Putting faith in mortal successes and good intentions could only lead to despair, for those successes and hopes are all too easily shattered by the iniquities of humanity. Working toward a healthy future without expectation of immediate change—the "seventh generation" principle common in pan-Indian circles—allows our current setbacks and losses to be put into a more hopeful context.

This is the central tenet of Oskison's expression of Beloved principles, one that, while to some degree cynical, still avoids the despair of Riggs's work. Oskison has no illusions about Whites or their attitude toward Indians and Indian lands: the struggle will always go on, and any hope of ending it will have to be based in clear, unromantic pragmatism. He's not always consistent; some of his nonfiction, such as the above-mentioned "Friends of the Indian," takes the United States and its agents to task for paternalism and presumption of Indian ignorance, whereas other essays, like the controversial 1907 piece, "Remaining Causes of Indian Discontent," advocate a rather sweeping divestiture of the United States' trust relationship to the tribes.[65] He points out in an essay that "It is not the despairing cynic who advises the Indian, 'For God's sake, get the ballot in your hands as soon as possible,'" while acknowledging in his fiction that the ballot isn't going to be enough to survive if your enemies have vastly greater numbers.[66]

Whatever the future holds for Native peoples in the Americas is, to Oskison, as much the responsibility of non-Indians as Indians. His Indian Territory isn't just about Indians—by the time of his birth, the growing White population was already alarming Indian leaders, and that growing population threat brought with it many challenges for the People. Yet it's still *Indian* Territory; it's still the land under the political jurisdiction and authority of the Real People; and it's still the place where they exercise their rights of self-determination and sovereignty, where they fight to determine their own way in the world without interference from the United States and its citizens. It's a place of possibility denied but not erased, a world of pain and joy, hatred and love, all inextricably mingled together in the land and the peoples who call that land home.

Throughout his work, Oskison provides neither easy answers nor grim predictions for an empty future; he simply shares the stories, neither optimistic nor entirely despairing, as certain of the righteousness of the Indian cause as he is of the inevitability of U.S. treachery and greed. Which will survive longest depends on the willingness of people to be led not by their unquenchable appetites or base fears, but by their better ideals. And that, Oskison suggests, is a question still very much without an answer.

WILL ROGERS, THE CHEROKEE VOICE OF AMERICA

In the middle of a series of stories about Will Rogers's 1935 death in a plane crash in Alaska, Richard M. Ketchum shares one of particular poignancy:

> In Locust Grove, Oklahoma, half a dozen Cherokees were building a fence when an old man drove along the road to tell them the news. Again, there was only stunned silence—people could find no words to express themselves in the face of this. After a time some of the Indians spoke of how they had known Will or remembered a favor he had done for someone. Then one said, "I can't work any more today," and all of them stacked their tools and slowly walked away.[67]

There has been no single Cherokee who influenced the world like Will Rogers, "The Cherokee Kid." He was the unofficial voice of the idealized United States, a man who gently but firmly held a mirror up to the American public and teased its excesses and failings while celebrating its virtues. He was honored by U.S. presidents and European royalty; he turned down calls for public office, choosing instead to be a "Self-Made Diplomat"; he reveled in the life of the stage and the public eye, but cherished his family and his privacy; and, consistently throughout his life, he honored his Cherokee heritage and was proud of his Indian Territory and Oklahoma roots: "My father was one-eighth Cherokee Indian and my mother was a quarter-blood Cherokee. I never got far enough in arithmetic to figure out just how much 'Injun' that makes me, but there's nothing of which I am more proud than my Cherokee blood."[68] Rogers walked firmly on the Beloved Path throughout his life, with occasional drifts into Chickamauga rebellion when his anger was aroused. His was the red center of the Beloved Path—patient in peace, but not a man to trifle with.

In his biography of Rogers, Donald Day observes that "Will was fantastically proud of his Indian blood and it may well have been the dominating force in heredity's contribution to his make-up."[69] Rogers saw no conflict between his identity as a Cherokee man and his embrace of many

Will Rogers. Courtesy of the Research Division of the Oklahoma Historical Society.

Eurowestern cultural values; in fact, he saw himself distinctly as a *true* American precisely because of his Native roots. This Beloved Path balance was, as biographer Ben Yagoda notes, "a kind of dual consciousness [that] he displayed all his life: the way he could be a hero to the forces of 'decency' and yet be a headliner in the all-but-pornographic *Ziegfield Follies,* the way he could present himself as a mere comedian and yet be an extremely influential political voice in the country, the way he could take strong stands without, usually, offending those on the opposite side of the issue."[70] Unlike Lynn Riggs, Will Rogers was largely unscathed by mixedblood angst, and he was ultimately more successful in reflecting the realities of the enduring Cherokee presence in the modern age than was John Oskison.

Some White commentators have argued that Rogers's embrace of his Cherokee heritage was little more than shrewd showmanship. Richard Ketchum asserts:

> Quite naturally, Will never possessed the same degree of identification his father had with the Cherokees. His upbringing and appearance were those of whites; he left home at a fairly early age; and his later associations were almost entirely with whites. Yet the Indian blood was there, and he became too much of a showman not to realize the appeal an Indian background had for an audience.[71]

Ketchum's claim ignores many realities: the private correspondence in which Rogers discusses his own understandings of himself as a Cherokee; the particular contexts of Indianness in the Indian Territory of the time, in which Rogers perceived himself and was perceived by others as Cherokee; the numerous references to both Cherokees and other tribal nations in Rogers's writings and radio addresses, most of which spoke against the stereotypes that would have been most appealing to a Eurowestern public that preferred antiquated Noble Savage stereotypes; Rogers's many Native friends and correspondents (most notably his childhood friend Charley McClellan, a vocal Cherokee nationalist, ceremonial traditionalist, and stomp dancer); his lifelong advocacy of Native causes and equity; the enduring Cherokee presence in Rogers's writings throughout his life; and the personal costs he endured as a result of anti-Indian bigotry.[72] Yagoda has a better understanding of Oklahoma Cherokee cultural values:

> How did [Rogers's fame] happen? The answer, as far as there is one, lies in the pages that follow. But a few points bear preliminary consideration. The first is that Will Rogers was a Cherokee Indian. He was scarcely more than a quarter Cherokee, to be sure, but in the Indian Territory (where he was born and where he lived for most of the first twenty-three years of his life) that in no way diminished his standing in the tribe. . . . Other than a gag or two, and an occasional barbed reference to [Andrew] Jackson, Will Rogers did not make much of his Cherokee heritage. But the weight

of that heritage, the sense that history can turn on you when you least expect it, surely helped forge in him an equanimity that colored everything
he wrote or said and that the [U.S.] nation appreciated as wisdom.[73]

While Rogers certainly didn't share the same degree of familiarity with
tribal traditions that his father possessed—most notably, a facility with
the Cherokee language—he shared a cultural history and experience
with many Cherokees of Indian Territory and Oklahoma. It's also important to note that Rogers has always been accepted by most Oklahoma
Cherokees as one of their own—a central tenet of Cherokee sovereignty.

Much of this criticism draws from a pervasive stereotype about Okla-
homa Indians, which W. David Baird addresses in his essay "Are There
'Real' Indians in Oklahoma? Historical Perceptions of the Five Civilized
Tribes":

> Presupposing that assimilation and "being Indian" are mutually contra-
> dictory, most historical studies of twentieth-century Native Americans
> make only brief references, if any at all, to Five Tribes people. When they
> do, it is usually to extol the tribal minority that resisted allotment, that
> now maintain the Sacred Fire, or that did or do live in rural isolation. Put
> differently, both popular and scholarly minds tend to categorize the vast
> majority of those Native Americans who have and still do occupy eastern
> Oklahoma as something other than "real" Indians.[74]

While Baird falls to some degree into the same trap of the strict binary
between acculturation and tradition—there is no room for Stomp Dance
Baptists or for those syncretic Cherokees who follow the Beloved Path—
his point is generally an apt one: if a person doesn't look like an Indian is
"supposed" to look and/or fight vigorously against Eurowestern cultural
values, s/he must not be "real," at least according to non-Indian cultural
purists who arrogantly presume authority based on stereotypical and
racist standards. This is another convenient erasure and removal of Native
presence that traps Indians as unchanging museum artifacts instead of
human communities with dynamic traditions and historically influenced
cultural contexts.

Contrary to Yagoda's aforementioned assertion, Rogers's references to
being Cherokee are more significant than "a gag or two": throughout his
adult life, Rogers frequently spoke from the position of a Cherokee—and
thus, a *real* American—when addressing issues of social concern. The family

of William Penn Adair Rogers was active in Cherokee political affairs long before his birth: his grandfather, Robert Rogers, was an Old Settler descendant of Chickamauga emigrants from the old Nation; his father Clem was a student at the Cherokee Male Seminary in the Cherokee capital, Tahlequah, and was, later in life, one of the Nation's delegates to the Dawes Commission, even participating in the Oklahoma constitutional convention.[75] From ranching, wheat farming, and livestock speculation, the Rogers family expanded their political and economic strength in the area, and by the time of Will's birth around 1879 were a well-established upper-class family in Indian Territory. Rogers's lifelong mystique of the "poor boy come to riches" was clearly more myth than reality, as he was the pampered only son of a wealthy Cherokee entrepreneur, but he always associated himself with the working-class issues of his native land, particularly those of other Indians.[76]

Just as the substance of much of his social commentary was rooted in the cultural concerns of his people, so too was his Cherokee upbringing the source of his particular brand of humor. Jack and Anna Kilpatrick point out that although "most [Cherokee humor] is hidden from outsiders behind a language barrier . . . the whole world had it in the most characteristic form, and for many years, in Will Rogers, the greatest humorist the Cherokee people ever produced." Rogers was, according to the Kilpatricks, "the archetype of the uncounted and unsung many of his tribesmen who skillfully practice the healing art of cheerfulness."[77]

The Kilpatricks go on to note that "the crowning glory of Cherokee wit is a scintillating satire couched in dry understatement," which would become the trademark of Rogers's observations about the world, particularly in reference to Indian issues.[78] For example, Rogers was clearly thunderstruck when, while visiting New York City for the first time, he was asked to provide proof of U.S. citizenship. He remarks:

> That was the first time I had ever been called on to prove that. Here my Father and Mother were both one-eighth Cherokee Indians and I have been on the Cherokee rolls since I was named, and my family had lived on one ranch for 75 years. But just offhand, how was I going to show that I was born in America? The English that I spoke had none of the earmarks of the Mayflower.[79]

Throughout his life, Rogers would try his hand at many things, from travels across the world as "the Cherokee Kid, the World's Champion

Lassoer," or "The Indian Cowpuncher" and "Indian Cowboy" as part of Texas Jack's Wild West Show, to his rope-trick act in the *Ziegfield Follies* and his frequent gigs as a banquet speaker, to comedy movies, to regular radio shows and his thirteen-year stint as a nationally syndicated social commentator for the *New York Times*. And as his fame as an entertainer and social humorist expanded, Rogers turned his critique of the United States and its imperialist policies into a well-honed instrument that amused yet never pulled away from the truth.

His targets were most often privileged social groups—politicians, lawyers, celebrities, European nobility—and he rarely let a chance go by to speak against those whose policies and practices worked to the detriment of the poor and the working class. Having seen the devastation that so many of those groups brought to his people and the neighboring tribes in Indian Territory, Rogers was in the ideal place to speak to these issues; as a light-skinned Cherokee well-loved in the United States, he was a stealth minority with access to a forum and a platform inaccessible to other Indians of his day. His walk upon the Beloved Path was one he strode with confidence.

Rogers often addressed his Indian ancestry as a more substantial link to the Americas than that claimed by the descendants of Pilgrims and other White settlers, as recounted by his wife:

> Will's pride in the fact that he was part Indian inspired a story that has been repeated as often as anything he ever said. He was appearing on one of his lecture tours in Boston's hallowed Symphony Hall, not long after his return from a trip abroad. With a rambling beginning Will solemnly announced to the audience that he was honored by the presence of so many descendants of the pioneer Americans, and admitted that his forefathers had not come over on the *Mayflower*—"But," he said, "they met the boat."[80]

Here he declares himself an Indian, one who came from the Indian Territory, where "we spoiled the best Territory in the World to make a State."[81] His critique of U.S. imperialist policies toward Puerto Rico, Hawai'i, Cuba, and the Philippines—policies which mirrored and perfected the brutal erasure of Indian sovereignty in the former Indian Territory—are particularly pointed and often utilize language familiar in Indian Country as the language of embattled tribal sovereignty.[82] Alaska, a region of particular (and ultimately fatal) fascination to Rogers, is "a great country," and if "they can just keep it from being taken over by the U. S. they got a great future."[83] As for the Philippines, Rogers is equally emphatic about that nation's sovereignty and independence:

> The U.S. Senate sentenced the Philippines to twelve more years of American receivership. Will you tell me one thing? How can one nation tell when another nation is ready for independence? But our government can do it. Yes, sir, there is not a dozen of 'em that's ever been west of the Golden Gate, but they could just tell you to a day twelve years from now, just when the "Little Brown Brothers" would be able to mess up their affairs as bad as ours.[84]

The insidious union between evangelical Christianity and commercial interests involved in the U.S. imperial exercise doesn't escape his keen eye or sharp tongue, either: "We send many missionaries there. Missionaries teach 'em not only how to serve the Lord, but run a Ford car. Then the American agent sells 'em one. You take religion backed up by commerce and it's awful hard for a heathern to overcome."[85]

Rogers generally gives Native peoples the moral high ground that drew not only on the unarguable treachery of the United States and its citizenry, but also simply from the cultural values of Indian peoplehood. Conversely, he sees Whites as having a lower moral fiber than Indians, noting more than once that, although Cherokee, he "had enough white in [him] to make [his] honesty questionable."[86] He claims that Arizona and New Mexico "have a romance in history that out dates anything we have in our own country, and there is just enough Indians to keep the whole thing respectable."[87] In a 1926 *Saturday Evening Post* article, Rogers writes of his less-than-successful meeting with Florida's Governor Martin, who lashed out after Rogers mentioned the word "California":

> A Seminole Indian who had starved there [in Florida] all his life led me away and apologized for the Governor's conduct. He said I just happened to approach the Governor wrong; that if I hadn't mentioned California perhaps the Governor would have answered me civilly, even affectionately, and perhaps sold me the Governor's office in the Capitol.
>
> Well, this seemed like such a nice fellow, this Indian, and such a Gentleman, that I asked him how is it that he was not selling lots in Florida, being a native and knowing the country and its possibilities. He could be a Star salesman.
>
> He said, "I am an Indian—I have a conscience."[88]

Rogers often asserts Native perspectives and the truths of history in his critique of cherished Eurowestern values and cultural assumptions, connecting them to troubling political issues of his own time. Some of his favorite targets in both radio and print are U.S. presidents. As has long been the case with many Cherokees, Rogers demonstrates a particular loathing for Andrew Jackson, and he never hesitates to condemn both Jackson and the president's particularly anti-Indian values. Rogers was the special guest at a Democratic dinner celebrating Jackson, and in a 1928 article he recounts the experience and his own distaste for "Old Hickory":

> Well, to tell you the truth, I am not so sweet on old Andy. He is the one that run us Cherokees out of Georgia and North Carolina. I ate dinner on him, but I didn't enjoy it. I thought I was eating for Stonewall. Old Andy, every time he couldn't find any one to jump on, would come back and pounce onto us Indians. Course he licked the English down in New Orleans, but he didn't do it till the war had been over two weeks, so he really just fought them as an encore. Then he would go to Florida and shoot up the Seminoles. . . . Then he would have a row with the Government, and they would take his command and his liquor away from him, and he would come back and sick himself onto us Cherokees again.[89]

Cowardice, deception, and alcoholism are all traits Rogers attributes to Jackson, but Rogers is just getting warmed up: "But old Andy made the White House. . . . The Indians wanted him in there so he would let us alone for awhile. Andy stayed two terms, and was the first man that didn't 'choose' to run again. He had to get back to his regular business, which was shooting at the Indians."[90] In a 1929 *Saturday Evening Post* article, "Mr. Toastmaster and Democrats," Rogers writes that "Jacksonian Democracy consisted of inventing the plan of giving everybody jobs according to how many votes they delivered to Jackson. . . . Then he would go back home, if he had happened to have been defeated, and pounce on the Indians and take it out on them. An Indian had no more right to live, according to old Andrew, than a Republican to hold a job during a Democratic Administration."[91] Although Rogers was generally an even-tempered man, Jackson was a topic that brought out a particularly visceral response, as Yagoda relates:

> One memorable eruption came during an appearance before a large group of Cherokee Indians. The beginning of his performance was like any other. "Then, suddenly, he became furious," reported a newspaper-

man who was there. "His transformation was terrifying, and for three minutes his astonished audience was treated to a demonstration of what primitive, instinctive hatred could be." The object of his hatred was Andrew Jackson, who in the distant past had started the chain of events that sent the Cherokees on the Trail of Tears. "The Indians listened, and then the quiet was ripped by the screaming war cry of the tribe, while Rogers stood, white, trembling and actually aghast at himself."[92]

Although Cherokee concerns dominate Rogers's comments about Indians, he also gives his voice to the struggles of other tribal nations, as when he critiques the theft of Apache land for dam projects created under the Coolidge administration:

> You know as you saw all those Indians you couldent help but think of the old days. Here was the old warlike Apaches that fought to hold all they had, and most of them wound up in jail, but there was a Washington that fought for his tribe against invaders and wound up with a flock of Statues and a title of Father of his Country. And yet I expect if the truth were known the old Apache Chiefs went through more and fought harder for their Country than George did. But George won, that's the whole answer to history, it's not what did you do, but what did you get away with at the finish.[93]

Not even the secular god of the United States, George Washington, is exempt from Rogers's critique. Yet not all Indians receive the same degree of praise; for example, he's quite critical of Atlantic coast tribes for what he sees as their failure to stop Invasion:

> If my tribe ever settled in New England with all the rest of North America to pick from, they certainly wouldent be known today as the most highly civilized tribe in America. That's the bunch of Indians up there that let the Pilgrims land. That showed right there they dident know anything. Why, it took the Pilgrims 300 years of constant education before we let them land in Oklahoma with us, and then we made one of our only mistakes.[94]

Osages in particular are a favorite target, reflecting deep-seated intertribal conflicts that stem from the early movements of Old Settler Cherokees into Osage territories prior to the Trail of Tears, and the U.S.-imposed land cessions to the Cherokees following the Trail. Osage oil money is Rogers's typical point of irritation: "Lots of people think 'cause the Osages have oil that all Indians are rich. Why the Pine Ridge Agency Siouxs eat so much horse meat, that they are wearing bridles instead of hats."[95] His silence on the brutal murder conspiracies against Osages by non-Indians eager to claim oil headrights—the "Osage Reign of Terror"—is quite telling, certainly more an issue of selective silence than ignorance.

Rogers also demonstrates a strong streak of Cherokee superiority, a national pride that then, as today, is often the subject of good-natured ribbing: "You know [Charley Curtis] is a mighty human kind of a cuss. He is a Kaw Indian. There ain't many of 'em. It's just a little tribe in Kansas and northern Oklahoma. But they are good Indians. Not as good as us Cherokees, but good enough."[96] This Cherokee-centrism does not, however, keep Rogers from being critical of some of the failings of his own people. In discussing the loss of the Cherokee Strip to allotment and White settlement, Rogers also gives a rare note of praise (albeit generally backhanded) for Osages:

> The Cherokees are supposed to be the highest civilized Tribe there is and yet . . . [we] sold a fortune in oil and wonderful agricultural land to get that little [$]320 apiece. Yet there was the Osages lived right by us and they get that much before breakfast every morning, and they are supposed to be uncivilized.
>
> So it really shows you it kinder pays not to know too much. I would trade my so called superior knowledge right now for an Osage headright. If you had their payments you wouldent need to know anything only where the payments was going to be held. But as a matter of fact the Osages got some mighty smart men among them.[97]

There are also moments of militant defiance in his writings, the warrior strain of the Beloved Path that accommodates just so far—even those upon the Beloved Path are called upon to defend the People. Charles Curtis, Vice President of the United States in the Hoover administration, was Kaw and Osage, and a politician who gained Rogers's support largely because of his Indian heritage; nearly every time Rogers mentions Curtis, he also mentions Curtis's tribal affiliation. On the eve of Curtis's selection as Hoover's running mate, Rogers writes:

> And don't forget Charlie Curtis. You Republicans owe him more than you do anybody outside of your Campaign contributors. . . . He has stayed with you through all your disgraces and never got mixed up in

any of them. He is an Indian. I wish he would get in. Us Indians would run these White people out of this country.[98]

In 1928, after Curtis's selection as the vice-presidential candidate, Rogers repeats the militant announcement: "I been telling you for days that Curtis would be the one. He is a Kaw Indian and me a Cherokee and I am for him. It's the first time we have ever got a break—the only American that has ever run for that high office. . . . Come on, Injun! If you are elected let's run the white people out of this country."[99] His 20 April 1930 radio broadcast concludes on a supportive note to Curtis: "So good luck to you, Charlie, old Injun, and I hope you are elected President some day and we will run the White House out of this country. That is what we will do. Good night."[100]

Another instance in which Rogers called for Indians to cast off White Invasion was in response to the controversy that surrounded Roberta Lawson, a Cherokee woman from Tulsa who, as vice president, sought the presidency of the General Federation of Women's Clubs (with whom Yankton Sioux activist Gertrude Bonnin/Zitkala-Ša worked in the 1920s and 1930s). A number of objections were raised solely based on her Indianness, which rankled Rogers so much that he addressed it at least three times in three different venues: his "Daily Telegrams," "Weekly Articles," and radio show. In the latter, Rogers announces his solidarity with her cause:

> And so, any of you women who are going to Detroit next week don't you vote my Indian out, or I'll be on you from now on, I'm telling you. Say, listen, don't get our intolerance reaching as far down as the Indian, 'cause you monkey around with her and I—I'm Cherokee, too, so's she—and I—we'll just get together and run you all out of this country and take it back over again.[101]

Rogers's sharpest criticisms of the U.S. government include some of his other favored targets, the Pilgrims:

> Our record with the Indians is going to go down in history. It is going to make us mighty proud of it in the future when our children of ten more generations read of what we did to them. Every man in our history that killed the most Indians has got a statue built for him. The only difference between the Roman gladiators and the Pilgrims was that the Romans used a lion to cut down their native population, and the Pilgrims had a gun. The Romans didn't have no gun; they just had to use a lion.

The Government, by statistics, shows they have got 456 treaties that they have broken with the Indians. That is why the Indians get a kick out reading the Government's usual remark when some big affair comes up, "Our honor is at stake."

Every time the Indians move the Government will give them a treaty. They say, "You can have this ground as long as grass grows and water flows." On account of its being a grammatical error, the Government didn't have to live up to it. It didn't say "flown," or "flew" or something. Now they have moved the Indians and they settled the whole thing by putting them on land where the grass won't grow and the water won't flow, so now they have it all set.[102]

Rogers's distaste of Pilgrims is here unvarnished and scathing, but often with a gently biting humor that reaches deeper than simple condemnation. He notes that "They were very religious people that come over here from the old country. They were very human. They would shoot a couple of Indians on the way to every prayer meeting."[103]

Additional comments by Rogers show him tearing the veneer away from the romanticized Eurowestern myth of the poor Pilgrims driven by their God and piety to tame a wild land. When analyzing the arrival of the Pilgrims on the shores of North America, Rogers notes:

I want to be broadminded, but I am sure that it was only the extreme generosity of the Indians that allowed the Pilgrims to land. Suppose we reversed the case. Do you reckon the Pilgrims would have ever let the Indians land? Yeah, what a chance! What a chance! The Pilgrims wouldn't even allow the Indians to live after the Indians went to the trouble of letting 'em land.[104]

He further tears down the myth with understated and scathing insight:

Well, anyhow, the Provincetown officials, they sent me a lot of official data, that when the Pilgrims landed they found some corn that the Indians had stored and that the Pilgrims were about starved and that they eat the Indians' corn. And they claim that the corn was stored at Provincetown. You see, the minute the Pilgrims landed they got full of the corn and then they shot the Indians, perhaps because they hadn't stored more corn. I don't know. . . . Of course—but they'd always pray. That's one thing about a Pilgrim. He would pray, mostly for more Indian corn. You've never in your life seen a picture—I bet anyone of you—have never seen a picture of one of the old Pilgrims praying when he didn't have a gun right by the side of him. That was to see that he got what he was praying for.[105]

By the time of his death in a plane crash near Point Barrow, Alaska, on 15 August 1935, Rogers had become America's goodwill ambassador, but not through blind, unreflective patriotism. Rather, Rogers spoke as a man of principle, a man who knew the dangers of such thought and spoke against it at all opportunities. The Cherokees had learned of the duplicity of the U.S. government and its agents; Rogers brought that awareness to a worldwide audience that might otherwise not be willing to listen.

It can hardly be a coincidence that, as he came into the world surrounded by Indians, so too did he leave it, as it was Inuit fishermen who discovered the wrecked plane in which the bodies of Rogers and his friend Wiley Post were found. In her biography of her husband, Betty Rogers gives a haunting account of the funeral boat that took Will and Wiley Post from the crash site to Point Barrow: "Dr. W. H. Greist, the medical missionary at Point Barrow, told me . . . how [the party from Point Barrow] started back with Will and Wiley a few hours later in the boat, the Eskimos [sic] chanting their songs for the dead, the strange, solemn words echoing across the still water and into the night."[106]

Will Rogers, as a Cherokee and a *true* American, was honored by the Cherokee Nation in death as in life. On a marble tablet at the Will Rogers Memorial in Claremore is inscribed the Seal of the Cherokee Nation, a brief aphorism by Rogers in both English and the Cherokee syllabary ("Live your life, so that whenever you lose you are ahead"), his enrollment number (11384) and blood quantum ("Quarter-Blood Cherokee"), and the following epitaph, which was "Presented by The Cherokee Nation, November 4th, 1946, the 67th Anniversary of His Birth":

We honor the memory of Oklahoma's beloved native son. A modest, unspoiled child of the plains, cowboy, actor, humorist and world traveler whose homely philosophy and superior gifts brought laughter and tears to prince and commoner alike. His aversion to sham and deceit, his love of candor and sincerity, coupled with abounding wit and affable repartee, won for him universal homage and an appropriate title, "Ambassador of Good Will."

Truly, Will Rogers walked many delicate paths. Of all those trails, however, his walk on the Beloved Path was the one he most honored, and it is the one for which Cherokees will long remember him: he remains the Cherokee voice of America.

"HERODOTUS OF THE CHEROKEES": THE CHICKAMAUGA DEFIANCE OF EMMET STARR

In *Heart of the Eagle: Dragging Canoe and the Emergence of the Chickamauga Confederacy* (1999), Cherokee historian Brent Cox notes that there are "four primary responses to imperialism: fight, flight, diplomacy, and reform." Of these, Cox chronicles fight and flight as the Chickamauga responses to White encroachments:

> From 1775–1792, Dragging Canoe and the Chickamaugans contested the advance of white civilization, and twice they retreated southward for reorganization. Though Dragging Canoe and his warriors never consented to reform, two primary responses to imperialism were evident. Their principal objective was the return of the Cherokee hunting grounds, and conquest was never a factor.[107]

Fight and flight; strike hard, then pull back to gather strength. This strategy served them well in their battles with the United States and its squatters. When fighting was no longer a viable option, many of the Chickamaugas moved west to avoid further White intrusions. There they rebuilt their towns and their homes and continued their old social and ceremonial ways.

Such strategies have been exercised by many Cherokees before and since, on many battlegrounds. Emmet Starr, the foremost Cherokee historian and genealogist of the late nineteenth and early twentieth centuries, drew on a Chickamauga consciousness in his own writing. His last work, *History of the Cherokee Indians and Their Legends and Folk Lore* (1921), stands today not only as his greatest literary achievement, but also as perhaps the most important volume on Cherokee history and kinship structures of the Indian Territory.

The first half of the book includes a brief early history of the Cherokees, which is followed by primary documents, generally treaties, laws, and letters that impacted the political affairs of the Nation. The second half contains a staggering collection of genealogical information, including

Emmet Starr, 1914. Courtesy of the Northeastern State University Archives, Tahlequah, Oklahoma.

thousands of individuals and hundreds of family names, along with their relationships, and hundreds of smaller biographies. Starr chronicled the histories and family ties of the Cherokee Nation to preserve vital cultural information and to stave off some of the more debilitating impacts of allotment and Oklahoma statehood, both of which exacerbated existing tensions within the Nation and helped to fragment much of the national consciousness.

There is little information about Starr available in the public record. As Rennard Strickland and Jack Gregory note, "[t]oday, there are many descendants of distinguished Cherokees who have no idea of the contributions which their Indian ancestors made to the Cherokee tribe."[108] This is certainly the case with Starr. *History of the Cherokee Indians* has been reprinted numerous times, but always by small presses with equally small press runs. His three other books—*Cherokees West* (1910), *Encyclopedia of Oklahoma* (1912), and *Early History of the Cherokees* (1917)—are rare and largely unavailable to anyone but scholars. Only a few articles have been written about the medical doctor–turned–national historian or his immeasurable contributions to both the written record and Cherokee cultural consciousness; the most insightful work dates back to the late 1960s and mid-1970s. Unlike the case of many of his contemporaries—the aforementioned Gertrude Bonnin (Yankton Sioux), Carlos Montezuma (Yavapai Apache), Charles Eastman (Santee Sioux), Sarah Winnemucca Hopkins (Paiute), Ella Deloria (Yankton Sioux), E. Pauline Johnson (Mohawk), and Alexander Posey (Muskogee Creek)—there is a dearth of critical discussion about Starr's contributions to American Indian intellectualism. While he may well have been "the Cherokee historian for all times," one would hardly guess this given the erasure of Starr from contemporary historical and intellectual criticism.[109]

Unlike White scholars of the time who tended to be either dismissive or patronizing, Starr was a clear admirer of the traditionalist Keetoowahs, and he was generally quite critical of those who would see the Cherokees as being a "civilized" people overcoming their "savage" Indigenousness. He was unhesitant in his criticisms of "two gun historians" (such as Grant Foreman) who wrote of Cherokee history as "a Republican tribute to acculturation," seeking instead to explore the multifaceted complexity of the Nation, traditionalists and acculturated Cherokees alike.[110] He wrote fiercely against both physical and textual erasure, with a primary commitment to the genealogical and documentary concerns of the People—

concerns that didn't find favor with the White gatekeepers of Oklahoma history—and as a result he has been largely removed from current critical discussions.

Starr was born in 1870 into a mixedblood family of the Cherokee Nation, over thirty years before Indian Territory became Oklahoma, and he was educated in Cherokee cultural traditions and history, as well as in both Cherokee schools and Barnes College in St. Louis. His work represents a clear focus on Cherokee tribal nationhood; this philosophy emerged during his young adulthood years, during which the Nation was besieged by Whites seeking Cherokee land and resources. His *History* is primarily a genealogical text; over half of the book chronicles the detailed family relationships of "Old Families" and people of influence in the Nation. This concern with genealogy is more than family ties; it's also an assertion of national presence through the living People. His biographers Strickland and Gregory observe that Starr's "genealogical notes were used as evidence by the Dawes Commission in establishing Cherokee settlements and for listing on the official tribal rolls"; in a very real way, his encyclopedic compilation of national ties have provided the current political Nation with its established citizenry.[111] His aim is made clear in the preface to the *History*:

> This humble effort is attempted for the purpose of perpetuating some of the facts relative to the Cherokee tribe, that might otherwise be lost. The object has been to make it as near a personal history and biography of as many Cherokees as possible.
>
> Without the assistance of the magnanimous, wholesoul membership of the nation, the work would not have been possible and for that reason I wish to thank each and every member, for their hearty collaboration and express my regret that the work has not the merit with which many others might have invested it.[112]

The structure and content of the text reflects the complexity of the Nation. The book includes sketches of ancient Cherokee artifacts titled "Echota," each of a warrior wearing either wings or a winged robe, bearing a war club in one hand and a human head in another.[113] The 1839 seal of the Cherokee Nation stands on the title page, neither dominating nor being obscured by the Echota warriors—ancient tradition and modernity in balance with one another. There is no hint of the "two gun history" that sees Cherokees as "progressing" from savagery to civilization; rather, the history and contemporary lives of the Nation are connected to one another and, indeed, exist alongside one another, neither given primacy.

Starr's work is an unflinching exercise of intellectual sovereignty, embedded fully in Cherokee culture and history and ignoring the conventions of the written histories of the time. Photographs and maps abound throughout the book, with over two dozen portraits in the genealogy chapters alone. Along with the main genealogical materials, the remainder of the book consists of syncretic Christian and premissionary traditional stories, the full texts of treaties, laws, proclamations, important and/or problematic issues that impacted the Nation (including strong critiques of missionary activities), lists of Cherokees who held particular political and social posts, short individual biographies of hundreds of individuals and many of their own family genealogies, and some historical treatises, including a chapter devoted to the Keetoowah movement. He was, as Strickland and Gregory note, "frequently an Indian at war with the Oklahoma historical establishment, especially with the land allotment, settlement and statehood historians who wrote with the obvious White bias of Dawes Commission and Oklahoma constitutional forces."[114] His histories defy outsider interpretations that demand Native removal from both the physical and symbolic landscapes of America. *History of the Cherokee Indians* speaks not simply to the continuing presence of Cherokees during the catastrophic era of allotment; it speaks to the kinship ties and relationships that have endured in spite of the devastating effects of White racism.

This isn't to say that there aren't tensions within the text, because in many ways the *History* is a study of contradictions, uncertainties, and the all-too-familiar dualism of traditional ceremonialism and Christianity. The diverse content is reflected in the absence of a single authoritative definition of Cherokee social life and values—perhaps one of the book's most unique features, and certainly one of its greatest strengths. There's an unwieldy struggle in the *History* between Starr's sympathetic portrayal of the non-Christian Keetoowahs and his embrace of the "lost tribe of Israel" thesis that was common among White commentators of the eighteenth century, in which perceived similarities between Cherokee cultural practices and those of biblical accounts were seen as indicative of a historical affiliation.[115]

Indeed, Starr even goes so far as to state that the political influence of early Europeans, such as French provocateur Christian Priber, was such that the Cherokees had replaced their own origin accounts with muddled fragments of biblical stories that were then "attributed . . . to legends that had descended from the mythical Kutani and their primal religion." Starr extends this odd claim, asserting that the Cherokees "thought that the missionaries were bringing back to them their old religion," and once the Cherokees "were converted, they, at the behest of the missionaries cast aside every vestige of their ancient customs to such an extent that not any of their mythology has ever been preserved, even among those of the tribe that speak the Cherokee language perfectly."[116] This assertion is strikingly inaccurate, especially in light of anthropologist James Mooney's voluminous 1900 collection of that very "mythology" among the North Carolina Cherokees, and the subsequent rich field work of Jack and Anna Kilpatrick in the 1960s (and that of Alan Kilpatrick today) that demonstrates the endurance of those "ancient customs" among Oklahoma Cherokees, even among professing Christians.[117] The claim is also contradicted by Starr's later discussion of the Keetoowahs, many of whom he acknowledges practice "ancient customs and usages" that are historically and substantively distinctive from Christianity, naming them the "ancient Keetoowahs" without any mention of his earlier presumption that they follow anything but aboriginal, non-Christian traditions.[118]

It's also important to remember that although Starr was connected to many ceremonialists by bonds of kinship and respect, he was also a southern Democrat and a member of both the Freemasons and the evangelical Methodist Episcopal Church, South, a conservative denomination that split with its northern counterpart in 1845 on the subject of slavery (but which also had a sizeable African American population in Starr's time). These facts all likely predisposed him toward sympathizing with the political aims of the ancient Keetoowahs without understanding or even consistently appreciating their spiritual practices. Most Cherokees in Starr's era, as today, were at least nominally Christians; this religious affiliation didn't necessarily reflect political affiliation.

The unifying principles of Cherokee peoplehood can be read at the heart of the tension here: while Starr fails to recognize the ancient stories and traditions that were still told among both Eastern and Oklahoma Cherokees during his time, he's also willing to acknowledge that the internecine tensions between the "ancient" and "Christian" Keetoowah groups emerged "only after the white Missionaries objected to and condemned what they termed 'the Pagan Form of worship' of the ancient Keetowahs, and designated it as 'The work of the Devil,'" without vilification of either.[119] In some ways Starr was the opposite of Will Rogers: while the former advocated a political Chickamauga consciousness rooted in a Cherokee nationhood that encompassed Christianity, Rogers's Beloved Path was one that fundamentally rejected the false security and monotheistic chauvinism implicit in so much of Christian practice. The attitudes of each man toward spirituality unsettle any easy conflation of politics, faith, and identity with principles of Cherokee nationhood, just as the mixedblood/fullblood binary is ultimately more complicated and unstable than popular discourses of blood quantum would suggest.

Starr was well known to his Oklahoma Cherokee kin; he gathered most of his genealogical materials from personal interviews and correspondence with a wide and diverse range of Cherokees. His personal papers, now held at the Oklahoma Historical Society, demonstrate the comprehensive detail and deep respect with which Starr approached his vocation. He knew the interrelationships and family ties of thousands of Cherokees, and within the community was famed for this knowledge, a fact to which Cherokee historian R. H. Fowler attested: "Dr. Starr was the best versed, on Cherokee history and old family geneological [sic] lines in the far back past, that has ever lived. It was his chosen life work from his young days. No one dare dispute or go back on Dr. Starr's records for he was considered the highest recognized authority living at that time."[120] Through this work, Starr insisted on the continued cultural presence of the Cherokee Nation. He wrote *of* the past, but he wrote *to* the future, to the never-quenched fire of the Cherokees.

And yet, after Oklahoma statehood and allotment, after the U.S. government declared the Cherokee government to be extinguished, Starr left the land base of his beloved Nation and lived in seclusion in St. Louis, Missouri. He died there "in a two room walk-up apartment in St. Louis suffering a self-imposed exile and convinced that he had failed his people."[121] For a man so defiant and cognizant of the necessity for symbolic as well as physical Native presence, this seems a sad and ironic end. What brought him to this moment? Had he surrendered to despair, as some have argued, or was this an extension of the Chickamauga defiance he had exercised throughout his life?

Strickland and Gregory posit a singular reason for Starr's exile: "The simple truth was that he was a man whose country was gone, destroyed as completely as if it had been bombed from the face of the earth. To Starr, and other Cherokees of his age, the end of the Nation was a catastrophic blow. In his case, it was a blow from which he never recovered." They cite Cherokee writer William R. Harper's similar observations:

> But finding that the parental fortune has disappeared and the education of his younger orphaned brothers and sisters about to be neglected, he magnanimously forsook his own plans and ambitions and took upon his own shoulders this task. By the time this was completed the old order of things had passed away and the new had passed in. Transformation from tribal government to statehood eliminated his opportunity—there was no more demand for the services he was so able and so anxious to render. So, like the "Last of the Mohicans," he passed out. Finding his occupation gone he wandered "off the reservation" only to be swallowed up in the maelstrom of modern "efficiency" and greed.[122]

This "parental fortune" is more than simple money; it also includes the rich cultural legacy of the Cherokee Nation, which many Cherokees saw as fading away before the invasion of the White settler hordes under allotment and statehood. Starr's historical and cultural vocation is to share this legacy with the People, both his literal "younger orphaned brothers and sisters" whom he helped to educate after the deaths of their parents, and those Cherokees who had turned their back on a community and traditions that they viewed as doomed to extinction anyway (much like the character of Viney in Lynn Riggs's *The Cherokee Night*). In his 1930 memorial to Starr, Micah Pearce Smith comments that "Doctor Starr told me that he had come to St. Louis some years before I met him because he felt that he could make a better living here. He said he never expected to return to Oklahoma to live," and adds with a dramatic flourish, "and he never did."[123] Thus, in this interpretation, Starr left Oklahoma with the sad certainty that there was no hope left for the Nation or the Cherokee people, and that they were, indeed, a "vanishing race."

This interpretation, however, ignores one important point: Starr published his two most important books *after* the passage of the calamitous events that accompanied allotment, and after the most visible devastation had taken place. The *Early History of the Cherokees* was published in 1917 and focused on the Old Settler Cherokees; the exhaustive culmination of his life's work, *History of the Cherokee Indians,* was published five years later. If he was convinced that his people were doomed to erasure, why would he continue fruitlessly working on books that were rooted in the concept of Cherokee continuity?

We can look to the second Chickamauga resistance strategy for an answer to this puzzle: retreat. In the Chickamauga context, retreat doesn't mean surrender. It's a falling back to heal, regroup, reassemble, and return on another front. It's a classic strategy of Cherokee guerilla warfare, one that struck fear in the enemy and minimized losses among the People. Starr didn't abandon his work when it was clear that Oklahoma statehood and allotment would become reality; instead, he continued compiling information, writing, corresponding and visiting with Cherokee families and historians, editing, and publishing. He was gathering strength on another front and preparing for the next volley.

It's difficult to quote Starr's voice directly from the *History,* as there is little authorial intrusion: most primary documents are printed without annotations or explanations. The short biographies are generally lists of facts and dates; the primary moments that Starr's voice appears are the early narration of Cherokee origins and migration stories and his four-page commentary on the Keetoowahs. Yet we can clearly connect with Starr's voice through those stories, photos, and documents he includes in the text, particularly in regard to the Keetoowah content, which is generally absent from those histories written by White historians of the Grant Foreman school. Starr devotes a full chapter to Redbird Smith and the Keetoowahs, composed mostly of letters and other primary documents, and he made clear in his brief commentary his deep admiration for the goal of their resistance:

> [Smith's] program covered not only the Nighthawks [Keetoowahs], but all people of Cherokee blood. His great ambition was to accomplish a united spirit of co-operation among all the factors of the Cherokee people. It was distinctly not his idea to reestablish the old and discarded regime of the Cherokee Government, but to awaken a racial pride, so that the more fortunate of the race may become great factors in helping their less fortunate brethren.
>
> It is this spirit and ambition of his that has prevailed even after his death, and that which his survivors in Office are carrying out in the selection of Levi Gritts as Chief of the Cherokees. It should be understood that it is purely a purpose of unifying the Cherokee people to a grand effort

of agrandizing [sic] the race that it may acquit itself as a contributor to
a grand race of men in America, as Redbird called it "The Mother of the
New World."[124]

These are not the words of a man who had fallen into despair about his
people. While clearly distressed about the political threats that the People
faced—as is evidenced in his preface to the book, when he states his goal of
compiling the information "that might otherwise be lost"—he yet retains a
certainty about Cherokee survival. That survival, as the Keetoowah movement proclaimed, required both a return to ceremonial traditions and a
development into a new type of community, one that would continue in
spite of the predatory hunger of the White U.S. citizenry. Although surprisingly quiet about the continuing state of these traditions, Starr nonetheless treats the Keetoowahs and their goals with remarkable sensitivity
and clarity.

Indeed, Strickland and Gregory themselves note that Starr directly
stated his reason for moving to St. Louis to be "because he felt he could
make a better living." Yet they then assert that "[m]oney is too convenient
an excuse although, after he abandoned his medical career, he moved
from job to job." He had long since given up on medicine to devote himself to his vocation as Cherokee chronicler. There was little tolerance in
Oklahoma for a historian who was critical of the White historical establishment, so Starr left to make a living elsewhere, going back to a familiar big city that he had known during his days in medical school. Why
wouldn't he return to a city to which he wasn't a stranger? He spent much
of his time in St. Louis trying to create his own book shop, even purchas-
ing letterhead (with his apartment as the business address) advertising
"Any Book Ever Printed in English Except Erotica."[125] He continued to
critique the Oklahoma "two gun historians" and to bemoan the lack of
Oklahoma news in his new home. A man convinced that his "country was
gone, destroyed as completely as if it had been bombed from the face of the
earth," would not likely be concerned with such matters, especially when
the publication process was both expensive and time-consuming.[126]

There is little evidence from either the published record or his correspondence that Starr left any other reason for such a move. Employment
difficulties and thwarted professional ambitions seem truly to have been
very much central to his life. Much of his rather ingratiating correspondence to Joseph Thoburn, noted Oklahoma historian and staff member of

the Oklahoma Historical Society, concerns appeals for public acknowl-edgment of his historiography and, in particular, assistance with finding employment. It seems that Thoburn was able to help a number of times, both by citing Starr in his own texts and helping with jobs at least twice: a three-year stint (1913–16) as the librarian for Northeastern State Normal School (now Northeastern State University) in Tahlequah, and a position with the Muskogee Office of the Indian Service from December 1917 until sometime around April 1919. An undercurrent of thwarted ambition flows through Starr's letters to Thoburn, both before and after his move to St. Louis, the latter punctuated with an occasional appeal for employment in Oklahoma (particularly with the Oklahoma Historical Society, a site of scholarly legitimacy that continually evaded him).[127] Through it all, he asserts his desire to find an institutional home where he could continue to share the true history of Cherokees and reclaim the field of Oklahoma history from "the Two Gun Historians and their bunch."[128]

The evidence thus far available doesn't support the idea that Starr re-treated into self-exile. Just as the Chickamaugas moved from areas where their survival was imperiled to regroup and rebuild, it's reasonable to posit that Starr, too, exercised this principle of strategic defeat. That he died away from his homeland shouldn't, by itself, be seen as evidence of "self-imposed exile." Death is generally an unexpected visitor, and it's un-likely that Starr knew he would die away from Oklahoma, in spite of what seems, in Micah Smith's memorial, to have been more an offhand com-ment than a firm resolution.

Besides, Starr didn't move very far from home; St. Louis is only about 370 miles on U.S. Interstate 44 from his old home of Claremore—a direct journey on the St. Louis and San Francisco line that cut diagonally through the Cooweescoowee District of the Cherokee Nation in Indian Territory. Betty Rogers notes too that St. Louis was a "great market" for cattle that, by her estimation, was "only 250 miles away" from Claremore by train. Starr could have been home on an overnight train that went right through both St. Louis and Claremore on its way west, a well-traveled and familiar route to many Cherokees, especially those involved in the cattle business (including, as Oskison notes in his autobiography, a group that included himself and Will Rogers).[129] It was a familiar route to most Cherokees, as one leg of the Trail of Tears went through southern Missouri.

A man in life-long exile would hardly be likely to be so conveniently located near his homeland. Such a location, however, would be ideal for a committed truth-seeker hoping to one day return at his community's call. Starr needed to make a living and found the means to do so in St. Louis, spending his last years as an employee at The Book World, a second-hand bookstore and gathering place of local scholars. But he never went far away from the People, or from his life's calling. Long after allotment had stripped the Cherokees of much of the national land base, Starr continued to compile and revise his genealogies and histories, to give the People a fuller sense of themselves as a continuing nation in spite of the U.S. insistence on fragmentation and assimilation. His work and life are anything but reminiscent of *The Last of the Mohicans,* in spite of William R. Harper's romantic assertion. Instead, Starr was a Chickamauga patriot in spirit and in deed.

Truly, as Strickland and Gregory claim, Emmet Starr "was the heroic Cherokee historian for all time," but not because he was a tragic victim of the political traumas of the age who managed to produce important texts before crossing to the Nightlands. He was no "vanishing Indian," no sad and lonely Native on a pinto riding off into the sunset. Reading his life and work through Chickamauga principles demonstrates instead that Starr was a dedicated scholar who gave up financial comfort and the respect of the Oklahoma historical establishment to dedicate himself to the task of providing an honest, dignified, and unyielding chronicle of Cherokee history. As with the early Chickamaugas, Starr didn't simply disappear into the obscuring shadows of despair. Instead, he lived, fought, and ultimately died in hopeful service to the future of the Cherokee people.

THINKING ABOUT HOME

One afternoon in the summer of 1997, as I was preparing to move to Nebraska for graduate school, my mom and I drove the sixty miles south from my hometown of Victor, Colorado, to Cañon City, where my grandmother Betty and her husband lived. I'd never been very close to my maternal grandparents, but we got along well enough, and on this day they were interested in my plans for my graduate education. They were particularly intrigued by my choice to go into American Indian literature, as they had no idea that Indians had much in the way of written texts. Eventually the conversation moved from literature to the larger state of colonization in the United States. To my surprise, Betty was quite receptive to the argument. She then surprised me further by acknowledging the horrors of colonization while simultaneously stating, with no small relief, "It's a good thing that didn't happen around here, since there weren't any Indians."

My mom and I were flabbergasted. After collecting my thoughts, I pointed out to Betty that our family wasn't exempt from being implicated in the processes of colonization: after all, traveling from Colorado Springs to Victor required going past *Cheyenne* Mountain, up *Ute* Pass, and past *Chipita* Park, which was named after the wife of the Tabeguache/Uncompahgre Ute chief Ouray. The geothermal waters of Manitou Springs, just west of Colorado Springs, made the area a hospitable gathering-grounds among the Cheyennes, Utes, Kiowas, and Arapahos before Whites drove the tribes out, and Manitou Springs is also the site of the Cave of the Winds, which features in both Jicarilla Apache and Ute oral traditions. The entire Cripple Creek–Victor mining district, where I, my mother, my maternal grandfather, grandmother, and stepgrandfather were all raised, is within the traditional territories of the Mouache Ute band of the Southern Ute Tribe. The Indian presence of the area is invoked in other ways, some more insulting than others: our hometown was built on the southeastern slope of Squaw Mountain, one of at least three such mountains in the state. Of the Indian nations who lived or traveled in this area before Eurowestern Invasion, only the Southern Ute and Ute Mountain tribes have reservations in what is known today by Whites as the southwestern corner of Colorado.

I was raised in Victor; it's the place that's most firmly woven into my thoughts when I speak the word "home." I've hiked, camped, and hunted with my dad all over the mountains, sat in the kitchen late into the night with my mom and shared my heart's hopes and fears, daydreamed with my pug dogs among fragrant pines and whispering aspens, and watched storms roll over the top of Pikes Peak to the northeast and brilliant orange and purple sunsets burn across the soaring Sangre de Cristo mountains to the south. The spirits of that place are a part of my consciousness. As Cherokees have long been mountain people, it seems fitting that we'd find our way to this place.[130] My dad often says that once the mountains are in your blood, you just can't be happy anyplace else. He's got a point.

Victor is my home, but the stark truth is that it's my home largely because the Mouache Utes were driven from the area by Eurowestern miners and ranchers, just as the chaos brought by White land-seekers drove my dad's parents away from Oklahoma in the years following allotment. My maternal family came to Victor as part of the great Cripple Creek–

Victor gold rush, and my dad followed in the 1960s, lured by the promise of a good job. My parents both worked for the mines when I was a child, my dad in various positions, including hoist operator of the Ajax Mine, and my mom as plant lab superintendent and assayer for one of the larger mining companies. Victor is our home, the site of multigenerational history and memory, with the bones of some of our ancestors buried in the red soil, but it's someone else's home, too. They've been removed and displaced, but they weren't erased from the memory of the place I call home. One hundred years of their absent presence doesn't change the fact that Victor isn't mine alone.

It never was.

Part III

REGENERATION

Regeneration

All Nations have had their rises & their falls. This has been the
case with us. Within the orbit the U. States move the States &
within these we move in a little circle, dependent on the great center. We may live in this way fifty years & then we shall by Natural
causes merge in & mingle with the U. States. Cherokee blood, if
not destroyed, will wind its courses in beings of fair complexions,
who will read that their ancestors became civilized under the
frowns of misfortune & causes of their enemies.

—John Ridge (Cherokee), letter to Albert Gallatin, 1826

Where will we be as a people five, ten, fifty, or one hundred years
from now? Do we talk only of ancestors or do we plan for our
descendants? Do we talk about our full-blood ancestors or do we
admire our Indian grandchildren? Do we live in the past or do we
focus on the future? Is being Cherokee a novelty or a way of life? Is
being Cherokee a heritage or a future?

—Chad Smith, Principal Chief of the Cherokee Nation,
"Introduction" to *Cherokee*

Cherokee nationhood didn't disappear with the end of the Trail of
Tears. It endured through the U.S. Civil War. Although many in Indian
Territory and beyond thought it lost during the allotment era, it survived
that storm, too. And now, in the first years of the *yoneg* twenty-first century, over 460 years after the Ani-Yunwiya first encountered Europeans in the

de Soto invasion force, over 330 years after the *Chalakee* first engaged with English colonists, the fires of Cherokee nationhood continue to burn.

Yet the spirit of Cherokee nationhood is a delicate thing, dependent as it is on the People's purposeful engagement with their kinship connections and obligations. Like all living things, this spirit withers when neglected, just as it bursts to strong life when given vital sustenance and attention. Vigilance and care are fundamental to our survival, a lesson that John Ridge and others too often forgot. Despair leads to a darkening path.

Hindsight can make us arrogant, and it's easy to read Ridge's words and forget the horrors that led him to a grim vision of the future in which Cherokee nationhood was nothing but memory. It shouldn't be forgotten that he and the other members of the Treaty Party waited to sign the Treaty of New Echota until after all avenues of appeal in the U.S. system were exhausted. The promises of U.S. magnanimity have always been lies when Indians are involved.

Hindsight can be instructive as well. It might not be as simple as the tired adage of history repeating itself, but we have seen again and again, as Chief Smith notes, that Cherokees "are a people who face adversity, survive, adapt, prosper, and excel."[1] The ability to emerge from devastation intact doesn't happen on its own; it requires the People to be willing to plant deep roots, to tend them with care, and to harvest respectfully with an eye toward the future.

The Cherokee literary tradition is intimately tied with these processes of cultural regeneration and recovery, for it remains a powerful assertion of continuity. Whether in oral accounts or written stories, interviews or letters, novels, poems, plays, newspaper articles, treaties, historical monographs, medico-magical notebooks, songs, dances, drawings, or sermons, whether in *Tsalagi,* English, or Spanish, Cherokee literature speaks to the fact that the People are anything but "vanishing Indians." The dead don't generally write; the humanity of Indians isn't locked away in museums to be poked and prodded in the objectifying name of Eurowestern science. With each addition to the Cherokee literary tradition, our living presence is renewed, and we give something to those generations that follow. As the title character muses in Robert Conley's novel, *Sequoyah,* "Let the white men write all the lies they wanted to about the Cherokees. He would write the truth, and it would always be there for Cherokees to read. It would not be forgotten. It would not be lost."[2]

The final section of this book focuses on contemporary Cherokee texts and issues. I've narrowed my textual attention a bit, choosing here a number of works that are a bit more "literary" in form than the texts of previous chapters, more because the chosen writers are most compelling in these particular genres than due to any genre preference. Chapter 4, "Readings in Contemporary Cherokee Literature," extends this study's Chickamauga and Beloved concerns to a diverse collection of contemporary writers: Marilou Awiakta (Cherokee/Appalachian), Thomas King (Cherokee/Greek), Wilma Mankiller (Cherokee Nation), Geary Hobson (Cherokee-Quapaw/Chickasaw), Diane Glancy (Cherokee), and Robert J. Conley (Keetoowah Cherokee).

In my study of these writers, I largely limit my discussion to a single work by each, pairing each text with that of another Cherokee writer within the spheres of cultural influence that I've identified in previous chapters. For example, I read Awiakta's *Selu: Seeking the Corn-Mother's Wisdom* (1993) in conjunction with King's *Truth and Bright Water* (1999) as two compelling manifestations of the Beloved Path principles, whereas Mankiller's 1993 autobiography, *Mankiller: A Chief and Her People,* shares attributes of the Chickamauga consciousness with Hobson's novella *The Last of the Ofos* (2000). My analysis of the work of the last two writers— Glancy and Conley—is quite a bit more focused; although each of these prolific writers has a far larger textual body for discussion than the others, their Trail of Tears novels—Conley's *Mountain Windsong* (1992) and Glancy's *Pushing the Bear* (1996)—provide another useful pairing for comparative analysis. Yet this particular section also brings together the Chickamauga consciousness and Beloved Path readings in a more immediate way, as these writers respectively represent the clearest literary manifestations of the war/peace cultural streams that have nourished Cherokee nationhood for ages. The pairings of these texts and authors is neither arbitrary nor reductive; rather, these connections place them into interpretive relationships that directly respond to the dynamic foundation of tribal nationhood.

My purpose here is twofold: to examine texts that seem most clearly to express the principles of Cherokee nationhood as they appear in contemporary Cherokee literature, and to provide a representative sampling of today's most compelling Cherokee writers. Such privileging of writers and texts will inevitably be judged deficient by some readers, and rightly so, as there are dozens of worthy Cherokee writers who could illustrate these textual concerns. My choice of the above authors shouldn't be read as a dismissal of others; indeed, I would have liked to have included more of the work of writers such as Gogisgi/Carroll Arnett, Betty Louise Bell, Gladys Cardiff, William Sanders, Ralph Salisbury, and Ron Welburn. Yet this study couldn't possibly be the authoritative work on Cherokee literature, nor is it intended to be read as such; rather, it's just one more contribution to a rich and growing body of scholarship. Its value, if any, is as part of a continuing discussion.

The concluding afterword, "The Stories That Matter," departs from the texts a bit to discuss current issues in the field of Indigenous literary studies which, like all areas of Native Studies, is experiencing a backlash against the increasing presence of Indigenous scholars and epistemologies into the field. Due to the tireless work of principled scholars of various backgrounds and blood quanta who work more for the continuity of Native peoples than for their own institutional comfort, the field has slowly shifted toward the privileging of American Indian voices and knowledge traditions, especially after the watershed publication of Robert Allen Warrior's *Tribal Secrets*. Yet each step has been a struggle, and the forces of backlash—whom James Cox has called "poachers"—continue to challenge every success with belligerent tenacity.[3] The afterword first places the larger text within the genealogy of American Indian literary studies, then draws on a range of sources to provide some strategies for the following: to examine through both Beloved and Chickamauga principles ways to meaningfully enrich the field that are ethically responsible and accountable to Indian communities; to privilege Indigenous perspectives and principles in scholarship and teaching while acknowledging the relevant good work done by non-Indians; to productively challenge the backlash without descending into the position of race-baiting and smug condescension that both poachers and Indian reactionaries fall back upon; and to reimagine the field as a respectful gathering grounds where all people of good heart and mind can come to share their intellectual gifts, first for the benefit of Indian nations and then for the larger world.

Contrary to the poachers' claims, to say "Indian first" is not to say "Indian only." Indigenous nationhood is distinguished from Eurowestern nationalism by its concern for respectful relational connection; so too is the best of Indigenous scholarship. The lessons of Cherokee history guide my reflections here, thus bringing the discussion firmly back to the larger concerns of the text: namely, the continuity of the People. Because the

Cherokee literary tradition is so deeply tied to the health of Cherokee nationhood, the state of literary scholarship also has an impact on the People. The afterword, then, examines the possibilities and complications of the future of Indigenous literary studies, as well as the role of Cherokee relational values in helping to shape the more hopeful contours of that future.

Readings in Contemporary Cherokee Literature

Writing prepares the ground for recovery, and even re-creation, of
Indian identity and culture. Native writers speak to that part of us
the colonial power and the dominant culture cannot reach, cannot
touch. They help Indians imagine themselves as Indians. Just as
there is no practice of Native religions for personal empowerment,
they write that the People might live.

—Jace Weaver (Cherokee), *That the People Might Live*

*W*hether by open resistance, defiant withdrawal, subversive accommodation, or enthusiastic assimilation, Cherokees have long interrupted
the Eurowestern narratives of removal and erasure, and, as a result, from
North Carolina to Arkansas, Oklahoma, and locations all over the world,
Cherokees continue to assert their living presence. It is quite heartening
to note that there are more Cherokees living today and actively involved
with the processes of nationhood than at any time in history.[1] As I have
proposed throughout this study, Cherokee nationhood, in all its complexity, is consistently grounded in enduring cultural traditions that have as a
central feature the necessary tension between the Beloved Path of negotiation and accommodation and the Chickamauga consciousness of rhetorical (and sometimes physical) defiance. Neither exists in a vacuum; just as
the peace chiefs were balanced by the war chiefs in the old ways of the
People, and as the war chiefs often became Beloved advocates of peace
when elders, so too must their descendants be seen within a historical
and cultural context of continuity, in which Cherokee identity in its many
complicated forms engages with the politics of the age.

While the surface of those politics may change, the roiling waters beneath attest to a sadly consistent reality: Eurowesterners still seek to dispossess and possess Indian people; if not tribal lands then Indigenous voices, identities, and relationships to the cosmos. Cherokee writers, past and present, speak with eloquence and dedication to that predatory current beneath the too-often deceptively smooth affairs of day-to-day life. The spirits of Nanye'hi and Tsiyu Gansini still endure, bound by one common truth: their unyielding dedication to the endurance of the People.

Between the principles of the Beloved Path and the Chickamauga consciousness, the former is perhaps hardest for contemporary readers to conceptualize, especially in the United States, where violence is the institutionalized foundation of national identity, religious expression, commerce, and territorial expansion.[2] The Chickamauga consciousness is rooted in principles of war and resistance, concepts familiar to the U.S. citizenry (even though Chickamauga values of conflict are not analogous to those characterized by Eurowestern militarism). The Beloved Path, on the other hand, requires a greater conceptual leap, for the actively peaceful resistance of this perspective is accorded a much lower status in U.S. contexts: while much lip service is given to the nonviolent protests of Martin Luther King Jr. and Mohandas (Mahatma) Gandhi, warriors who advocate the shedding of blood have far more cultural capital in the United States.

To be sure, both the war and peace spheres have their complement within them: the Chickamaugas didn't fight all the time, and their battles were for the ultimate cause of a lasting peace; nor were the Beloved leaders always willing to accommodate their antagonists, especially as most had been fiery warriors in their younger days. The one exists in relationship with the other; indeed, it's through attention to such an active and complementary red/white relationship that the historical and contemporary complexity of Cherokees is best understood. As I discuss in chapter 1, the Eurowestern fascination with an assumed oppositional dualism in Cherokee cultural history is an inaccurate and grossly limited concept. Although Cherokee ceremonial and cultural traditions have long had an affinity toward a dualistic worldview, such a worldview is rooted much more in a war and peace complementarity than in conflict, a point that Rennard Strickland made nearly thirty years ago:

> Too much of Cherokee historical scholarship is stagnant. We are producing a truncated history written too much from the political acculturation-

civilization viewpoint and too little from the traditional tribal and broader national-policy perspective. And this, too, is tragic. The Cherokees'
great achievement was not that they adapted so well to white culture but
that they exerted so great a national impact and yet, being on the beach-
head of white expansion, were able to preserve so much that was traditional. Large numbers of nativistic Cherokees retained their Indianness. Their
right to do so was vigorously defended by the more acculturated members
of the tribe. Cherokeeness never became a blood issue. . . . The interplay
of cultures and the resilience of the old Cherokee ways has generally been
ignored.[3]

Although Strickland perhaps overstates the point about the defense of
ceremonial traditionalists by their acculturated kin, his larger message
is undeniably accurate: Cherokees have never been a simple people. It
isn't surprising that this cultural and philosophical complexity has been
erased in favor of an oppositional dualism based on old ideas of "savagism
vs. civilization," but such erasures do nothing to inform a more accurate
understanding of what it is to be Cherokee, and it certainly has negative
implications for Cherokees today and in the future. We have already seen
how, in the allotment era, such a limited worldview was the underpinning
of that devastating sociopolitical policy; if we, too, forget the richness and
diversity that have contributed to our survival as a people today, we risk
losing many of our most vital constituent elements. Eurowestern eugenics
movements have always been, at their core, an attempt to simplify, to literally *remove* from the body politic those deemed "undesirable" by the
latest fear-mongering politician. Simplification is just another word for
genocide, and that philosophy is fundamentally antithetical to relational
principles of kinship, respect, and mutual accountability.

Each of the writers discussed in this chapter understands Cherokee
complexity, and although each approaches the issue and its manifestations differently, this respect for the deeper realities of Cherokee life is a
shared intellectual and artistic principle. A common theme that all the
writers address in their Chickamaugan and Beloved reflections on this
principle is the ever-present shadow of removal. How do we survive the
apocalyptic ravages of colonialism, both those of the past and those to
come? How do we realign ourselves to a cosmos that has been fundamentally thrown out of balance? Is there a place in the present and future for
an acknowledgment of that trauma that extends beyond it to a balanced
place of remembrance *and* healing?

Whether as professional writers, educators, scholars, politicians, speakers, or cultural workers, these Cherokees demonstrate in their lives and on the written page that the Cherokee spirit is a dynamic, adaptive force rooted in the timeless principles that Marilou Awiakta identifies as "strength, respect, balance, harmony. . . . adaptability, cooperation, unity in diversity."[4] It's in living that the People endure the removals of the past and those to come, not in the frozen timelessness of death.

BELOVED READINGS

At first glance, little but their Cherokee affiliation seems to connect the lives and work of Marilou Awiakta and Thomas King. Awiakta's poems and essays are deeply rooted in the Appalachian soil of her Cherokee and Celtic ancestors; King's novels and short stories focus on the Blackfoot peoples of what is now Alberta, Canada, rather than on the cultural specificities of his Cherokee, Greek, and German heritage. Awiakta's work frequently crosses temporal boundaries, passing far into the historical past as much as focusing on concerns of the present day, whereas King's work is largely attentive to contemporary pan-Native realities and imaginative possibilities. Awiakta melds hope with pragmatism in her poetry and prose, always pushing toward positive change while acknowledging the difficulties of such a task; King, on the other hand, has a more cautious view of humanity, and he sometimes leans more toward grim acceptance of human frailty than any real hope for its transformation.[5] The Cherokee spirit Little Deer—Awi Usdi, the chief of the deer peoples who cripples disrespectful hunters—stands as Awiakta's stable symbol for the ordered laws of the Spirit World and this world, whereas the erratic, destructive, creative, and ever-unpredictable Coyote—the trickster spirit of many prairie tribes, distinct from Rabbit (Jisdu), the Cherokee trickster—dances wildly through King's fiction, leaving chaos and uncertainty in his wake.

Yet far more connects these writers and their work than divides them. Both are strongly connected to the broad concerns of Indigenous survival and (re)connection to the web of relationships between humans and other animals, spirits of this world and those beyond, and all participants in creation. They've each acknowledged pan-Indian issues as significant and important connecting threads between tribal specificities. Both have given significant attention to a gender realignment that emphasizes the traditional respect among Cherokees and other tribal peoples for the wis-

Marilou Awiakta. Photograph by Carol Marrow.

dom and strength of women. And, perhaps most significantly, both have directed their work toward unraveling the tangled strands of cultural and historical dislocation that affects all Indian peoples and, indeed, all of humanity. It's this latter point that I want to emphasize here, for it's here that their tread on the Beloved Path is the most certain. Awiakta and King

Thomas King. Photograph by Dean Palmer / The Scenario.

both reach past the specifics of their own diverse Cherokee contexts to explore the connections with other peoples, giving respectful attention to these extended relationships without turning away from their particular tribal roots.

In pursuing these connections, Awiakta gives much of her attention to the relational reality that Louis Owens (Choctaw/Cherokee) has called "ecosystemic," the understanding that Indians "[are] not removed from and superior to nature but rather an essential part of that complex of relationships we call environment," as opposed to the toxic fragmentation at the "egosystemic" heart of modern industrialized nations.[6] In her 1993 multigenre book, *Selu: Seeking the Corn-Mother's Wisdom,* Awiakta centers her Beloved Path approach on the issue of respect—between humans, between humans and other peoples, and between all constituent elements of creation. It's a gentle defiance that accommodates the realities and experiences of others, one that is willing to negotiate with her audience—but only as far as that respectful negotiation is reciprocated, for she understands all too well the crouching shadow of dispossession and dislocation that threatens not just Cherokees but all peoples. An ecocentric ethic of respect—the communitistic Cherokee spirit taken to a global level—is an active challenge to future removals.

In *Truth and Bright Water*—the most explicitly Cherokee of all his work due to its richly textured consciousness of Cherokee Removal and its legacies—King, too, attends to the issue of respectful relationships with the cosmos, but he moves from the living world to the Spirit World and its influence. Just as we can't disregard our responsibilities to the living relationships of which we are a part, neither can we ignore the links we have to those who have passed to the Nightland, or those spirits of other realities outside life and death. The young protagonist of the novel, Tecumseh, struggles to understand his place in the tangled secrets, love, pain, and shadows between the small border towns of Truth and Bright Water. There life and death bleed together, and it's only through the gradual and respectful understanding of the full complexity of these relationships that Tecumseh emerges from the narrative, touched by tragedy but now fully integrated into the stories that make up his world.

Born and raised in what was known before the Trail of Tears as the Overhill country, from which Nanye'hi rose to prominence in Cherokee political affairs, Awiakta's Cherokee/Appalachian heritage is the foundation of her creative life, rooted as it is in both kinship and geographic contexts. This is clearest in *Selu,* her most encompassing work, in which she explores the metaphoric, philosophical, and physical reality of the First Woman and Corn-Mother of the Cherokees, Selu, through an interweaving of tradition, physical and spiritual place, personal experience, contemporary sociopolitical contexts, and poetry.

Awiakta describes herself as both Cherokee and southern Appalachian, thus linking her Indigenous identity inextricably with the physical land of her people. Her life exemplifies her gentle but firm refusal to be defined by Eurowesterners' views of Natives as primitive throwbacks to a static wilderness utopia. As a child Awiakta grew up in Oak Ridge, "the atomic frontier where the atom had been split, where it still was splitting," and where her father worked as an accountant from 1943 until 1973.[7] Nuclear power, then the newest and most challenging "frontier" of Western science and technology, and its devastating environmental legacy—as well as its immense potential for healing and many other positive forces—were defining images in her life, as they still remain. They are joined together without true conflict, no mixedblood angst or bicultural torment; she's at once a woman of the atomic 1950s (when the high-tech trend began) and a Cherokee of the early twenty-first century. She has stated that she actually recognizes three different heritages: Cherokee, Appalachian, and Scientific.[8] She expresses this melding in the poem "Where Mountain and Atom Meet":

> Ancient haze lies on the mountain
> smoke-blue, strange and still
> a presence that eludes the mind and
> moves through a deeper kind of knowing.
> It is nature's breath and more—
> an aura from the great I Am
> that gathers to its own
> spirits that have gone before.
>
> Deep below the valley waters
> eerie and hid from view
> the atom splits without a sound
> its only trace a fine blue glow
> rising from the fissioned whole
> and at its core
> power that commands the will
> quiet that strikes the soul,
> "Be still and know . . . I Am."[9]

In this stanza, Awiakta stands beside the immense "swimming pool" nuclear reactor, where forty feet of purified water shield the reactor's core.

Dark and cylindrical, the core emits a phosphorescent, flame-like blue mist that scientists call "Cerenkov's Fire." The second stanza intimately connects the energy and beauty of the atom with the Indigenous understanding of the same attributes of nature: "the Creator made them."[10] The last line is unequivocal: "'I Am' is what God calls him/herself in the Bible"; Awiakta here interprets the transformative energies of the atom as reflecting the essential nature of the Creator, who is self-named by a verb of dynamic *being*, fully outside of human attempts at imposing definition on the sacred.[11] Elsewhere Awiakta connects atomic energy with the Cherokee deer spirit, Awi Usdi, a "white stag leaping at the heart of three [electron] orbits," who "embodied the sacred law of taking and giving back with respect, the Sacred Circle of Life."[12] Little Deer cripples hunters who killed deer without praying for their forgiveness; nuclear energy also cripples the foolhardy and disrespectful.

Such concerns aren't limited to Cherokee writers. Bay of Quinte Mohawk poet Beth Brant explores the connections between Native women writers, their cultures, and their relationships to the spirits of creation. To Brant, the overwhelming subject that Native women write about is "the land, the land, the land. This land that brought us into existence, this land that houses the bones of our ancestors, this land that was stolen, this land that withers without our love and care. This land that calls us in our dreams and visions, this land that bleeds and cries, this land that runs through our bodies."[13]

This loving, painful, and expressive relationship with the land is certainly the focus of much of Awiakta's poetry. She embraces the woman-earth connection, seeing nothing disrespectful in being linked to the living world, while also bringing men into the fold:

> To me, "The Feminine" conjures up ruffles and little fingers crooked in the air. I'd rather use "The Womanly." It has sinew and suppleness. "The Womanly" is strength, nurture, patience, wisdom—a force of nature. But if you mess with her, expect strong repercussions. The Womanly is life force, like the atom and like Mother Earth herself. The Manly is a different but equal "force majeure"—the warrior force. These concepts are based on a primary dynamic of nature: continuance in the midst of change.[14]

Awiakta's poetry works toward the full integration of her Appalachian world and her identities as a Cherokee, a woman, a mother and grandmother, a poet, and all the names, titles, and perspectives between. There is no separation between them; like the Beloved Path and Chickamauga consciousness, each depends upon the others, and each is embraced in balance and respect. The text reaches toward the restoration of that balance, thus bringing a long-needed healing back to the people. Hers is a tribal emphasis, one that is intimately Cherokee but which accepts the responsibility of a healing for *all* peoples, Native and non-Native alike, for one wounded strand weakens the entire web. Such a healing comes from a balanced relationship with the world. Nature is the physical manifestation of spirit. The world in this view is fully alive and sentient, inhabited by spirits and personalities (such as Selu and Awi Usdi, who together anchor so much of Awiakta's work); thus, it is imperative to participate in a mature, respectful relationship with all the peoples of this world—the standing people (trees), the four-footed and winged, the swimming and the flying, the crawling and the still—for true Beloved balance to be achieved.

Awiakta explores the radical difference between a worldview that privileges relationships and one that dismisses such connections throughout her poetry, but nowhere more explicitly than in "When Earth Becomes an 'It'":

> When the people call Earth "Mother,"
> they take with love
> and with love give back
> so that all may live.
>
> When the people call Earth "it,"
> they use her
> consume her strength.
> Then the people die.
>
> Already the sun is hot
> out of season.
> Our Mother's breast
> is going dry.
> She is taking all green
> into her heart
> and will not turn back
> until we call her
> by her name.[15]

There's no objectification, no attempt to subsume Earth to an egosystemic philosophy. Rather, Awiakta is advocating an ecosystemic understanding that rejects human supremacism by taking into account not only the physical world but its many peoples. When people lovingly and generously give of themselves to this familial community, then "all may live," but without that acceptance of personal and community responsibility, "the people die." The message is clear: we must mend the injuries inflicted upon ourselves, one another, and the world, before we've gone too far for a healing. There's a message of hope, but it's always tempered with the gravity of the problem.

Gender relations, intimately tied with attitudes and philosophies about nature, are also addressed by this perspective:

Conservation

An irreverent man
looks at earth
as he looks at woman.
"Feed me," he says.
"Receive my seed
and recreate me.
Soothe me
with cool waters.
Shelter me
then let me soar
as I will."

Earth says,
"Look again."
Woman says,
"I too have wings."[16]

The warning from the previous poem has echoed traces in "Conservation": as Earth *(Eloh')* is "taking all green / into her heart / and will not turn back / until we call her / by her name," she also says to look again, to reevaluate, to reconnect.[17] The spirit of *Eloh'* is linked to the spirit of Selu. Gender is fully a part of these relationships. This multilayered interrelatedness and intimacy maintains all Creation in a balanced embrace, a point that Inés Hernández-Ávila (Nez Perce) identifies as a foundation of Native women's perspectives:

For many activist Native women of this hemisphere, the concern with "home" involves a concern with "home*land*." Even when Native women activists no longer reside on their ancestral land bases (though many still do) they continue to defend the tribal sovereignty of their own communities as well as communities of other indigenous peoples. Sovereignty encompasses the cultural, spiritual, economic, and political aspects of the life of the communities and of the individuals who comprise them. Issues of sovereignty are intimately interwoven with issues pertaining to the land(base) of each people.[18]

In this principled perspective there is no separation between one's opinion of women, one's treatment of the Earth and her children, and the politico-social life of the community. Sovereignty at its heart is the ultimate political extension of this philosophy of interconnectedness.

Awiakta is concerned with confronting those forces that seek to alienate us from our world, such as the greed and corruption that resulted in the destruction of Chota, the sacred mother-city of the Cherokees that was flooded in 1979 by the ill-conceived Tellico Dam that destroyed the Little Tennessee River.[19] Just as ecocide and misogyny are intimately connected, so too are racism and environmental devastation; these aren't abstract concerns, but rather real traumas. In the days before the Native American Graves Protection and Repatriation Act (NAGPRA), the desecration of Chota was particularly onerous, as the ancient burial mounds of the Cherokees were bulldozed open and their remains taken to the University of Tennessee in Knoxville, while Eurowestern graves were disinterred and reburied with honor.[20] Tellico became, as Awiakta writes, "a Lake of Tears":

Tears from "the folk," from conservationists, historians, archeologists, scholars, lawmakers. Tears from farm families, poets, writers, artists, musicians. Tears from everyone who loved the beautiful valley of the Little Tennessee and had tried in vain to save it. And tears welling up from the bottom of the lake, from the eyes of the Cherokee ancestors. We are all part of the web. What affects one strand affects us all. In time, even the fish of Tellico Lake would have cause to weep.[21]

Awiakta's mission of bringing balance to her people and the world also brings an energizing anger. She's angry about the greed and selfishness exemplified by events like the flooding of Chota, by racism and self-satisfied bigotry. And, notably in a Beloved Path reading, her anger is for all people who are abused, not just Cherokees. She takes care to explain that the descendants of the White settlers who claimed the land after the Trail of Tears—who were generally poor family farmers—were also displaced by the Tellico project, thus demonstrating further the interconnectedness of human communities and the shared experiences of displacement and oppression. Not just Indians are harmed by a disregard of Native rights and connection to a particular landscape, and part of her hope for the future comes from emphasizing the knowledge that "Mother Earth may go down for a while, but she always comes back. . . . When you've done all you can, stand and wait."[22]

One section of the book—"Amazons in Appalachia"—provides a powerful illustration of the ways in which these concerns of balance, respect, gender complementarity, and care for the rest of the world come together in a Beloved assertion of Cherokee continuity. Significantly, this section—coming shortly after a lengthy and emotional analysis of the drowning of Chota beneath the Tellico Reservoir—concerns Nanye'hi and Ada-gal'kala (here Nanyehi and Attakullakulla), thus explicitly invoking the Beloved political structure of the ancient peace city. The section follows the narrator into "'the time immemorial,' a spiritual place we enter to commute intimately with all that is, a place abidingly real," where the barrier between the past and present disappears. Here she travels to 1765, to the time of Henry Timberlake's visit to the Nation, where she walks "with the strong Cherokee grandmothers" and hears Ada-gal'kala ask, "Where are your women?"[23] It's a powerful question that reaches through the ages, from the British trade delegation through to "the Congress, the Joint Chiefs of Staff, the Nuclear Regulatory Commission," and even "the hierarchies of my church, my university, my children's school." The white chief's question is as pointed in our time as his own: "Implicit in their chief's question, 'Where are your women?' the Cherokee hear, 'Where is your balance? What is your intent?' They see that balance is absent and are wary of the white men's motives."[24] Whether in the intimate sphere or in the larger political arena, the absence of balance carries the same danger—it separates people from the meaningful relationships that keep selves and communities whole and healthy.

This extension of Beloved principles from the imagined re-creation of a historical gathering to the tangible dangers of the nuclear age helps us better understand the links between social history and the creative text.

This is particularly the case when the narrator—whom we can quite safely assume is Awiakta herself—is on her way to meet with the great Beloved Woman herself, Nanye'hi of Chota:

> She works ceaselessly for harmony with white settlers, interpreting the ways of each people to the other. From her uncle and mentor, Attakullakulla, she has learned diplomacy and the realities of power. She understands that the Cherokee ultimately will be outnumbered and that war will bring sure extinction. She counsels them to channel their energies from fighting into more effective government and better food production. To avoid bloodshed, she often risks censure and misunderstanding to warn either side of an impending attack, then urges resolution by arbitration. In the councils she speaks powerfully on two major themes: "Work for peace. Do not sell your land."[25]

The narrator isn't sure of the moment in which she'll meet Nanye'hi, but there are many to choose from: the young woman's elevation to War Woman in 1755 at age seventeen, her 1776 rescue of Lydia Bean from execution, the 1781 speech she gives at the Long Island Treaty Council, the negotiations of the 1785 Hopewell Treaty, her domestic life with her family, or even her final act as Beloved Woman in 1817, when she insists, "My children, do not part with any more of our lands . . . it would be like destroying your mothers."[26] Each of these historical moments reinforces the knowledge of Nanye'hi's full involvement in the sociopolitical life of the Nation and enhances the role she played as a leader both in times of war and in negotiations for peace. Nanye'hi's full Cherokee specificity emerges with each memory. The narrator's participation in this remembrance, and her movement through time to attach those moments to both her personal life and the concerns of the current age, make manifest the principles of the Beloved Path—principles that extend beyond imaginative texts into the social life and historical heritage of the People.

That the narrator's meeting with Nanye'hi becomes instead an immersion in a "cornfield in bloom," where "there seems no division between self and green," is a meaningful development of this balance, seeking the strength of Cherokee womanhood within the representation of the Corn-Mother as spiritual and physical source of the People.[27] It's the Beloved understanding of kinship and negotiation taken to an ecosystemic level. Nanye'hi lives in both the past and the present; Selu continues to give us life; and the poet finds strength to fight the dangers of her day through the legacies of Beloved balance from the past.

Throughout *Selu,* Awiakta makes the connections, and although aware of the danger of ecological devastation, she keeps one eye to the East in hope for the sunrise. She offers an "arrow of warning and hope," a promise of balance and connection, and she emphasizes the promise with Selu, Spirit of Survival.[28] The interweaving connections of life draw all of creation together into a complex web of communities, whether we accept that reality or not. As Awiakta says, "I think my work helps people remember what they already know deep down—that all life is interconnected and every life is important."[29] To deny this truth brings all things closer to destruction, to the final tipping of the balance into catastrophe, but to accept it brings a healing, a cleansing that may be painful but will serve us well.

Awiakta has said that, "I have a sign on the bumper of my car that says 'Poets sing for you.' All people have poetry in them. Some can't write it, but the poet can listen intently to what people say and send it out into the world. It's a process of translation for the people."[30]

As her poetry demonstrates, Awiakta has spent a lifetime listening to the people and spirits around her, and she has consequently crafted a sensitive and distinct body of work that brings together her varied perspectives—Cherokee, Appalachian, "womanly," scientific. In the doubleweaving of tradition, community, identity, and place, Marilou Awiakta sings for the People, spinning a vision of a balanced life between humanity and our human and nonhuman relations.

Another Cherokee text that grapples with the continued realignment of Cherokee understandings of community identity in the face of cataclysmic removals is *Truth and Bright Water* (1999), by Canadian Cherokee Thomas King. King's exploration of these issues can be read as an extended comment on a single question, but one that ripples outward with urgency: How do we reestablish bonds of nationhood when they have been damaged or severed for generations? Although on the surface King's work seems to focus almost entirely on non-Cherokee subjects, I argue here that a closer reading demonstrates a profoundly Cherokee sensibility at the heart of his literary texts that goes beyond the use of the syllabary in the section headings of *Green Grass, Running Water* (1993) or the novel's organization as a Cherokee divining ceremony. Unlike Awiakta, whose sense of Cherokeeness is rooted in the land of her ancestors, an outland Cherokee like King, raised far from the home and land bases of the People, has had to reconnect to the familial and cultural bonds of nationhood in a different way, but one that's no less Cherokee. It's just a different kind of Cherokee experience than that of Awiakta, made particularly difficult as a result of the demographic scattering of so many Cherokees by the policies of removal.

Truth and Bright Water is a particularly instructive text in this regard, as King reconnects to those bonds and communities through the direct evocation of the Cherokee spirits—both those of the dead and those of the *Eloh'*—and through these spirits asserts a living link with the people. My reading of this novel reflects on King's walk along the Beloved Path through a reconnection with these spirits, bringing them into the present day and giving voice to his Cherokee ancestors, and thus his own Cherokee perspective, in a narrative world far from the old mountains of the southeast.

In his many works, including *Medicine River* (1990), *One Good Story, That One* (1993), the aforementioned *Green Grass, Running Water,* his 2002 mystery novel, *Dreadfulwater Shows Up* (written under the pseudonym "Hartley GoodWeather"), and his 2003 essay collection, *The Truth About Stories: A Native Narrative,* King melds the worlds of the living, the dead, and the imagined to reveal the contradictions, absurdities, and tragedies of a world that tries to erase Indigenous peoples and their stories and replace them with colonialist lies. *Truth and Bright Water* is, in some ways, a slight departure from the tone of the others. The humor that marks the earlier works is largely veiled in this text; it's a darker book, physically haunted by spirits of the past and present, and offers what is perhaps King's most textured and personal exploration of the power of imagination to rewrite history of the self, the community, and the cosmos.

The novel is also King's most direct evocation of the Spirit World— the Cherokee Ghostland—a tangible haunting, which works to evoke his Cherokee roots in the borderland space within which he "Cherokee-izes" Native Canadian literature. Just as Awiakta draws on the spirit-beings Selu and Awi Usdi to more fully root her narrative within Cherokee concepts, the spirits of the Cherokee dead make King's Native Canada explicitly Cherokee in ways that none of his other texts to date have attempted. On an imaginary Canadian reserve, King crafts a distinctly Cherokee sensibility that is informed by Cherokee traditions and history, and one that provides a tentative tribal center for an outland Cherokee writer far from the land base of the nation and its grounded tribal memory.

Truth and Bright Water are twin communities separated by the Canadian-American border, and are inhabited respectively by the narrator, Tecumseh, and his cousin Lum. Truth is a railroad town on the American side of the border; Bright Water is the reserve on the Canadian side. The tribal nation of which both boys are members is unnamed, though buffalo, teepees, and discussion of Canadian politics stand as the primary markers of prairie Indian traditions; this vague tribal specificity is one of many expressions of King's stated interest in pan-Indian issues and concerns.[31] The narrative straddles the United States and Canada, as do the boys. From the start of the novel the boys and their personalities conjure two similar figures in some versions of Cherokee cosmology: the Thunders, sons of Selu and Kanati, Corn-Mother and the Lucky Hunter. Tecumseh (named for the Shawnee resistance leader) stands in for Selu's birth son, Tame Boy: quiet, mildly curious, and devoted to his brash cousin Lum. Lum's adventurousness brings a painful wisdom to his family, much as Wild Boy—adopted after emerging from the blood of game Selu washed in a stream—brings knowledge of the hunt and crop and their associated pain to humanity. In those old stories, Tame Boy and Wild Boy spy on their parents and, as a result of this direct violation of respectful standards of conduct, bring the risk of starvation and suffering to the world. Their actions force them to become responsible for their own lives—a passage into manhood, albeit a painful one. Just as the curiosity of the Thunders results in a suffering that brings mature wisdom, so too does the curiosity of Tecumseh and Lum bring, by the end of the novel, a painful but ultimately significant awakening into the responsibilities of adulthood.

King is a descendant of removal policies and Cherokee diaspora who now lives and writes in Guelph, Ontario. How does he work to bring a Beloved healing to this legacy? How does he exercise the moral imperative of tribal continuity, especially given his stated preference for pan-Indian narratives that reflect a "more urban and rural existence than a reservation one"?[32] One distinct way is through the haunting of his created community by the *consciousness of Removal,* the full embrace of history, pain, and continuing existence. The shadows of the Trail needn't kill us or drive us to despair, but we must understand the spirits who still travel in our world before we can reconcile that history.

This approach extends beyond Cherokee concerns. In the countless

Native poems, stories, and novels in which spirits appear, their presence is rarely considered *super*natural—rather, it is *fully* natural, the logical extension of systems of belief in which the cosmos is fully sentient and alive, where nothing is without spirit. And these spirits are often angry, as in *Ghost Singer,* by Anna Lee Walters (Pawnee/Otoe), *Eye Killers,* by A. A. Carr (Navajo/Pueblo), *Chancers,* by Gerald Vizenor (Anishinaabe), and *Almanac of the Dead,* by Leslie Marmon Silko (Laguna Pueblo/Sioux). Wendy Rose (Hopi/Miwok) struggles with the anthropological legacies of grave-robbing in many of her poems, including "Three Thousand Dollar Death Song," "I Expected My Skin and My Blood to Ripen," and "Notes On A Conspiracy," while Cherokee speculative fiction writer William Sanders invokes a more benevolent (although cranky) spirit in *The Ballad of Billy Badass and the Rose of Turkestan.* Haisla novelist Eden Robinson's *Monkey Beach* is a richly textured study of the interweaving of the Spirit World into a troubled young woman's life, with occasionally tragic consequences. In each of these texts, and many more, the presence of spirits breaks down the barriers of the worlds between the living and the dead, but they are still a natural part of those worlds.

Rather than conforming to the Eurowestern philosophy of dualism that splits the cosmos into differentiated fragments that can be designated, as per religion historian Mircea Eliade, either "sacred" or "profane," most Native spiritual traditions (and thus literary traditions) draw upon a perspective that experiences *all* existence as sacred. The fragmented worldview of sacred/profane fits nicely with imperialist claims to cultural and racial superiority—the Linnaean hierarchy of species, the social Darwinian apologetics for cultural genocide—but it is incompatible with Indigenous traditions that not only recognize life as what Wendat scholar Georges Sioui calls "a vast system of kinship" within "a sacred circle of relationships among all beings, whatever their form, and among all species," but also recognize that the borders between the worlds of the living and those of the dead are arbitrary and all too easy to cross, if they exist at all.[33] These crossings can often be devastating to the living—as in the books by Silko, Vizenor, and Walters mentioned above, in which the spirits of the dead return to the land of the living to wreak havoc upon those who violate the earth and the sanctity of the grave—or benign or educational, as with Sanders's story of a beloved grandfather returning in the form of a blue jay to give guidance to his wayward grandson. Whatever the nature of the haunting, it comes as a result of natural events or human actions, and as such is as fully a part of the natural order as a thunderstorm.

The beginning of King's tale—the onset of this particular haunting—rests in the mystery of a child's skull, "a long red ribbon through the eye sockets," found by the boys when exploring with Tecumseh's dog Soldier on the bank of the Shield, the river that separates Truth and Bright Water.[34] They watch a strange figure on a cliff throw bones into the river, then later discover the small skull with its scarlet ribbon. The skull catches Lum's attention in particular, and he remains fascinated with it through the course of the story, an unhealthy interest in death and the unknown that ultimately drives him toward self-destruction.

Most of the narrative focuses on the dramatic events that surround the family lives of Tecumseh and Lum during the Indian Days festivities, but the true heart of the text—the haunting remembrance of things past, and the foreshadowing of things to come—emerges upon the arrival of a group of Cherokees from Georgia. Rebecca Neugin, the only Cherokee who speaks in the novel, is at first an enigmatic presence. When Tecumseh meets her, "[s]he's standing in the shadows of one of the trailers," with a red ribbon tying back her hair. She wears "a long dress that is torn and frayed at the hem and at the sleeves, as if the material has been ripped rather than cut. It looks a little old-fashioned, but probably a new style that hasn't gotten this far north yet. It's okay, but I don't think it's going to be a hit in Truth or Bright Water."[35] Rebecca wears a Cherokee tear dress—fabric torn into strips because scissors were unavailable after the travels on the bloody road; a *tear* dress—the weeping remembrance of loss on that long trail. Her name is that of a childhood survivor of the Trail of Tears who was interviewed and photographed when in her nineties by Grant Foreman (the Oklahoma scholar whom Emmet Starr dismissed as a "two gun historian").[36] In history and in fiction, Rebecca stands as the representative survivor of Removal.

The Beloved negotiations of self and others that find common bonds and transform the surface without loss of the center are fully at work in this novel, particularly in the scenes where Rebecca and Tecumseh enter one another's worlds. She doesn't engage in idle chitchat: she's a girl on a mission:

> "I'm looking for my duck," says the girl. "Have you seen her?"
>
> Down at the tent, my father and Franklin are still working on the motorcycles. "This is kind of a dangerous place for a duck," I say.
>
> "Some people think a duck is a silly thing," says the girl. "But it was a duck who helped to create the world."

"Ducks are cool," I tell her. "I have a dog and he's pretty silly."

"When the world was new and the woman fell out of the sky, it was a duck who dove down to the bottom of the ocean and brought up the mud for the dry land."[37]

Ducks are a frequent image that appear in King's work, and often replace other spirit beings in various story retellings, a shape-shift that realigns the narrative to King's pan-Indian perspective.[38] His fame is as a Canadian Native, and his books center on the geography with which he is most familiar. But as an outland Cherokee, King is also exploring the complications of living as a Cherokee in a distant land. In this narrative, the duck takes the place of Dayunisi, the Little Water Beetle of Cherokee tradition who dives below the great waters of the Middle World and brings up muddy earth, but is spoken of as a creator by a Cherokee spirit, thus melding the traditions of King's ancestry with other mud-diver traditions.[39] The Beloved Path quality of adaptation is fully in operation here. In some other Cherokee versions of the story, a duck or other animal does dive for the mud, but s/he drowns in the depths; only Dayunisi survives to emerge with the foundation for the world.[40]

It should be noted here, too, that King is drawing as much from the historical record as from his own imagination in associating young Rebecca with the duck. Following his interview with the flesh-and-blood Neugin in *The Five Civilized Tribes,* Grant Foreman notes with his characteristic narrative distance:

> Mrs. Neugin, who was a small child when her people removed from the east, could recall only one incident of that experience and that was of her pet duck that she cherished and would not leave behind. She carried it in her little arms until she squeezed the life out of it and grieved to see it thrown by the road side. The poignant memory of that childish love and grief remained with her more than ninety years.[41]

Although Rebecca mourns her duck's loss in the novel, the bird is more than another lost Cherokee spirit. King's concern with survival literally surfaces again in the novel, and it's the duck, not Dayunisi, who is named the worldmaker. But while the duck resurfaces to create the world, it vanishes from the narrative once the Cherokees start for Oklahoma, and its guardian, Rebecca, searches still.

King repeatedly draws on Cherokee history to inform the novel's emotional landscape; although Tecumseh doesn't understand the true nature of the girl's oddness, her arrival heralds a meaningful shift in the narrative toward the storied burdens of history. In a remarkable analysis of the multiple contexts of the novel, Robin Ridington notes that "each story the narrator hears makes sense in relation to the larger story of which it is a part. One good story articulates with every other story. Every story is at once a fragment and an entirety. Each one hints at every other. Stories function as metonyms, parts that stand for wholes."[42] The stories of history merge with those of the present, and although Tecumseh isn't initially aware of the significance of his interactions with Rebecca, each meeting builds on the next, inexorably revealing to the reader the relationships between these worlds. When Rebecca emerges from the shadows, she is "strange, pale and transparent"; Tecumseh asks about two of the men with whom she travels:

> "That your father?"
> "No," says the girl. "That's Mr. John Ross. He's got the big red trailer."
> "So, your father's the other guy?"
> "No, that's Mr. George Guess. He reads books." The girl steps back into the shadows as if there's a line drawn in the ground past which she is not willing to go.
> "Indian Days are this weekend. Maybe you'd like me to show you around."
> "Watch out for my duck," says the girl, and she turns and disappears among the trailers.[43]

Ross and George Guess (Sequoyah's English name), like Neugin, survived the period of Removal, but their lives ended far from the ancient homelands of the Cherokee Nation: Ross died in Washington, D.C., fighting until the end against U.S. intrusions and land claims, while most accounts hold that Sequoyah died in Mexico while seeking scattered Cherokee communities, with the intent of convincing them to return to Indian Territory.

All three of the historical Cherokee personages named by King in the text—Rebecca Neugin, Sequoyah, and John Ross—lived much of their lives and died far from the lands of their ancestors, the lands from which they had been torn by the U.S. government and the White citizens of Georgia. Yet in doing so they speak across the ages to the reality of Cherokee survival. It's not John Ridge or Elias Boudinot—two famous Cherokees who also "read books"—who show up at Indian Days, but rather Cherokees who weren't destroyed by the events of the Trail of Tears.

Here is where the red and white paths intersect, where the spirit of Chickamauga defiance crosses through time—not unlike the narrator in Awiakta's "Amazons in Appalachia"—to speak to the strengthened presence of both the living and the dead. Ridington notes that other historical figures are invoked by the novel, and most feature quite prominently in the history of both the Cherokees and Indian Removal: the Shawnee warrior Tecumseh—a subject of John Milton Oskison's own biographical interest, as noted in chapter 3—whose failed dream of a lasting Indian confederation made physical relocation of the eastern tribes possible, but who had been inspired in that dream in his youth by the earlier confederation forged by the great Chickamauga war leader himself, Tsiyu Gansini; the Cherokee medicine maker, Swimmer, who was James Mooney's primary informant for his comprehensive *Myths of the Cherokee*; U.S. President James Monroe, a leading proponent of Indian Removal, among others. At one point in the novel, too, Monroe sings the "title song from *Oklahoma!*"— the musical version of Lynn Riggs's *Green Grow the Lilacs*—and removes a kitschy black wig in respect as he and Tecumseh sing. It's a ceremony that mixes a traditional honor song and a Broadway musical while invoking the spirit of a Cherokee playwright in the Canadian prairie.

These invocations offer a challenge to the erasure of Indians from historical memory, even in their tragedy. Pain might be healed, but it can't be forgotten. These spirits live again in Beloved memory; there will be no vanishing in forgetfulness. Rebecca's search is for realignment, the balance that comes with creation and healing. She walks upon the Beloved Path, seeking balance in a world between life and death, the past and present, remembrance and erasure. Later, when Tecumseh encounters Rebecca while camping with his dog, she reveals more of her origins:

> "You and your folks staying for Indian Days?"
>
> Rebecca nods. "Then we have to go." She looks tired, as if she's walked a long ways today and still has a long ways to go. I wonder if she is one of those girls who eat and then throw up after each meal in order to stay skinny.
>
> "Your duck will probably be back by then."
>
> "If she's not," says Rebecca, "Mr. Ross says we'll have to go without her. He says the soldiers won't wait for a duck."
>
> "So, your folks are in the military?"[44]

The soldiers won't wait for the world-maker, and devastation is the result. Rebecca has come at a time when a healing is needed in Bright Water, especially within young Tecumseh's family: his divorced parents are battling fiercely; his wild Aunt Cassie seeks to reestablish contact with her family; Lum grows more estranged from his abusive father and a mortal world of pain. Tecumseh doesn't understand what's going on any more than the soldiers did; this state of ignorance doesn't last, but knowledge comes at a cost.

Rebecca is the storyteller, the one who carries the sorrow of the Trail in her heart. That she's a spirit is made clear by her association with the skull (she wears the same red ribbon in her hair that is threaded through the eye sockets), the fear experienced by Soldier at her presence and his awareness of her otherness—"Rebecca kneels and looks at Soldier, as if she is trying to find something in his eyes, as if the two of them have a secret that they're not going to share with anyone else"—as well as her emotional distance and her frequent association with shadows, a hint of the Nightland of the Cherokee dead.[45] She's a spirit of the Cherokee past who walks in the present, brought back by a haunting of history as well as the unearthing of her skull. She says far more than Tecumseh realizes at the time, and her presence lingers even when she's no longer in the narrative:

> "Now the rules are," says Lucille, "if you're a guest, we have to feed you, and you have to tell us all about the Cherokee."
>
> Rebecca tries to smile, but she looks as if she's going to cry, too. Not so you can see unless you're up close.[46]

Her sadness lifts when she begins to tell a creation story in the Cherokee language. Though a spirit of the dead, she's still part of the making of the world, still accompanied on her journey by the Chickamauga spirits of unbroken Cherokee leaders. If, as King states elsewhere, "The truth about stories is that that's all we are," then hope inhabits young Rebecca to the core as much as grief and loss.[47]

One of the important things to remember about stories is that they are never limited—they can be told again and again, and new ones can be added. Grief isn't the only possibility here. Monroe Swimmer, a long-absent but recently returned painter and cosmopolitan Indian eccentric whose name evokes both the medicine man Swimmer and the former Cherokee Nation Principal Chief Ross Swimmer, reveals himself near the end of the novel as the one who rescued the bones and spirits from museums and cast the bones into the Shield, including the small child's skull with the red ribbon. When asked by Tecumseh why he brought them to Bright Water, Monroe replies, "'Look around you,' he says. 'This is the centre of the universe. Where else would I bring them? Where else would they want to be?'"[48] King, a Canadian now, brings his Beloved sensibility and community north, without erasing either the cultural distinctiveness of the Cherokees or the geographic placement of Truth and Bright Water.

At the end of the novel, after Lum's fascination with death brings him (and Soldier) to its embrace, after Tecumseh's reconciliation begins, and after the bones retrieved by Monroe are all returned to the land:

> [T]he people from Georgia loaded up their RVs and headed out. Lucille Rain said they were heading for Oklahoma, but that they were going to take their time and see the sights. . . . I would have liked to have said goodbye to Rebecca, to tell her that I was sorry about her duck, that it might turn up yet, that I knew what it was like to lose things.[49]

The Cherokees continue the long journey, as does Tecumseh—familiar now with loss and pain, likely strong enough to survive it. There are, however, no guarantees, and Tecumseh must find his way through this story and others. The duck is still gone, and Lum is still dead; King doesn't rewrite these stories or mitigate their loss—or avoid the possible permanence of that loss. The present tense of the narrative, and its first person perspective from Tecumseh's point of view, undermines any easy determination of an ending, either tragic or happy; it's not the past-tense recollections of a wise man looking back on an episode of his life. Rather, it's the living story of a fallible human boy, and thus one that endures and carries on beyond the written text.

Bright Water's Cherokee presence is that of Removal, and of the survival of those scattered by the Trail. King's deliberate and frequent connections of characters and events to those connected to the dark death march of 1838–39 bring the narrative much of its dark pall. Yet survival is the ultimate Cherokee story King tells as a Cherokee who lives far from the Nation but who fully embraces the stories, the histories, and the traditions of the People. This is no Chickamauga text, centered deeply in the landscape and memoried presence of the People; rather, it steps lightly on the Beloved Path, where continuity *through* change is the underlying understanding of Cherokee presence. Distance is arbitrary; geography is less binding than its perception. The Indian Nations continue. Through the

Cherokees—living and dead—who populate *Truth and Bright Water,* King breaks down the illusory borders between nations, between times, and between the ancestors and their descendants—without, as Ridington points out, ignoring the contextualized particularities of each. Just as Awiakta shares her hope for the possibility of Chota's renewal—in spirit, if not in physical form—through stories of remembrance and responsibility, so too does King share his hope in the possibility of Indian continuity through the power of story. The nature of our stories determines the nature of our survival; they're "all we are." Through memory strengthened by a humble view of the future, the stories will go on—and so will the People, in all our pain and possibility.

Chickamauga Readings

Although their battlefields have generally differed in appearance, both Wilma Mankiller and Geary Hobson have spent decades fighting against similar forces of dispossession, dismissal, and racism. As the first woman to lead the Cherokee Nation as Principal Chief, Mankiller has participated in some of the Nation's most challenging and transformative years in the twentieth century, gaining international recognition in the process. Far less public, but no less dedicated to the cause of Indian nationhood, Hobson's long tenure as a professor of English at the University of Oklahoma has helped to guide and shape Indian-centered literary scholarship since the 1970s.[50] In their respective political and scholastic struggles, Mankiller and Hobson have consistently demonstrated that the Chickamauga consciousness of defiance is a strong and defining characteristic in the literary expressions of their lives. In spite of imposing and sometimes vocal resistance, these Cherokees have helped to transform the political and literary landscapes of Indian Country and, in doing so, have made it easier for the next generations of Indian leaders and scholars to work for necessary change.

But the battle is far from over, as Chickamaugan vigilance continually reminds us. Both Mankiller and Hobson have remained active in the struggle against the forces of removal that consistently cast a shadow over Cherokee continuity, from Mankiller's public campaign against the policies of her successor, Joe Byrd, particularly during the 1997 constitutional crisis, to Hobson's published warnings about the enduring appeal of "whiteshaman" poachers and the dismissal of Indian voices in academia by

Wilma Mankiller. Photograph by Charlie L. Soap.

many non-Natives, especially those who claim to be modern-day "friends of the Indian." Their work celebrates the enduring spirit of Indian nation-hood while cautioning us against becoming complacent or imagining that anti-Indianism (to borrow a phrase from Elizabeth Cook-Lynn) is in any way fading from the social or political fabric of North America. More than five hundred years of the Columbian Invasion have given us adequate evidence of the dangers of believing that the larger Eurowestern presence in this hemisphere has any benign interest in Indian well-being, as Mankiller notes: "People who refuse to put any stock in the adage that history repeats itself undoubtedly do not know any Cherokees. Although most Native Americans have learned hard lessons from the experiences of the bygone years, it seems that as often as not, we are still doomed to revisit some of the bleakest episodes from our tribe's past."[51]

These "bleakest episodes" are the subject of my inquiry here, for it's these particular historical moments of physical and cultural displacement that act as both narrative catalyst and source of Chickamaugan resistance. I have chosen for this section to focus largely on one book by each writer: Mankiller's autobiography, and Hobson's fictionalized autobiography of Thomas Darko, the last of the Mosopelea tribe of Louisiana (known as

Geary Hobson. Photograph by Robert Taylor, University of Oklahoma.

Ofos to local Whites), drawing as I go from a few other relevant texts. Although the lines of fiction and tribal subject highlight some of the differences between the texts, I am interested here in the ways that each writer employs the Chickamauga consciousness as both the explicit narrative center and the energizing force of principle behind that narrative. In Mankiller's autobiography, the formative removal is the recent U.S. policy of Indian "relocation," which she has explicitly linked with the Trail of Tears as another manifestation of that brutal legislation. Her family's move to urban San Francisco when she was a girl helped to politicize her as part of a larger Red Pride movement as well as a Cherokee nationalist, and helped prepare her for the challenges of returning powerful female voices to the center of Cherokee politics. While the protagonist of Hobson's *The Last of the Ofos,* Thomas Darko, isn't forcibly removed from his family's traditional lands, a number of historical events and personal tragedies realign his relationship to the world in every bit as complicated a manner as those of Mankiller's experience.

Although this analysis begins with these rather grim events, it doesn't end there, as Cherokee nationhood isn't defined by conflict, but rather by the remarkable ability of Cherokees not only to endure such times but to emerge with a renewed sense of community and purpose. Rather than just linger on the present and historical injustices of U.S. society—what James Cox has reminded me is an act of sadism intended to obsessively reaffirm to audiences that Indians were brutalized and massacred—I am interested here in the Chickamauga strategies of response that proactively align Cherokee nationhood toward the needs and concerns of the community and away from a reactionary relationship to outside forces. If we stop with removal, we stop with death, and the Cherokee literary tradition is about far more than that.

The most striking structural feature of Mankiller's text, as explained in the authors' note, is the interweaving of her own history with that of the Cherokee people, "much as traditional Cherokee stories weave together the unbroken threads of tribal history, wisdom, and culture preserved by each generation."[52] Unlike many autobiographies, which place the individual subject at the narrative center, *Mankiller: A Chief and Her People* emphasizes tribal relationships of interdependence and mutual definition—neither exists in its fullest sense without the other. As she relates her familial origin, she parallels the account with Cherokee origin stories; her own uprooting during the U.S. "relocation" policy of the 1950s reflects that of the Cherokees during the Trail of Tears; the book ends with a fifteen-page Cherokee history chronology that only briefly mentions her political achievements. Her own personal struggles are given context—and hope—through the survival of her people through the ages. It's a relationship of peoplehood, of kinship and accountability, of remembrance and possibility.

This relationship, by extension, belongs to all tribal peoples, thus shifting attention yet again from the individual to the community in all its complexity. She begins with her family name—Mankiller—and traces it back through blood ties and cultural function, where the name has long served to indicate the responsibilities incumbent upon a red-sphere warrior of the people. She is, from the beginning, first and foremost Mankiller, not Wilma, and thus one of a *people*, not simply an individual *person*. "Especially in the context of a tribal people," she writes, "no individual's life stands apart and alone from the rest. My own story has meaning only as long as it is a part of the overall story of my people. For above all else, I am a Cherokee woman."[53]

These principles of peoplehood are also embedded within *The Last of the Ofos,* although no author's note remarks on this point. An aged Thomas Darko is speaking into a tape recorder as he gives the account of his life, but he claims little authority of his own life's events; rather, the story becomes immediately one about relationships, specifically those with his homeland and his family. He doesn't talk of his earliest childhood, because those stories were known to his now-dead family, and he refuses to speak for them (just as he later refuses to tell their Mosopelea names out of respect). Trying to invoke his early memories, he finds that "it would be easier to separate the bark from the tree trunk—or stink from shit, as my papa used to say—than it would be for you to set me aside from my land and all my earliest memories of it."[54] When he returns again to talking about his individual self, he moves from his name to his hometown, to his Mosopelea name, to his clan, to his family and their extended clan relationships. Self, family, and land are interdependent concepts throughout the novella, and when they appear in isolation they do so to highlight the devastation of those fragmented relationships. When Thomas reveals that his is "a nation of one," the statement is one of deep, lasting pain.

This pain of fragmentation features heavily in each narrative: it begins with the attempts by colonialist authorities to undermine tribal identities through language, then moves into a literal fragmentation of community. Mankiller begins her own account with her name, but goes on to relate her father's struggles in the U.S.-run Sequoyah Training School near Tahlequah, Oklahoma, where he was whipped for speaking the Cherokee language. Sharing a fictionalized generational relationship with Charley Mankiller, Thomas Darko, too, undergoes this brutal conditioning in the U.S. educational system under the cruelty of his teacher Old Lady Mitchell, forcing him eventually to abandon that system entirely and to instead receive his full early education from the "School of Hard Knocks," knowledge gained through personal experience, which includes knowledge of the old Ofo ways from his mother and grandfather:

> A Indian person jist ain't born a Indian—like a Ofo, or a Tunica, or a Choctaw—and let it go at that. That person need to learn to be a Ofo, or a Tunica, and such-like, and it is that learning makes them Ofos and such-like. It's learning comes through the community, even if it's jist a tiny community of three older folks or so, like ours was. We are born, we grow, and we learn—first, that we are in the Ofo world, a place made the good place it is by Sun Father, and the ground we walk on is our Mother. We have to do things right, keep everything on a even keel, don't rock the foundations, do our part to keep the world we live in and on in a good balance with the sky world above and the underworld below. Everything about being Ofo begins with this sense of evenness.[55]

Though Thomas learns to speak and read English fluently, the education he values most is the one that respects his humanity, not the one that threatens to break him into pieces. "So now maybe you can see that I might have said so long to Old Lady Mitchell and her pine-wood paddle," he remarks wryly, "but I never really said no good-byes to learning and knowing." He adds, not quite as an afterthought, "They's a lot to be said for the School of Hard Knocks."[56]

Mankiller discusses the 1950s termination and relocation policies by presenting them as both formal policy analysis and as a personal recollection of the legislation's impact on her own life, her own "school of hard knocks." Connecting these lessons to the lessons of history not only gives her narrative a sense of larger significance, it also demonstrates the ripple effects of historical politics on the lives of people today. Relocation of rural and reservation Indians to major U.S. cities—where they were expected to integrate into the individualist/capitalist ethos of urban life—was another manifestation of the assimilation directive that inspired the allotment era, given strength by the anti-Communist hysteria of the United States at the time. This time, however, the policy went back to one of the prime features of the Indian Removal Act, which involved moving Indians from their homelands to an alien environment. In that early removal, the tribes were generally expected to remain somewhat cohesive for a while, at least until missionaries were able to fully "civilize" them; through allotment, the tribes were expected to be physically broken apart and be dispersed. Relocation was the unholy union of the two policies, involving land dislocation and cultural fragmentation. Its proponents hoped that this new monster would, at last, result in full Indian assimilation and the end of "the Indian problem." As Mankiller points out, the policy of relocation—and its sibling, "termination," which involved the federal erasure of trust responsibility to sixty-one Indian communities—was another attempt by the U.S. government to "destroy tribal governments." Such action would, once again, "break up native communities and put tribal land on the market by abolishing its status as nontaxable trust land," and, as with most laws imposed on Indians by U.S. politicians, "Native Americans would soon lose control of their land."[57] Without Indians on the land, there would be no obstacle to speculators and other commercial interests.

When BIA representatives came to her family's house on their allotment (known as Mankiller Flats) with an enthusiastic proposal for moving out of Oklahoma—"a wonderful opportunity for Indian families to get great jobs, obtain good educations for their kids and, once and for all, leave poverty behind"—Mankiller notes that it was "poverty [that] prompted the move," a poverty tied to the earlier allotment of Cherokee lands.[58] After much discussion and contemplation, the family chose San Francisco, only to find that the promises of good financial opportunities were more government lies, and that their poverty was now compounded with the shock of living in a frantic, noisy, and often very hostile alien environment. "Everything was new to us," she recalls. "For instance, we had never seen neon lights before. No one had bothered to even try to prepare us for city living."[59] Her family, along with many other Indians of the relocation period, discovered to their misfortune that "the 'better life' the BIA had promised all of us was, in reality, life in a tough, urban ghetto."[60] It was an early but galvanizing lesson in the tidal endurance of U.S. promises and Indian policy.

Thomas Darko, too, finds cultural dislocation when he moves from home to work in the Little Bayou Oil Field of New Iberia, Louisiana, to get money to send home; the deaths of two brothers and his father's stroke have been brutal blows to the family's survival. His own alienation is more gradual than that of the Mankillers. He falls in love with a greedy young Houma woman named Sally Fachette; her desire for the latest commercial goods and his own pride lead him into bootlegging during the Great Depression and, eventually, into a five-year sentence at Angola Prison. As an Indian "in a state where they's not sposed to be no Indians," neither Black nor White, Thomas is generally isolated from the other prisoners, a state of being that foreshadows his solitude as the last of the Mosopelea speakers.[61] While in Angola, Thomas learns that most of his family died when a train car jumped the track and crushed their truck. This event wipes out not only his immediate kin, but also his link to their cultural knowledge, a grievous loss that recalls his sadness as a child upon hearing the story of another imprisoned Indian—Ishi, the so-called last of the Yahi, who, his family dead and land in the possession of Whites, spent his last days in the University of California Museum of Anthropology under the proprietary eye of anthropologist Karl Kroeber:

> Hearing Papa read about it out loud from the newspaper, that sounded near-about like the end of everything. I remember Papa got a faraway thoughtful look on his face and said, "Well, pretty soon all us Indians gonna be gone. This ain't our world no more." It was hard for any of us to spute his word, so we all jist changed the subject, started talking about our mink traps or something like that.[62]

When he leaves prison, Darko goes back to the home place, but finds that he's now not only "alone—really alone—for all the rest of [his] life," but he's also poor for the first time, poor as only a person without relatives can be: "Like I say, I was a poor man, but not jist cause I had no property. No, I was poor cause I no longer had a family. This is real poorness. It can't never git no worse than that."[63]

The fear of such poverty—cultural dislocation that extends even beyond death—runs through both texts, and this is the site of the strongest Chickamauga statements. Neither Mankiller nor Hobson pull away from the pain of removal, but neither do they imagine that removal is the end of the story. For young Wilma Mankiller, San Francisco is a strange and frightening place to the Mankiller family, but it's also a site of broad pan-Indian politicization, where the Oklahoma emigrations of the Great

Depression join with the post–World War II population explosion and the BIA relocation efforts to bring a diverse range of American Indians into the urban centers of California. It's there that she and her family become involved with the San Francisco Indian Center, and where, as a teenager, she begins connecting to the diverse racial and political communities that would strengthen her growing Cherokee nationalism and give her resources from which to draw during her terms as Principal Chief.

For Hobson, Thomas Darko's subsequent experiences as a soldier in World War II, as a field worker and Hollywood extra, and as a participant in an anthropological language-preservation project at the Smithsonian Institution reflect on the state of Indian Country in the first half of the twentieth century and one man's dignified representation of a people whose values transcend death. It's in Thomas's work as a language informant for the Smithsonian that Hobson's strength as a cultural warrior is most compellingly revealed, and in a way that is fully respectful of the Ofo values embedded in the narrative. Of the three White scholars who work with Thomas, two are men he respects; in particular, Dr. William Allerton Payne is "in all respects, a real gentleman. He had some of that old Indian way about him, probly cause he had spent so much time with Indian old-timers who practice respect on a daily basis."[64] The third, Dr. Matthew B. Smight, takes pride in being "known as the main authority on [Thomas's] tribe and language and other Indian tribes in Louisiana," but is clearly displeased to have an actual Ofo around to challenge his scholarly pronouncements.[65] Invoking the specter of Karl Kroeber, Smight is, in all respects, an academic poacher, for whom the privileges and accolades of the academy are the motivation of his scholarship, and for whom the authoritative presence of Indian people is a threat to be minimized, dismissed, or manipulated. He has no humility or respect in either speech or behavior, and the earliest lessons Thomas learned about Whites—"they was always the danger of what some white men would do to us if they was to have they way about it"[66]—reveals Smight to be cut of very nearly the same cloth as the Chicago mobster Frankie McErlane and the murderous Bonnie and Clyde gang, whom Thomas meets in his youth and barely escapes from with his life. Smight is just one more necrophilic anthropologist whose robbery of the Indian past for "scientific" study is of far more benefit to White academic careers than to the communities from which they steal.[67]

Although greatly suspicious of Smight's intentions, Thomas is no one's fool, and he contributes to the project on his own terms until Payne's death, when he returns home to the bayou country. He understands that there's a fundamental difference between Payne and Smight: Payne's motivation comes from a living engagement with real human beings. When Thomas and Payne first meet, the scholar shares a photograph and stories of his earlier conversations with Thomas's grandfather. It's a moment of simple generosity that marks the measure of the man. Payne isn't entirely removed from the dehumanized aspects of academia, as Thomas discovers when he asks "about the good of saving a language on records and in a dictionary when they wudn't nobody but me left to talk it," and Payne's response is "In the Name of Science was the reason, almost like he was talking about a church or something."[68] Still, Thomas is treated with respect and returns it in kind. He practices the old Ofo ways of respect, a behavior expressed in Cherokee contexts as the harmony ethic, where kinship connections are privileged over individualist ego, and where intergroup conflict is (ideally) kept to a minimum.

Thomas maintains these old ways even though all but his most distant human kin are dead, and in this way Hobson reveals a compelling truth: although Thomas is lonely as the only living Ofo speaker, he's not without relatives, for beyond the Tunica-Biloxis to whom he's related by blood, he's still connected to Sun Father, to Mother Ground, and to all the spirits of the world, thus lending a degree of irony to the novella's title. His Tunica family still lives; he's asked by Chief Joe to "make some tapes . . . for all our cousins and relations," tapes that will help keep both Thomas and the Ofo ways alive among his blood kin.[69] He's taught as a child "to balance out," but "not only for yourself, but for all your close ones, blood and not blood," and although he sometimes forgets these lessons, especially during his years of bootlegging and prison, he honors them again in his later years.[70] The Ofos continue on in a way of balance with the world because of Thomas.

This is nowhere more evident than in the conclusion of the first-person section of the novella, in which Thomas wades into the night swamp among nightbirds and other unseen animals, with the bright moon "like a nighttime reminder of Sun Father's promise" above:

> For a while I try to play the switch-cane flute, but I know I got a lot of
> practicing to do before I git the hang of it. Then I begin to talk real low
> and slow in Mosopelea. I had a great-big lump in my throat, and soon

my low-talking become kind of loud, and then I wudn't so much singing
as yelling. My face and eyes was wet, but I keep on singing till my voice
become raspy, like a old lady's with a real-bad cold. I was beginning to get
tired and also kind of chilly, but I sung on, and the lump got smaller and
smaller and then it was gone. When I finally stopped, it seem to me like I
could still hear me in all the trees around and out over the water. I turned
and walked back to the bank, and I knowed pretty good that things was
alright for the time being. But, if they wudn't, then I figgered I could
come back out here tomorrow night and sing again.[71]

Thomas isn't fading sadly into the sunset—he's lifting his voice in song,
finding strength in the language and giving it out into the world. His voice
continues on into the far distance, and hearing the Mosopelea language
come alive again with his extended animal kin and the Mother Ground
around him, he finds strength for his continuing struggle. The book
ends with Thomas's obituary in the coldly unemotional *Contemporary
Anthropology,* but his life has passed beyond this grasping narrative; his
swamp-song puts the lie to the obituary's claim that "from the time he
returned to Louisiana after his stay in Washington up until his death,
Mr. Darko was never known to have uttered a single Ofo word publicly."[72]
Thomas, in true Chickamauga fashion, remains both strong and respectful in withdrawal, and a defiant Mosopelea voice lives on in his last days
in the swamp.

Mankiller draws on a similar ethic of respect in her narrative; coming
from a larger community, she here gives voice to many different Cherokee
perspectives, even those of which she's quite critical. The principles of relationship define the text as much here as in *The Last of the Ofos.* Nationhood
depends on more than one viewpoint to survive; it's nourished by many
sources. The 1960s and 1970s brought a renewed sense of Indian nationhood to Indian people across the United States, particularly among urban
Indians, among whom a pan-Indian Red Power movement emerged in response to anti-Indianism, most visibly during the Alcatraz occupation and
the U.S. government's draconian siege on Wounded Knee in 1973. During
these contentious years Mankiller returned home to Oklahoma with her
daughters, where her liberalized urban activism and grass-roots democracy on behalf of Indians and other disadvantaged groups faced the living realities of rural Cherokee country. As usual, the assimilation directive of the
relocation policy was a failure: Mankiller was more connected to Cherokee

concerns than ever before. Throughout her life in California and through her return to Oklahoma, years of service within the Cherokee government in economic revitalization and program development, a catastrophic car wreck, and the diagnoses of both myasthenia gravis and kidney disease, Mankiller found her greatest strength within the ceremonial and medicine traditions comprising "what our elders call 'a Cherokee approach' to life," which worked to put her back into balance with both the material and ceremonial aspects of her world—not unlike Thomas Darko's own rebalancing.[73]

Mankiller returns to this idea in her short story "Keeping Pace with the Rest of the World." The protagonist, Pearl, is taking her Grandmother Ahniwake to a *yoneg* Indian Hospital for the first time. The young woman is deeply concerned about her grandmother, whose various ailments—including diabetes and heart disease—are beyond the art of most traditional Cherokee doctors to help, as "the secret of the blood medicine" has largely been lost in this age of materialism and imbalance.[74] The old ways are under siege, as much from neglect as from condescension and fear: Pearl, fearing that Indian medicine isn't, in the end, as effective as that of Whites, ignores Ahniwake's clear discomfort in the hospital and convinces her grandmother to remain overnight for tests and observation. That evening, without the protections of her own home, Ahniwake has a terrifying nightmare:

> in the moonlight was a young blond man wearing a white jacket. He moved toward her and she somehow knew she had to dance with him so she managed to shakily stand up and wait for him to join her. She linked her left arm through his right arm and they began to dance. But instead of the familiar Cherokee songs she had heard earlier, he sang a fast, loud cowboy song while twirling her around so rapidly she tripped and fell to the ground. She was out of breath, there were sharp pains in the left side of her chest, she could not get on her feet again. He jerked her up, laughing in a way that frightened her even more and told her that she had to keep pace with the rest of the world.[75]

In the morning, after being told by the icy Dr. Brown that her leg will have to be amputated, Ahniwake insists that Pearl take her back home. The old woman notes, "He did not know my clan, my family, my history. How could he possibly know how to heal me?"[76] To Ahniwake, the hospital is a place of absolute disconnection—the separation of people from themselves, from their histories and families, from their very limbs. To the White doctor at the Indian Hospital, she's a body that's been diagnosed with a disease, but she's more than this to Charlie Christie, her former Indian doctor, and others like him—she's a Cherokee woman with a family, with a history, with kinship relationships, and all these things must be taken into account when determining not only her ailment but also her treatment.

Pearl learns of a Seminole doctor, Billie Joe Harjo, who might be able to help her grandmother. But on the day he is scheduled to meet Ahniwake, the old woman slips into unconsciousness, and rather than call Billie Joe, Pearl again surrenders to fear and rushes to the Indian Hospital, in spite of her grandmother's explicit desire to stay away from the place. This time, though, Ahniwake doesn't recover, and in a brief moment of consciousness is so frightened by the alienness of the hospital and its staff that she has a heart attack and she dies, far from the safety of her home. The next evening, as Pearl is staring into the wood stove, she sees her grandmother among the flames, looking back in comfort, reminding her granddaughter that "As long as the Cherokee people honor our ancestors and our Creator, the roots, herbs, and medicine songs will be available to us. These things will be shown to our people again. They are never really lost as long as we are not lost."[77] Pearl commits herself to recovering the old ways, thereby healing the rift of disrespect between the People and the cosmos.

Reflecting the spirit of Mankiller's autobiography, this story is firmly embedded in Chickamauga defiance. Invoking the memory of Tsiyu Gansini's dismemberment after death, Ahniwake's wholeness is also cut into pieces—first by her diabetes, a health condition resulting from colonialism's dramatic impact on Indigenous diets, then by the disrespect for the older medicine ways that has left the People vulnerable, then by Ahniwake's well-meaning but fearful granddaughter, and finally by Dr. Brown and the Indian Hospital. Both her intimate domain and the larger world are out of balance; though Ahniwake finds peace after death, it's now left to Pearl to work toward reestablishing balance by eschewing negotiation and dedicating herself to becoming strong in the old ways. The right way of things sometimes requires a radical response to correct a system left too long out of balance.

Like the fictional Pearl, Mankiller sought to correct the imbalance in her own life through returning to the values of the old ways, a personal commitment that strengthened her in challenging the sometimes violent sexism of many Cherokees during her campaign as deputy chief in 1983, where "some people claimed that [her] running for office was an affront to God," and others feared that "having a female run our tribe would make the Cherokees the laughingstock of the tribal world."[78] Faithful to Chickamauga principles, she didn't back down from the challenges; indeed, her narrow first election as Ross Swimmer's running mate and strong popularity during her own later service as Principal Chief were reminders of the ancient importance Cherokees put on the words and wisdom of women in political matters. Although a self-avowed liberal Democrat in modern U.S. politics, Mankiller's autobiography demonstrates that she's also a defiant War Woman whose integration of modern political activism with Cherokee values of kinship, respect, and unwavering dedication has worked to rebalance her relocated youth. "Women can help turn the world right side up," she reminds us. "We bring a more collaborative approach to government. And if we do not participate, then decisions will be made without us."[79] While it was the eighteenth-century Beloved Man Adagal'kala who "appeared before the South Carolina Governor's Council" and "demanded to know why no women were in attendance," it's no small irony that the assertion of the presence of women in political matters has become a feature of contemporary Chickamauga resistance by a Cherokee War Woman of the modern age.[80]

This, too, highlights the adaptive and fluid nature of both the Beloved Path and Chickamauga consciousness, which respond to the needs and concerns of the living people, not just historical representations. Adaptive human communities require adaptive responses to conflicts, or cultural stasis and death are inevitable. While *The Last of the Ofos* intentionally invokes "vanishing Indian" narratives like James Fenimore Cooper's *The Last of the Mohicans* (1826), Theodora Kroeber's *Ishi in Two Worlds: A Biography of the Last Wild Indian in North America* (1961), and Asa "Forrest" Carter's *The Education of Little Tree* (1976), Hobson does more than simply invert the stereotype: he explores one man's personal history and tragedies through an attentive respect for the cultural, relational, and cosmological composition of that man's existence. Thomas Darko isn't just another sad and lonely Chingachgook. He takes responsibility for his place in the world, and for his duties to his people, and becomes more than the last Ofo: he becomes a *good* Ofo, and that's every bit as important.

Being good as well as responsible is a driving feature behind the Chickamauga consciousness. It's not enough to be a living Cherokee—it's much more important to be a *good* Cherokee. Neither Mankiller nor Hobson pretends that the Removal period is over; if anything, complacency over past victories is a more immediate danger than Eurowestern oppression, because it leaves us weak and vulnerable. Mankiller tells the story of the early nineteenth-century Cherokee prophet, Charley, who warned the People to return to the old ways or risk being destroyed by White culture. His words, she writes, are a reminder "of the need for contemporary Cherokees to be on guard" and "to do everything we can to hold onto our language, our ceremonies, our culture."[81] Hobson, too, insists on vigilance in a commentary on the state of current Native scholarship, as much against those ostensibly well-meaning people who would speak for us as against those who would silence us entirely: "I mean no disrespect to all our White colleagues by saying these things, but, the bottom line for me is, damnit to the White Man's Hell, let Indian people speak for Indian people." If readers find offense at his words, he apologizes, but also notes without hesitation:

> I decided a few years ago, as I came into elderhood (or dufferdom, as the less kind would have it), that I wasn't going to be just another "nice" old guy sitting in the corner collecting dust. I still have a bark—and a bite. There is still an incredible amount of very important work to be done in academia, and I have great hopes that many of the younger Indian scholars now making their marks will eventually go on to accomplish much that the Elizabeth Cook-Lynns and Vine Delorias were addressing a few years ago. This is our real and best hope.[82]

It's a challenging red sphere mandate and a heavy responsibility that both Mankiller and Hobson give to their readers, but they ask for no less commitment than they have given themselves. Nationhood is a living thing, as are the stories, the ceremonies, the histories, and the relationships. They must be treated with respect, both for the continuity of the People and for the balanced ordering of the world itself. The People go on, but so do the struggles. We can't afford to let our guard down. Not now. Not ever.

To propose a particular Beloved or Chickamauga reading of each text doesn't preclude other readings; it simply opens the texts to a contextualized Cherokee-centered conversation. The principles behind these readings are necessarily relational and very often complementary; as noted before, the peace and war spheres are fluid and context-dependent concepts, and few writers or texts will be limited entirely in one sphere or the other. Such intentional instability makes all readings conditional, as they should be, given the ever-changing dynamics of the relational principles on which they are based. Would, for example, Awiakta approach Thomas Darko's story as a teaching meant to explicitly realign the reader's relationship to the world through Beloved Path principles? Would Hobson's account of Tecumseh's coming-of-age include the Chickamauga naming and privileging of tribal specificity? Rather than presume to know what these writers would do with the stories of others, I would rather present these readings as partial but nonetheless meaningful in their application of Cherokee principles to the texts. They're not the only principles possible, nor always exclusively Cherokee, but in their relationship to diverse Cherokee histories, ceremonial traditions and intellectual expressions, cultural values, and sociopolitical structures, they represent an active participation in something that can fairly be understood as the living Cherokee literary tradition.

Red and White Together

To this point I have tried to untangle some of the distinguishing characteristics between the Beloved Path and Chickamauga consciousness readings by pairing writers whose work seems to best represent those expressive elements within that tradition. In many ways these pairings—and, indeed, the very untangling process itself—are admittedly rather subjective, if ultimately rooted in cultural values that have more durability than

Diane Glancy. Photograph by Dave Scheele.

personal analytical opinion. Still, following Thomas King's suggestion that "literary analysis is not about proof, only persuasion,"[83] it seems to me a useful reflection on the links between Cherokee writers and their literatures, especially in thinking about the work of Robert J. Conley and Diane Glancy.

Of all contemporary Cherokee writers, Conley and Glancy most clearly represent the Chickamauga and Beloved spheres in their literary manifestations. From his Real People series of novels that chronicle Cherokee

Robert J. Conley. Courtesy of Robert J. Conley.

history from before European Invasion, to his Spur Award–winning westerns, western-mysteries (the Go-Ahead Rider series), Cherokee-themed horror *(Brass)*, short stories (notably the 1988 collection, *The Witch of Going-snake and Other Stories*), and essays, Conley's literary concerns have consistently involved the endurance of ceremonial traditions and Cherokee nationhood in the face of often brutal oppression from the United States and its citizenry. Even his scathing satire of academia, *The Meade Solution* (1998), follows a practical, no-nonsense male graduate student in his subversive assault on the assimilative hypocrisies of the professors in his department. His most compelling protagonists have been traditionalist Cherokee warriors in both outlook and deed: the "outlaws" Ned Christie in *Ned Christie's War* (1990) and Zeke Proctor in *Zeke Proctor: Cherokee Outlaw* (1994), the Chickamaugas Dutch/Tahchee in *Captain Dutch* (1995), Dragging Canoe/Tsiyu Gansini in *Cherokee Dragon* (2000), and Jack Spaniard in *Spanish Jack* (2001), and even Sequoyah in the eponymous novel (2002). Although women tend more often to be highly idealized romantic wallpaper or unpredictable bitches than worthy protagonists in Conley's work, the one novel where a female character is in center stage (Whirlwind in 1997's *War Woman*) follows a similar thread of Chickamauga defiance.

An accomplished poet as well as a novelist, essayist, dramatist, and short story writer, Glancy focuses most of her narrative energies examining the insecurities of being a Christian mixedblood woman in the United States, struggling between the varied legacies of her cultures, faiths, and histories. She writes, "I think I speak for a lot of Native Americans who have mixed blood and who know little of their culture and language. But the heritage shows up now and then like the Indian ancestors, whom I know sometimes, when I wake in the morning, have been there in the night."[84] In contrast to the male center of Conley's work, Glancy's work is both female-centered and first-person, more personality driven than Conley's action-oriented novels. Genres, forms, and voices constantly merge and diverge throughout her texts, often in the same narrative, as in her autobiographical collection of short vignettes, photos, poems, essays, and lectures, *The West Pole* (1997), as well as her novels *The Mask Maker* (2002) and *Stoneheart: A Novel of Sacajawea* (2003). There's a vulnerability to her work, an insecurity of self that reflects the scattered experiences of many contemporary Cherokees who live far from the lands and cultural centers of their respective communities. Whereas Conley asserts a complex but determined vision of Cherokee nationhood and self-determination, Glancy is distrustful of firm pronouncements: "If I say I am an Indian part, what do I do with the white?" she asks. "And what do I do with the hollowness where the Cherokee language should have been?"[85]

Rather than examine these writers' work in isolation, I would like to build on the earlier discussions in this chapter to finish with a brief reflection on the mutual engagements of both red and white traditions; a comparative analysis of these two writers together can provide a particularly enriching reading that will reveal the vitality of contemporary Cherokee literature. This will bring the discussion full circle, back to the dynamic relational connections that give life to Cherokee nationhood.

Although any number of texts could be examined here, two in particular highlight the Chickamauga consciousness and Beloved Path in starkest terms, particularly as both chronicle the same traumatic event in Cherokee history: the Trail of Tears. Both Robert Conley's *Mountain Windsong* (1992) and Diane Glancy's *Pushing the Bear* (1996) share the subtitle "A Novel of the Trail of Tears." This is quite fitting, as neither text purports to be *the* authoritative account of that period, and each speaks to very different experiences and perspectives. Conley's novel is, at its core, a Chickamauga text that chronicles the defiance of Cherokees to the injustice and brutality of the Trail through a synthesis of historical fiction, documents of the period, and historical accounts. Glancy's book, on the other hand, travels the Beloved Path, choosing to tell a much different story of survival and the difficult and complicated choices the survivors must make to accommodate their new realities.

There are multiple narratives in *Mountain Windsong,* but all are framed within the reflections of the narrator LeRoy (most often called *chooj*—"boy"—by his grandfather). He's Eastern Cherokee, and through the stories of his grandfather and, later, his grandmother, he learns not just about the history of the Cherokee Removal, but also of the continuation of Cherokee culture in the current age.[86] The book starts with Sonny and his grandfather in the sweetgrass- and dogwood-covered hills above the Cherokee community of Big Cove on the Qualla reservation. There, his grandfather begins to tell the story of Oconeechee and Waguli (Whippoorwill), two young Cherokee lovers whose dedication to one another will be tested by the turmoil of Removal. The grandfather tells traditional stories and history in his own voice; these accounts are supported at various times by the story of Oconeechee and Waguli themselves, then by historical accounts (generally by the Eurowestern ethnographers Charles C. Royce and James Mooney) and documents (the entirety of the Treaty of New Echota and a letter from Ralph Waldo Emerson to President Martin Van Buren in defense of the Cherokees), but the primary authority rests with the grandfather's storied memory. Those stories give shape and function to the text—they drive the narrative, even when interrupted by ethnographic and historical documents. It's essentially a conversation between the old man and his grandson, and together they speak memory to life.

While Glancy spends much time on the life and experiences of one character, Maritole, there's no central figure in *Pushing the Bear*. As thousands walked and experienced the death march of the Removal, so too do many voices speak in this text—a powerful and often discordant din carried through the ages. It's much more a broad range of voices speaking to the experience than is *Mountain Windsong*—at least fifty characters are chronicled in the text, both Cherokee and non-Cherokee. Some voices are collective or of the community—"The Soldiers," "Voices as They Walked," "Voices in the Dark," "Healing Song (Holy Men)," "Story of the Bear"—while others are anonymous, such as the newspaper article "From *The Baptist*" or "White Traveler from Maine" and "Government Teamster's Journal."

Although the range of voices in Glancy's novel could lead to a muddling of perspectives, her narrative skill encapsulates intense emotion in a small space, drawing the trauma forward and challenging any distancing response, as when Maritole is suddenly struck by mourning for her lost family members: "My voice stuck in my throat like a knife. I bent over as though I had a terrible pain. The heaving started in my stomach and rose to my chest. Soon it was in my throat, and I wailed for my baby and mother. Wailed for them in their graves on the Cumberland Mountains, their bones carried off by wolves."[87]

As Glancy states in the author's note, "I knew this wasn't going to be a good Indian/bad white man story. You know there has to be both sides in each."[88] Reading the novels together provides a much more complicated understanding of Cherokee experiences—and the issues of just who is "good" and "bad"—than would a reading of a single text. Just as Chickamauga consciousness and the Beloved Path work in tandem to best represent the diversity of the People, so too do these novels, when read together, draw out the social and political complexities that emerged from the upheaval of Removal. *Pushing the Bear* presents the Treaty Party in a rather positive light, and holds a much more critical view of Ross than does Conley's book. While Chief Ross is given room to speak three times and is, in the first, somewhat sympathetic, most characters who speak of him do so in a spirit of fear. This is most clear when Reverend Bushyhead remarks: "My brother-in-law had been killed by James Foreman, one of John Ross's men. Nancy had never spoken of it, but now in her delirium, she called it out. If you crossed Ross, you feared for your life."[89] Earlier, the character Knobowtee states, "Chief John Ross was not among [the men in the stockade]. He was as much white as Indian. Ross was preparing to leave on the steamship *Victoria* with some of the sick and elderly. Ross wouldn't walk the trail with us."[90]

Glancy writes from the perspective of the Treaty Party and their allies in representing Ross as a tyrant, but more than this, she writes from the perspectives of everyday Cherokees who are split between many worlds and perspectives. While the Chickamauga way is certainly difficult, there are no easy answers on the Beloved Path either; indeed, the latter's emphasis on creating harmony through cooperation, negotiation, and accommodation carries its own share of risks. The choices and deaths of the Treaty Party members are seen as tragedies—"Elias Boudinot had signed the New Echota Treaty because we were being killed by the white man"—but Ross is depicted as assimilated, scheming, grasping, and dangerous.[91] Conley's narrative, on the other hand, acknowledges the sacrifices Ross endured along with his people, including the death of his wife.[92]

The executions of the Ridges and Boudinot also feature in *Mountain Windsong*. Waguli, after walking the dark road to the West, finds himself immersed in alcohol and anger, and he accompanies Elias Boudinot's killers on their bloody mission. Conley avoids clear moralizing when narrating the circumstances that lead to the executions: even while leaving little doubt that signing the Treaty of New Echota was an act of treason against the People, he also makes clear that the act emerged out of the brutal oppression the Cherokees were facing from the U.S. government and the ravenous Georgia rabble who wanted Cherokee lands. The small group of Cherokees who plot the killings through their rage, pain, loss, and passion for *wisgi* (whiskey) have decided that they will mete out justice to the signers of the Treaty: "The law said that anyone who sold Cherokee land must die. These men had decided that they were the ones who would carry out the law."[93] As we've followed them through their agonizing journey, we can't help but be compelled through the narrative to respond sympathetically to their pain. But Waguli resists such a brutal resolution, in spirit if not in action. He and the others require *wisgi* to fully divest themselves of their hesitation, tribal allegiances, and kinship ties:

> Their faces were grim, and even though the *wisgi* still burned slightly inside, their long walk and the nature of their task had sobered them. Waguli's head was throbbing. His stomach churned. He had dreamed of being a warrior and achieving honor and respect by killing the enemies of the Cherokees, but the warrior days of the Cherokees were gone before his birth. Now he was going with these others—men, excepting Pheasant, he did not even know—to kill another Cherokee. He tried to recall the misery he had gone through, the suffering he had witnessed, and to blame it all on this man, to focus all his hatred and resentment on this man, but he could not call up much hatred. Inside he was still numb.[94]

These men are clearly acting out of a potent mixture of desperate emotions and liquor. They blame the Treaty Party signers for all their losses, but Conley reminds the reader that Boudinot, the Ridges, and Watie are Cherokees nonetheless, and that the true enemies are in Washington City and in Georgia.

Boudinot's execution is swift and gruesome, drawn from historical accounts. Lured from his home by men claiming to need assistance for a sickness, he emerges from his home, where they pin his arms and continue, "too soon for Waguli":

> Dirt Thrower sprang from hiding, raised the old hatchet high above his head, and with a mighty swing, buried it between Boudinot's shoulder blades. Boudinot screamed once, not long. Waguli thought the single blow must have killed him. Nevertheless, Thigh stepped out of the darkness and swung his ax, smashing Boudinot's skull. The victim's body hung lifeless between its two supporters for an instant, then they let it drop. Dirt Thrower, with great difficulty, wrenched his hatchet from the body's back, and he swung it again and again. Thigh did the same, and Pheasant and Swim [plunged] their knives into the body over and over.[95]

Waguli's horror in the aftermath of the killing is telling. No matter the justification, the execution is still the death of a Cherokee at the hands of his kinfolk, and this goes against the old ways of law and family bonds. Boudinot's killing haunts Waguli: "The bloody scene he had witnessed kept running through his mind. He heard the scream and the vicious chops and stabs over and over again, and he saw the blood. Boudinot was a traitor, he told himself. But he still felt sick, and he wanted to vomit."[96] Again Conley points to kinship connections as bearing a more fundamental value than political philosophies. While the Treaty Party members are held accountable for their actions and some measure of the responsibility of the Trail of Tears, the bulk of the burden belongs to a Predator state and nation. It is not an issue of race or ethnicity, either—just as there are wicked *yonegs,* such as Andrew Jackson, so too are there kind ones who support the Cherokee cry for justice, such as Wil Usdi (Little Will), a man born White but raised as a Cherokee, as well as Ralph Waldo Emerson.

The novel fully embraces a moral purpose of tribal continuity by highlighting the centrality of community, even over fundamental and unbridgeable philosophical differences. The issue is less one's genetic "race" than it is one's moral allegiances and kinship duties. Both texts include rich traditional elements, integrating the Cherokee language in many ways: Glancy through the inclusion of Cherokee names and untranslated Cherokee words written in the syllabary as well as dialectical transcriptions of Cherokee stories that include both the syllabary and English; Conley through Cherokee names and words, along with their English equivalents. Glancy's, however, true to the Beloved Path, is grounded more in the negotiations with Christianity and those who walked the Trail than is Conley's novel, which places a heavy emphasis on indigenous ceremonial traditions. While Glancy's work does make mention of some aspects of the clan system and medicine people, she pays most attention to the growing impact of Christianity among those who are walking the Trail, regarding the Cherokee "conjurers" with a fair bit of suspicion.

Yet Christians are also the object of distrust and struggle, especially for Knobowtee, who is flailing for answers in a world thrown completely into chaos:

> There was a voice somewhere. With all the voices on the trail. Ancestors. Conjurers. People. Even the voices of the animals and the land. I was almost sure I heard a voice. *You brought us through fire and through the water*—Maybe it was [Reverend] Bushyhead preaching in his sleep. It sounded like one of the Psalms. Maybe it was a voice beyond hope. A certainty I could hear in the ministers' voices. It woke me in the night. There was something that made sense. I just couldn't see it. But look at

the churches in the towns we passed. It was their God. Those people who made the Cherokee walk. It was men like Schermerhorn. Chief Justice Marshall. Though Marshall tried to be just. Andrew Jackson himself probably sat in church Sunday morning near the comfort of a woodstove. A hearth fire and supper waiting in his house. How could I understand? It churned in my head like Maritole's dasher stick in the milk. How could God allow men to walk a trail? Should I just swallow my pride and say their God was my God? How my brother would laugh.[97]

The old answers, for Knobowtee, no longer apply as they once did, as the world itself has changed. But he's still a Cherokee; he's still alive, and it's the Cherokee minister whose words touch him, not those of the White missionaries among the exiles. It's important here to return to Craig Womack's understanding of *tradition*—"anything that is useful to Indian people in retaining their values and worldviews, no matter how much it deviates from what people did one or two [or five] hundred years ago"—as for many contemporary Cherokees there's not always a sharp distinction between being Christian and being traditional.[98] Tradition, like any viable philosophy, changes and adapts to the changing needs of the community.

All these complications are realities of contemporary Cherokee life, and the varying emphases demonstrate again the necessary reciprocity of the Chickamauga and Beloved readings, which move together to propel a complex and heterogeneous people into a future of Cherokee presence. It's in both the red stability of the Chickamauga consciousness and the white adaptation of the Beloved Path that we are able to read the richness of Cherokee continuity in community. Each reading has great strengths as well as problematic aspects; to understand the costs and benefits of each, to weigh them and seek a balance we can live with, uncovers a much clearer understanding of Cherokee diversity and its role in our survival.

Community through continuity, continuity through change: these are the enduring legacies of Cherokee survival. As bloody and tragic as each removal has been, each purge and displacement, each act of genocide and terrorism against the Ani-Yunwiya, we've endured, survived, and continued on. The Beloved Path is a way of living through adaptation, through changing what can be changed while holding on to that which is central to the spirit; Chickamauga consciousness holds us to the old ways, those songs that keep the world whole and in balance. Together, these ways of viewing the world have guided Cherokees through devastation, and they will continue to guide us in the times to come.

The Cherokees discussed in this study have all participated in this circle of celebration and endurance, each giving a bit of their own stories to the rushing flow of Cherokee history, as have the untold thousands of Cherokees and allies unnamed but essential to our understanding of who we are today, and who we will be in the ages to come. Those stories join the great fire that stands at the center of Cherokee existence, each flame feeding the others, burning through both adversity and peace.

Awiakta recounts that, "In 1838, when soldiers herded Cherokee families from Red Clay [Tennessee], someone secretly carried the sacred fire, tamped and hidden in moss. The fire signified the spirit of the Creator, of the sun, of the people—and the Cherokee have kept it burning for centuries."[99] Our understandings of ourselves will change over time, as they have time and again through our rich history, but the fire will remain. As long as we tend it, give it fuel, protect it from wind and rain, and share as much as we receive, it will endure.

Afterword

The Stories That Matter

Who, then, are the Cherokees? The best answer seems to be that there are many different Cherokee populations. . . . Differences have always existed. Initially these differences were defined culturally and linguistically. They represented the geographical populations—the different towns—that gave rise to cultural and linguistic differences. Historical events, to which the Cherokees responded and ultimately adapted, produced other differences in the Cherokee population. Cultural and linguistic differences still exist. Some Cherokees actively participate in Cherokee cultural life; some speak the Cherokee language, often as their "mother tongue." . . .

But common to all the Cherokees is an identity as Cherokee. . . . They are distinct from the total United States population; they are distinct from the total United States American Indian population. Like all peoples of the world, they are the products of history, response to history, and adaptation to history.

—Russell Thornton (Cherokee), *The Cherokees: A Population History*

Cherokee nationhood—communitism in action—is embedded in the dynamic and adaptive significance of all that it means to be Cherokee. In her 1991 inaugural speech for her second term as Principal Chief of the Cherokee Nation, Wilma Mankiller reminded her people of a vital truth: "We've managed not to just barely hang on, we've managed to move forward in a very strong, very affirmative way. Given our history of adversity

I think it's a testament to our tenacity, both individually and collectively as a people, that we've been able to keep the Cherokee Nation government going since time immemorial."[1] The Cherokee people have endured numerous assaults—geographic dislocation, war, assimilation pressures, among others—and as each new antagonist announces the end of the Cherokees, from Governor Wilson Lumpkin of Georgia and Andrew Jackson to Henry Dawes, Hugh Cunningham, and all their philosophical descendants, the sacred fire of nationhood is rekindled, and we rise from the ashes, stronger and more defiant.

If "the truth about stories is that that's all we are," as Thomas King asserts, then the work of the literary scholar has profound ethical implications. Our vocation is the telling, preservation, interpretation, and creation of stories. Stories are what we *do*, as much as what we *are*. Stories expand or narrow our imaginative possibilities—physical freedom won't matter if we can't *imagine* ourselves free as well. As individuals, our words shape us, give us form and substance; they provide a depth of purpose that can strengthen us, or a corrosive pain that eats away at our humanity or makes us destructive and violent.

My own passion for storytelling began at a young age, and it so fully inhabited me by kindergarten that by the middle of the school year my veteran teacher, Ms. Chambers, refused to ever have "show and tell" again because of the disruptive impact of my stories: when I wanted sympathy, my stories made some students cry; when I preferred to be clownish, the classroom erupted in hilarity. At one point I even told the class that my dad had died from drinking "poison water," taking the opportunity from their stunned silence to weave a plausible but entirely fictional story about falling into one of the local mining company's cyanide leaching ponds. There was no ill intent to the story, as I was entirely devoted to my parents, but being the center of attention was too appealing to resist. I'd already become targeted by the bullies in class, and this was one way to defuse their cruelty. Yet I learned at that young age that stories can impact not just our own lives but those of others, and not always in good ways. After this last incident, which apparently traumatized a number of students, Ms. Chambers made me stand in front of the class and confess through humiliated tears that the story was a lie. The power I'd possessed with my story evaporated, and in its place came the derisive scorn of my classmates.

It had never seemed important to me whether or not the story was true; I just wanted to tell the most interesting stories I could imagine, and share them with others. But after talking with Mom and realizing that the story about my dad could be a hurtful thing, I understood that stories are never just dramatic entertainment—they have power that can be used to heal or harm, and we can't always be sure of the impact at the time. To be a keeper and sharer of stories is to take on a sacred trust, whether we assume that responsibility ourselves or are given it by others.[2]

Words are no less important to tribal communities. The stories told both *by* and *about* Indian people are vital to the processes of peoplehood, as they help to give shape to the social, political, intellectual, and spiritual dimensions of tribal life. Stories are never far from their contexts, as words give shape to the world. "Sovereignty" is a story, as are "self-determination" and "nationhood." These stories challenge others, like "Manifest Destiny," "savage," "assimilation," "genocide." Audiences will often help to determine the substance and meaning of that story; as my sister-in-law Diane has made clear in our occasional discussions about Indian issues, White folks who've claimed South Dakota as their own generally have a much different interpretation of the stories of Indian sovereignty than do the Lakotas of Pine Ridge. The stories we tell ourselves and share with others determine the quality of both our present and our future; they're the meaningful center of our lives, and the one thing that endures.

Elizabeth Cook-Lynn (Crow Creek Sioux) has pointed out that academics are, to a large degree, self-ordained in their role as "expert," and it's this presumption of authority that places us in a precarious position in our relationship with tribal communities.[3] This is true whether we're Indian or non-Indian. Here I distinguish *scholar* from *academic,* which aren't inherently the same thing. A scholar is one to whom knowledge and wisdom traditions are of substantive and purposeful concern; an academic is a professional who participates in the institutional structure of resources and privileges of the Eurowestern academy. Not all scholars are supported by universities in their intellectual endeavors, and not all academics are committed to the intellectual life. The academy gives a particular type of ordination and validation to its participants, largely through the processes of promotion and tenure, and these aren't necessarily bad things. I'm fully implicated in these processes myself, as I work at a large research university that places enormous value on the Eurowestern academic enterprise. Yet being implicated in those processes doesn't mean being determined *by* them—we have choices, and we can use the academy's resources and cultural capital to serve both the pursuit of truth and the dignified decolonization of Indigenous peoples. At its best, the academic enterprise is a good and worthy thing, especially when it provides a safe space of cultural recovery for those who are estranged from that knowledge. It's a part of the *process* of intellectual and spiritual development, not the end place of exploration.

Such growth, however, requires something more significant than a driving interest to be a fully connective link between self and community, no matter how smart or well-read a person might be. No matter how much you study, no matter how much you read, you have to go home, because that's where theory becomes story and moves into your bones.

TRIBAL-CENTERED SCHOLARSHIP AND THE WORK THAT WE DO

When I was about ten years old, my dad took me out shooting. We generally went with our .22s, but this time he brought along a shotgun for me to try out. As I'd been raised with guns since infancy, I knew how to handle them, but this time I was a bit careless and didn't pay attention to his words as he explained the recoil of the shotgun and the proper placement of the stock against my shoulder. My mind was likely wandering toward the He-Man toys in the cab of the truck. So, being cocky and sure of myself, I took the shotgun in hand, loaded and aimed, and pulled the trigger, only to collapse in tears as the butt of the gun smashed me in the face and sent blood flying.

My embarrassment was worse than the pain, and I threw the shotgun to the ground. Dad stood by the truck, his expression unreadable. Knowing full well that it was my own fault, but unwilling to take responsibility for ignoring him, I sobbed with dramatic angst, "Why didn't you *tell* me that was going to happen?"

Dad responded calmly, "Nobody has to tell you now."

I've since learned to look before I shoot, and to be prepared for the kickback.

Native literary criticism has a long genealogy. What were the Indigenous lawkeepers of old if not partially textual interpreters? Text and interpreter work together; the relationship between the two is a living one. Wampum belts transmitted messages about the political relationship of one people to another, and understanding the alignment of images on these texts determined whether the People were at war or peace. The Mayan codices were interpreted by trained authorities to help determine not just political and spiritual issues, but to help the people understand their history and place in the cosmos.[4] Cherokees interpreted both the nationalist Cherokee Constitution and the accommodationist Treaty of New Echota very differently than did their White antagonists; these competing readings were the source of both great pride and great pain for the People. Sequoyah's syllabary and written English alike gave Cherokees powerful tools in their textual arsenal against Removal, but they also provided the People with a new way of communicating concerns other than the overtly political that would extend beyond the Trail of Tears: love letters, friendly correspondence, daily news, Indian medicine of both benign and malignant intent, property lists, genealogies, histories, philosophical ruminations, poems, stories, novels, autobiographies . . . and books of literary criticism.

This book is a story that draws on Cherokee stories from the ancient times to the present that have helped to define our relationships to one another and to the rest of creation. To study these stories—written *by* Cherokees who are in conversation with Cherokee history, cultural practices, and politics—gives us a sense not just of the Cherokee literary tradition but also of the principles underpinning Cherokee nationhood and the continuing significance of the red and white paths. Our literature is both a product and an extension of our nationhood; to assert oneself as a Cherokee is to locate oneself in relationship to all these complex and multidimensional discourses—stories—of community. Craig Womack's words give me guidance here:

> Native literature, and Native literary criticism, written by Native authors, is part of sovereignty: Indian people exercising the right to present images of themselves and to discuss those images. Tribes recognizing their own extant literatures, writing new ones, and asserting the right to explicate them constitute a move toward nationhood.[5]

The centrality of Cherokee voices to this project is both an exercise of intellectual sovereignty and a matter of ethical accountability: Cherokees are in the first and best place to speak about who we are and what's important to us; to deny these voices, or to marginalize them in favor of those whose assumed authority is embedded within the ideologies of colonialism, is to add strength to the Eurowestern assimilationist directive from within.

Yet the decolonizing possibilities of literary criticism written in a tribal nationalist vein have been rather recent in coming to the broader field of Native literary studies. Tribal-specific criticism has its red roots both in the histories and traditions of tribal nations as well as in the work of critics (both Native and non-Native) over the past thirty years or so. There are many ways of exploring this genealogy, but a rough mapping might be from the early establishment of a fully formed field of Native American literature by such writers and scholars as LaVonne Brown Ruoff, Kenneth Roemer, Kenneth Lincoln, Simon Ortiz (Acoma Pueblo), and Leslie Marmon Silko (Laguna Pueblo), to the "crossblood" and mixedblood criticism of Gerald Vizenor and Louis Owens, the historicized woman-centered cultural recovery work of Paula Gunn Allen (Laguna Pueblo/Sioux), the land- and treaty-focused scholarship of Elizabeth Cook-Lynn, and the tribally contextualized storytelling-based literary criticism of Greg Sarris (Pomo/Miwok).

The current point of this genealogy is a tribal-specific criticism that takes seriously the intellectual and political sovereignty of the People. Robert Warrior's *Tribal Secrets* heralded the beginning of this body of work, emphasizing in his study of the work of Vine Deloria Jr. (Standing Rock Sioux) and John Joseph Mathews (Osage) not only the ability of Native peoples to intellectually engage with their own texts, but also their right to do so *on their own terms.* Jace Weaver's *That the People Might Live* extended this concept to a broader study of Native literature and the activist articulation of cohesive Native community that shapes so many of the texts in the field—a direct challenge to the tired cliché of the fragmented and angst-ridden Indian subject as the normative representative of Indianness. Both of these texts take as their first framework the intellectual traditions of Native peoples, as Cherokee literary scholar Christopher Teuton explains: "Weaver and Warrior are primarily concerned with understanding the function of Native literature and literary discourse, but their commitments to studying Native written literature, literary history, and critical theory are informed by the concepts and traditional values articulated within tribal oral traditions."[6] Craig Womack took these concepts homeward in his revolutionary study of Creek national literature, *Red on Red.* This book responded to Warrior's concern with intellectual sovereignty and Weaver's discussion of communitism and went further, linking these ideas to the specific relationships between Creek social and political history and Creek literary texts.

There's a traceable and hopeful genealogy of Indigenous critical thought that moves from the *self* to the complications of *community* to what I see as the central concern of Native literary nationalism: *community-in-relationship*.[7] The latter is both the strength and challenge of tribal-centered scholarship. It focuses on the ways by which the People understand themselves and their relationships with the rest of the world. It's necessarily political, and brings with it a burden of responsibility not just for the quality of the work but for its uses. This model places the People into the web of familial rights and responsibilities that define that particular tribal community, while acknowledging the realities of changing historical experiences and their impacts on the various threads of that relational web. It builds on the strengths of previous scholarship that located Indian concerns within broader historical and political influences, while shifting the critical lens from a central concern with mediation with Whites or finding pan-Indian commonalities to looking first at the particular experiences of the People in their world. It's a pragmatic model of scholarship that doesn't presume that change is synonymous with erasure, nor does it pretend that the People are without flaws. Above all, tribal-specific criticism links the critic and her/his work to a living kinship community with a political, cultural, and historical specificity, and it connects those concerns to the People's dignity and continuity in ways that are offered by no other mode of criticism.

In spite of the rich potential of this school of thought, some scholars like Elvira Pulitano, Louis Owens, and Arnold Krupat have characterized work by tribal nationalists as naive or parochial at best and racist at worst for its emphasis on the relationship between the central principles of nationhood and the literatures that emerge from specific community contexts.[8] Pulitano, in particular, trumpets cultural and racial "hybridity" and "cosmopolitanism" as the privileged theoretical center of contemporary Native identity, while ignoring or minimizing the historical, political, and cultural importance of nationhood and communitistic principles to the long struggles of Indian nations against the tangible ravages of colonialism.

I linger on this point because it reflects what seems to be a growing backlash against the development of tribal-centered scholarship, and one that too often emerges from either a misunderstanding of the critical tribal texts, a deliberate misrepresentation of their arguments to protect the assumption of privileged access, or both; either way, the "hybridity" argument misses the point that nation-centered writers and scholars are making. To privilege Indian perspectives in discourses by and about Indians isn't to claim that those perspectives exist in a vacuum, or that they're disconnected from historical and cultural influences beyond one's own nation(s); it is, however, to insist on the ethical repositioning of Indian voices from the margins of that discourse firmly to the center.

An example might be the controversial issue of blood. Throughout Native literature, blood marks Indigenous identity in various forms: genealogical, legal, political, and literary. Its shifting rhetorics and meanings carry an often heavy weight, as it often symbolizes authenticity and connection, as well as the now well-established burden of mixedblood angst, where the writer/protagonist is torn between the Indian and White worlds—as though either are monolithic realities. These blood burdens have been seized upon as *the* defining feature of Native identity by many critics and no small number of Indian writers themselves. In this model, to be fully Indian one must apparently suffer the agonies of mixedblood angst; Indianness can thus exist only through the fragmentation of the Indian self by Whiteness. It's a particularly sadistic (sometimes masochistic) variant of the "vanishing Indian"; the Indians aren't necessarily gone, but they exist only as dislocated and washed-out halfbreeds—not unlike the grim state of affairs in Lynn Riggs's *The Cherokee Night.*

I don't mean to minimize the difficulty that many mixedblood Indians have as a result of their multiple ancestries; those stories deserve to be told, too, as Owens argues eloquently (if somewhat unevenly) in *Mixedblood Messages.* And there's certainly room for variant ethical and intellectually defensible opinions in the charged debate about whether focusing on nation-specific scholarship is an effective tool in challenging colonialism in this hemisphere. But Pulitano's assertion that mixedblood criticism is inevitably the more mature, sophisticated, and intellectually defensible approach ultimately silences and displaces Indian nationhood in favor of those Native voices that privilege the constitutive influence of Whiteness. She can't imagine a viable literary criticism that isn't intimately concerned with talking back to the colonizers—in other words, that doesn't concern itself fundamentally with White folks. When critics imagine nation-specific scholarship as unreflective cultural chauvinism rather than as the engaged intellectual and political expression of tribal self-determination and sovereignty, then *Whiteness* is once again privileged as the foundational influence of enlightenment. It's the age-old story of Eurowestern civilization over Indigenous savagery all over again.

Cultures affect one another, and they intersect in unexpected and often complicated ways—this is a given and natural consequence of being alive in the world, whether the cultures are human, four-legged, winged, plant, stone, or otherwise defined. Yet while influence is, to varying degrees, a reality of existence, so too is some measure of internal cultural coherence, the ability of cultures to define and recognize themselves in whatever way seems best to them. This doesn't mean that such definitions are beyond critique, as every human culture expresses values that are antithetical to dignity or life, and it doesn't mean that such definitions aren't always in flux from influences both within and without, as change is the nature of living, dynamic communities. Most importantly, it doesn't deny the experiences of Métis, mestizos, Creoles, mixedbloods, and crossbloods in defining for themselves identities between and beyond those of their ancestral communities, for each of these groups asserts definitions of themselves as *peoples* with principles and histories of cultural affiliation—they are not simply random collections of disparate and disconnected individuals.

The concept that identities are both stable and in constant motion is hardly debatable in Indigenous contexts, especially in the United States. Of all people, American Indians are painfully familiar with the complexities of identity, as sociologist Eva Marie Garroutte (Cherokee) points out: "[Indians] are a group about which the question of racial identification and classification—its legal, social, economic, political, biological, and other dimensions—has been carefully contemplated by a variety of institutions for hundreds of years."[9] Similarly, the idea that identities are conditional and influenced by social contexts isn't particularly alien to Indigenous epistemologies, given historical and contemporary kinship relationships that often included, through adoption, the "sacred transformation of the individual that brought into being what nature had originally wrought otherwise."[10] Yet when Indigenous scholars assert a critical scholarship that draws from specific cultural contexts that privilege a distinctive Indigenous nationhood (and which are understood to be influenced by the above realities), we're variously condemned, dismissed, or simply pitied for being, among other things, parochial and unsophisticated, racist, naive, essentialist, disrespectful, ungenerous, or otherwise disagreeable and unmanageable. To state that the significance of our culturally rooted intellectual traditions is in some way less valid than the assimilative universalism of traditional Eurowestern scholarship is an exercise intrinsically linked to the intellectual, political, and economic colonization of the Americas.

Asserting the importance of Indian subjectivities to the study of Indian literatures is the driving ethical concern of tribal-specific criticism, and one that provokes surprising reactions. Pulitano's baffling assertion on this point merits attention here: "To insist, as Womack does, that seeking out a Native perspective is 'a worthwhile endeavor' amounts to a dismissal of the mutual interdependencies that for more than five hundred years of history have thrust on the American continent[s]."[11] Such a comment—coupled with her straw-man arguments against the idolatry of cultural "authenticity" or "purity" that none of her primary targets actually claim (and, in fact, take great pains in avoiding) and her consistent focus on the "interdependencies" of Indian/White contact that require Indians of the past and present to be nothing more than mediators of White influence—makes one thing clear about Pulitano's argument: Native people don't exist because they've changed since Invasion. Change equals erasure, and non-Native "authorities" stand as the final arbiters of all things Indian.

Extending this analysis further, if real Indians can *only* exist in this pre-Invasion state of grace, then why does Pulitano even bother formulating a "Native American literary theory"? Wouldn't this be a fundamental contradiction to these assumptions? To whatever degree "hybridity" is a human reality, one thing is certain from the work of most Indian writers: being Cherokee, Creek, Choctaw-Cherokee, or Anishinaabe, or any of the other self-designations of the Indigenous peoples of this hemisphere, includes a fundamental affirmation of the Indian nationhood of a specific community that expresses a tribal-specific identity that's rooted somewhere in a tribal-specific language, sacred history, ceremonial cycle, and geography. Why else would we cite tribal affiliation? Why would we acknowledge kin, ancestors, and spirits if not to acknowledge their specificity? Why would so many use their Indigenous language to name particular spirit beings, or give geographic details of a particularly meaningful place, if not to locate them in a specific linguistic, geographic, and sometimes historical relationship?

No matter how much Vizenor emphasizes crossblood discourses in his writing, he still notes his kinship relationship to the Anishinaabe people; although Owens's self-identification was primarily as a mixedblood, not as an Indian, he nonetheless asserted his relationship to Choctaw and Cherokee specificities. Hybridity is all the rage, but the political expression of *peoplehood* remains the central principle of Indian literatures. Without understanding these tribal-specific concerns and their influences on the writers, a reader risks a fundamental misreading of the texts.

For example, how are we to understand Wilma Mankiller's life's work if not to some degree as an assertion of Cherokee nationhood? Taiaiake Alfred's political theory is stripped of its heart if a reader ignores the Mohawk specificity of his work, just as the geographic and cultural specificity of Kitamaat Village and its oolichan harvest shapes Eden Robinson's Haisla sensibility. If Nanye'hi and Tsiyu Gansini are removed from their Cherokee context, they're nothing more than an Indian Princess and a doomed Indian warrior fading before the Manifest Destiny of Eurowestern civilization.

Native peoples are never just "Native": we are Cherokees, Creeks, Cherokee-Creeks, Mohawks, Eastern Miamis-Shawnees, and all distinctions and combinations between and beyond. Collapsing all these affiliations and relationships into a generic claim of between-the-worlds Native hybridity is yet another act of colonialist displacement that has, as its ultimate aim, the symbolic and physical erasure of Indigenous nations from the very memory of this land.

Again, the assertion that the People should come first is *not* a claim that the People are the only ones who matter; it is, however, to say that we have both the right and the responsibility to intervene in the five-hundred-year process of being defined by others to our detriment. Ignoring the ethical dimensions of literary criticism and its relationship to the processes of colonization is intellectually dishonest and lazy, as well as morally bankrupt. As colonization has consistently erased or dismissed Cherokee voices, then any responsible, ethical criticism demands the assertion of Cherokee voices and traditions in that project.

This isn't an issue of race—although the rhetoric of race has come to dominate American Indian Studies—because at its core nationhood isn't about genetics: it's about kinship, our rights, responsibilities, and relationships as a people, about our sacred relationships to one another, to other peoples, and to all Creation. Robert Conley gives an unhesitant red sphere analysis of this issue:

> People want to say it's not fair for Indians to have special privileges, and they're thinking in terms of race: black, white, Indian, whatever. "No *race* should have special privileges." And they're either ignoring on purpose or unaware of the issues of Indian tribes and the relationship of Indian

tribes to the federal government. Too often we make simple issues into racial issues.[12]

Nationhood is, fundamentally, the *political* expression of a people's understanding of themselves as a people. In both the United States and Canada, Indigenous communities have relationships with their respective nation-state oppressors foremost as political entities, then as racial or ethnic groups. How those entities are constituted will always be a struggle, especially given the unyielding interference by nation-states to influence membership in the most politically and economically expedient way possible. Even within the community there will rarely be unanimity in those definitions—dynamic nationhood in fact requires some measure of dissent and interior movement, because stasis and death are the only other alternative. At its best, tribal nationhood is a proactive union of biology and political principle, one that can absorb complexities into the strengths of the kinship network. Most of the Indian scholars I know are, like myself, of varying degrees of mixed ancestry, but tribal commitments and connections aren't determined by blood quantum. John Ross was every bit the nationalist patriot that Tsiyu Gansini and Nanye'hi were; his Scots ancestry didn't change the fact that he was, first and foremost, a Cherokee.

Nationhood is a commitment, not just an inheritance. According to both documented and oral family history, my family tree includes, along with Cherokees, various links to Shawnees, Scots, German Jews, French, and (according to contested allotment records on my mom's side) Chickasaws, but as a Cherokee citizen who's involved in various expressions of Cherokee nationhood, that's where my primary cultural affiliation is located. I'm proud of all my other kinship connections, because they all contribute to my history and my humanity, but my first duties are to the Ani-Yunwiya.

Tsiyu Gansini and Nanye'hi weren't respected leaders simply because they were Cherokees by heritage: they were respected and sometimes feared because they were also *good* Cherokees who were attentive to both their kinship and political responsibilities as members of their communities. Blood is meaningful to contemporary Indian definitions of identity, but we must be careful to avoid conflating blood with nationhood, because they're not inevitably the same thing. When nationhood—or scholarship—isn't only about blood, non-Indians aren't inevitably excluded from the circle of kinship, and Indians aren't inevitably inside that circle. Returning for a moment to literary scholarship, no Native scholar I know has ever said that non-Natives don't have a place in the study of Indian people, but most of us have insisted that such a place be earned through respect, not presumed through the unreflective exercise of privilege.

This respect is as much a responsibility of Native scholars as it is of non-Natives; indeed, the pressure on us is greater, as we're often held to a higher standard of behavior than are our non-Indian colleagues. It's one of the fundamental responsibilities of doing work in this field. It's part of being a responsible family member.

It's part of being one of the People.

Nationhood requires a lot of things from us, especially attentiveness and the hard work that goes with living responsibly in the world. The Chickamauga war chief and Beloved Woman were part of a living web of relationships that responded to the actions of all its members, and they understood that even their smallest actions would have profound influences on the rest of their world. The red and white spheres of influence aren't fixed, unchanging states of being. They're vital guiding principles that live as we do; they suffer when we're neglectful, but they burn brightly when we put them into mindful practice, as Robert Thomas points out: "It is the word of the spirit that nourishes our humanness. Our elders passed on that torch of the spirit to us. We must keep that torch burning not only for ourselves, but for other peoples as well. The world needs such a vision in these times."[13]

This vision—an ethical commitment to the health and well-being of the People—guides many who study and teach works by and about Indigenous peoples, but such a vision demands to varying degrees that we reevaluate our relationship to the mechanisms of academia. Scholars in Native literary studies—both Indian and non-Indian—are increasingly being asked a simple but provocative question by Indian people: "Why do you do this work?"[14] It's both a challenge toward accountability and an invitation to a more substantive relationship with the people whose lives and literatures we study.

So, why do *I* do this work? For lots of reasons, but primarily to challenge in my own small way those discourses that continually try to erase Cherokee voices (and those of other marginalized peoples) from both the living reality and the memory of the world. My grandmother Pearl died long before I was born, and she suffered for being a Cherokee in ways that I'll thankfully never know. My dad, too, has had to deal with a lifetime of indignities simply because he's an Indian, and while he's always been a scrapper and proud to be Cherokee, when his mother died he lost his strongest connection to the Nation, as my grandfather cut off all ties to my grandmother's family. These links have taken years to reestablish, but Dad never forgot who he is, and now we're both remembering for those who have gone before, and for those who come after. It's cultural recovery at its most basic: a return of the self *to* community through remembrance and integration into the web of kinship. As Linda Hogan (Chickasaw) reminds us, "memory is . . . a field of healing that has the capacity to restore the world, not only for the one person who recollects, but for cultures as well. When a person says 'I remember,' all things are possible."[15]

To do this work isn't just an academic exercise or a mark on the vita, nor is it a way to divest myself of the privileges that come from my light skin and maleness. I was raised working class but now work at a major research university, so I can't claim class marginalization now. To do this work isn't to pretend to be a fullblood—which I'm not—nor is it to assert some essential Indian spirit that gives me a magical connection to the Spirit World—which I don't.

The reason I do this work is simple: I do it to add more fuel to the healing fires of Cherokee nationhood.

It's the fire that keeps us warm and drives away the poachers and predators in the shadows. It's the fire that has led so many of us away from the darkness of self-hatred and assimilation back into the circle of community. The spirit of this particular fire helps us see ourselves as part of something more, to understand that being Cherokee isn't just recognition by others of that connection, but our own recognition of the responsibilities we have as Cherokees to ensure the continuity of the People.

One of those responsibilities is to know not only our lived history, but also our *intellectual* histories, to understand the legacies of story and thought that speak across the ages to strengthen our survival today. It's not enough to simply be alive; knowing the depth of our intellectual and cultural accomplishment helps us to be both alive and *whole*. It's to bear witness to the struggles and victories of our ancestors—from the clash of national vision between John Ross and the Treaty Party, to Lynn Riggs's eloquent battle for wholeness, John Milton Oskison's balance between the ambitions of his father and the political legacies of his mother, Will Rogers's unyielding affirmation of Cherokee pride, and Emmet Starr's Chickamauga challenge to the "two gun" historians who were Whitewashing his people's history. The healing fire of nationhood is also fed by our recognition that the old ways endure in new forms today, such as in the Beloved texts by Awiakta, King, and Glancy, and the defiant work of Mankiller, Hobson, and Conley. Yet we need to extend the analysis even further, to follow examples like Virginia Carney's work on Eastern Cherokee women's writing. We need more exploration of the textual production of particular and underexamined points in Cherokee history; more work about sexuality and Cherokee literary erotics; more analysis of Cherokee genre texts; more connections between language and faith-based concerns and Cherokee literature. There's so much to treasure, and much work left to do.

The struggles will go on, as Cherokee Nation Principal Chief Chad Smith warns us: "Our history tells us that the federal government changes policy toward Indians every twenty to forty years. That means in the next hundred years, we can expect the United States to abandon us two or three more times. Are we ready?"[16] Robert Thomas, too, cautions us to be vigilant, because much is at risk: "We must keep that fire of our own humanity, our Indianness, alive or we will perish without a whimper, and the North American earth will prevail without us."[17]

As the political winds shift and storm clouds gather on the horizon of U.S. Indian policy, we'll see reflections of those struggles in Indigenous literary studies, too. I'm often hopeful that this field will be a respectful gathering grounds where Indians and non-Indians can work together to better understand Indian literatures and their intellectual, cultural, historical, and artistic contexts and influences. I'm hopeful, but not optimistic, and the weight of history is not in our favor. Indians will always have true, much-honored non-Indian allies, friends, and kin who stand beside us through the hardest work and the most difficult of times, who suffer our setbacks and join us in our celebrations. On the other hand, we'll likely always be inflicted with various "friends of the Indians" who see living Indians as obstacles to the established traditions of exploitative Eurowestern scholarship, who see all areas of Indigenous life as resources to be claimed rather than as meaningful ways of being in the world that ensure the continuity of the People.

Still, the struggle itself is cause for great optimism as well as hope, for we're not going anywhere—we're here to stay. Europeans and their Eurowestern descendants have predicted the end of the Cherokees and other Indians for centuries, but our fires burn brightly still. Like all human beings, we've changed over time and suffered setbacks as well as successes, and though sometimes the sacred fire has dimmed, it has never been extinguished.

Drawing on the strengths of our history and our visions for the future, we'll continue on, red and white together, with the Chickamauga fire to give us strength for the battles to come, and Beloved patience to see the hope that lies beyond our enemies. We're aiming truer each time, and holding steady. Each time we're knocked down, we rise up again stronger and wiser than before. The winds are fierce, but our deep roots hold tight. We emerge from the ashes renewed and ready to greet the dawn.

These are the stories that matter the most. They're the stories that remind us of who we are today, where we came from, and who we'll be in the generations to come. We might not all look the same as we did or as we will, some of us might speak a bit differently, dress a bit differently, but as long as we tend the flames of nationhood, the Ani-Yunwiya, the Real People, will endure.

Today, as yesterday and tomorrow, our fire survives the storm.

Notes

A NOTE ON TERMINOLOGY

1. Keetoowah Cherokee writer Robert J. Conley writes, "Today, many Native Americans feel that the term 'Five Civilized Tribes' is inappropriate, in that it implies that those tribes were uncivilized before they began to imitate the white man, when in fact their traditional civilizations were simply much different than those that Europeans brought with them to America" (Conley and Fitzgerald, *Cherokee*, 54–55).

PART I. DEEP ROOTS

1. Warrior, *Tribal Secrets*, 118.

2. Churchill, "Walking the 'White Path,'" ix.

3. Weaver, *That the People Might Live*; see in particular 37–47.

4. Womack, *Red on Red*, 4.

5. Meredith and Meredith, *Reflections on Cherokee Literary Expression*, 1.

6. Ibid., 18.

7. Kilpatrick, *Night Has a Naked Soul*, xviii.

8. Harjo and Bird, "Introduction," 25–26.

9. Amanda J. Cobb provides insight into similar issues affecting the Chickasaws during the late nineteenth and early twentieth centuries: "However, living cultures do change, and customs and traditions do evolve into new traditions.... For many Chickasaws, [Eurowestern] education had become a tradition, and celebrating it may have enabled them, significantly, to continue the traditional rituals of coming together as a community, sharing stories, and feasting. 'New'

traditions may not have been all that new; they may have been very important links to old ways and, consequently, to continuance. By changing, the Chickasaws were not becoming 'less Indian' but were proving that their culture was dynamic and thriving. For that matter, how could Chickasaw people be any *more* Chickasaw? Chickasaws lived on their own land in the Chickasaw Nation. They were self-governing and, to a great extent, self-sufficient. In the sixty years since their removal, they had rebuilt their nation and achieved a tremendous and truly unique level of autonomy. The Chickasaws, in control, defined what it meant to be Chickasaw" (*Listening to Our Grandmothers' Stories,* 64).

10. Womack, *Red on Red,* 12.

11. In "A New Form of Royalty Rises in Indian Country," Lakota commentator Tim Giago reflects on the Cherokee Princess phenomenon: "Good heavens! We (Indians) have heard it so many times in our lives. A white man or woman approaches (this usually happens after I have given a speech) and says, 'My great grandmother was a Cherokee princess.'

"Never a Cherokee prince, but always a princess. I suppose that is because none of these descendants of royalty wish to admit that their great grandmothers had an affair with a Cherokee male. Heaven forbid that a nice young white lady would ever cast an eye about at an Indian man.

"The people most offended and embarrassed by this are the Cherokee. I recall joking about this with Wilma Mankiller when she was Principal Chief of the Cherokee Nation. 'Every time I hear somebody say this I want to just choke them,' she said with a half-smile, half-scowl. And believe me, you don't want to be on the wrong side of a Mankiller."

Giago's main concern in the column is to discuss the inequitable distribution of wealth in Indian Country as a result of gaming, which has created what he sees as a new economic elite (royalty), with a particular biting emphasis on the Oneidas in New York. He finishes with the following wry comment: "Perhaps the next generation of wannabes will say 'My great grandmother was an Oneida princess.' That would sure come as a relief to the people of the long suffering Cherokee Nation" ("New Form of Royalty," 9).

12. Weaver, *That the People Might Live,* ix.

13. Brant, *Writing as Witness,* 12.

14. Weaver, *That the People Might Live,* x. It's important to note here, however, that an "experiential" or "community-based" reading doesn't keep one from criticizing aspects of that community—all communities have flaws, after all, and the scholar's duty is to truth, as much the negative as the positive and value-neutral— nor does it demand that the reader avoid referring to relevant Eurowestern values when evaluating literature.

15. Cobb, *Listening to Our Grandmothers' Stories,* xv.

1. BEYOND THE CIVILIZED SAVAGE

1. Cunningham, "History of the Cherokee Indians," 440.

2. In her study of the history of the United Keetoowah Band, Georgia Rae Leeds notes: "In 1925 in a joint convention in Tahlequah a Tulsa group, mostly half-bloods and known as the Cherokee Executive Committee, joined with the Eastern and Western Cherokee council, the Keetoowah Society, Incorporated, and the NightHawks and elected [Levi] Gritts as Chief of the Cherokees. Operating as a business organization, the four groups transacted the business of the Cherokee Nation" (*United Keetoowah Band*, 13). This was a direct challenge to the assumed authority of the U.S. president to appoint Oklahoma Cherokee chiefs for a single day or limited term to "represent" the Cherokees in business transactions that generally involved transferring fee simple land rights. About fifteen years later, as Wilma Mankiller chronicles, Cherokees again took control of their political future: "Ignoring the federal government's system of appointing what some of our people called 'chiefs for a day' as token leaders, a council made up of several Cherokee organizations met in 1938 and chose its own candidate. The council elected J. Barley Milam of Claremore, Oklahoma, as our tribe's new principal chief. History was in the making. On 16 April 1941, President Roosevelt solidified the relationship between the two governments by appointing Milam as chief of the Cherokee Nation. For the first time ever, the elected chief of the council and the presidentially appointed chief were one and the same. And this time it was not just temporary. Chief Milam, subsequently reappointed by Roosevelt and later by President Harry Truman, would remain our leader until his death in 1949, when we returned to chiefs by presidential appointment for some time" (Mankiller and Wallis, *Mankiller*, 177). There is controversy between the United Keetoowah Band and the Cherokee Nation about which convention establishes contemporary Cherokee governmental authority and, consequently, which of the two is the most legitimate government for the Oklahoma Cherokees. Rather than take a particular stand on this thorny and occasionally internecine debate, I am interested here in these events as overtly defiant expressions of Cherokee nationhood and sovereignty.

3. Cherokees were, before Eurowestern Invasion, a confederation of autonomous towns connected by language, ceremonies, cultural traditions, and kinship ties. By the early nineteenth century, however, the unified Cherokee Nation had centralized its political structure into a Eurowestern republic-style government consisting of separate executive, legislative, and judicial branches. Small groups of Cherokees (the Old Settlers) began migrating west to Arkansas, Texas, Mexico, and beyond to escape the endless waves of Eurowestern settlers, but the largest emigrations took place in 1838 and 1839, when the U.S. government and Georgia state militia drove most Cherokees on a devastating journey to the Indian

Territory. Those Cherokees who managed to remain in their eastern homelands became the foundations of today's Eastern Band of Cherokee Indians in North Carolina. The descendants of the Old Settlers are today generally considered to be the nucleus of the United Keetoowah Band of Cherokee Indians in Oklahoma and Arkansas, while the larger Cherokee Nation in Oklahoma asserts primary descent from the 1838–39 emigrants under the guidance of Principal Chief John Ross.

4. For a few insightful histories of this period, see Burton, *Indian Territory and the United States, 1866–1906*; Debo, *And Still the Waters Run*; Fixico, *Invasion of Indian Country in the Twentieth Century*; McConnell, *Dispossession of the American Indian, 1887–1934*; and Washburn, *Assault on Indian Tribalism.*

5. Sam Smith, notice of election of Levi Gritts as Chief of the Cherokees, quoted in Starr, *History of the Cherokee Indians,* 485.

6. For a roughly chronological account of the crisis, see the following: "Former Leader Addresses Tribe's Internal Problems," *Indian Country Today,* 11–18 August 1997, A3; "Cherokee Leaders Trying to Bring Order to Unrest," *Indian Country Today,* 1–8 September 1997, A2; "Cherokee Nation Rehires Former Cherokee Marshals," *Indian Country Today,* 15–22 September 1997, A2; Will Chavez, "Tribal Powers Pitted against Each Other in Controversy," *Cherokee Advocate,* March–April 1997, 1 and 6; Lisa Finley, "Cherokee Controversy . . . the Facts behind the Crisis," *Cherokee Advocate,* March–April 1997, 1; Tim Giago, "Integrity Fuels Newspapers," *Indian Country Today,* 22–29 September 1997, A4; Linda Turnbull-Lewis and Dan Agent, "Chronology of Events in the Cherokee Nation Crisis," *Cherokee Observer,* 17 September 1997, 1–9; "Boycotts Lead to Employee Layoffs, Angry Cherokees," *Cherokee Advocate,* May–June 1998, 1 and 8; "Four Vie for Top Seats in Runoff," *Cherokee Advocate,* June 1999, 1 and 10; "Smith Sworn in as Chief," *Cherokee Advocate,* August 1999, 1 and 4. Dan Agent, editor of the *Cherokee Phoenix,* was the primary compiler or author of the most comprehensive chronologies of the Cherokee constitutional crisis, and he remains an authority on the events of that time. The charges against Smith were dropped in 2003.

7. According to the BIA 2001 Labor Force Report, the most recent enrollment numbers of the Eastern Band of Cherokees in North Carolina was 12,139; that of the United Keetoowah Band was 7,953. As of July 2004, an editorial by Dan Agent in the *Cherokee Phoenix* listed the Cherokee Nation citizen population as 248,813 (Agent, "Reflections on the Elections," 13).

8. In "A White Paper on Cherokee Community," Dr. Richard Allen, policy analyst for and citizen of the Cherokee Nation, posits the distinction between being recognized as a Cherokee *citizen* and being recognized as a *Cherokee,* for they will not always be perceived as synonymous concepts by all concerned parties. For Allen, as for many Cherokees raised in small, close-knit communities throughout northeastern Oklahoma and in North Carolina, "to be truly identi-

fied as a Cherokee, one must be reared in a family and social environment of a Cherokee community that extends back into history and exemplifies attributes and characteristics that have been retained and adapted over several generations. It is this environment with associated attributes and characteristics that define what and who is Cherokee." He points out, "tribal membership may have little relevance to how one may be defined by the Cherokee community as a whole" (6). While this does beg the question of what *the* Cherokee community is, particularly if much of the acknowledged body politic is excluded from that definition (or even if there is a monolithic Cherokee community or culture), Allen's point is an important one, especially for the purposes of this study, as there are competing definitions even among Cherokees about just what constitutes the community. As Allen notes, "One might suggest that there are Cherokees and there are Cherokee citizens" (7)—those raised within the geographic, linguistic, and cultural center of the traditional Cherokee settlements would be the former, with the latter being those assimilated/acculturated into largely non-Cherokee cultural experiences but tied to Cherokee citizenship largely through genealogy and history.

9. See Alfred, *Heeding the Voices of Our Ancestors* and *Peace, Power, Righteousness*.

10. This kinship foundation was as much linked to relationships with other human communities as it was with those of the People themselves, as Theda Perdue points out: "For southern Indians, human beings fell into two camps—relatives, who belonged within the community, and enemies, who did not. If a person had no ties of kinship to the community and no position within it, Native southerners regarded that person as an enemy, and enemies had no rights, not even the right to live. Only the formal incorporation of an individual into the community through ritual transformed an enemy into a relative. From the Native perspective, [adoptees] literally became Cherokee and Creek respectively because they became relatives, and the Indians expected them to remain permanently in the community with their new kin. Circumstances, however, sometimes demanded that a tribe convert enemies into relatives in order to open the door to peaceful relations between the two peoples" (*"Mixed Blood" Indians,* 9). Kinship, then, is as much a tool of diplomacy and an exercise of sovereignty as it is a way of ensuring good behavior within the community itself.

11. Minges, *Slavery in the Cherokee Nation,* 12–13.

12. Even those Eurowestern political movements that have asserted a more community-based social structure—such as civic republicanism in the past and communitarianism today—have been weakened by their exclusive focus on human peoples and relationships at the expense of a more expansive understanding of ecological interdependence, as well as by their replacement of sacred kinship histories with patriotic assimilation into the political narrative of the nation-state.

13. Weaver, *That the People Might Live,* 163. *Communitism* should not be read

as synonymous with the political movement of Communism here. To Weaver, Native literature "is communitist to the extent that it has a proactive commitment to Native community, including what [he] term[s] the 'wider community' of Creation itself" (xiii).

14. McLoughlin, *After the Trail of Tears*, xv. Keetoowah writer Robert J. Conley also asserts a Kituwah source for the People: "We Cherokees came from Keetoowah, an ancient Cherokee town. In those early days the People called themselves *Ani-Kituwagi,* meaning Keetoowah People, or *Ani-yunwi-ya,* the Real People. As the population grew, some people moved out of Keetoowah and built new towns" (Conley and Fitzgerald, *Cherokee,* 27). Not all Cherokees agree with this idea of origination, or with a concept of a generic shared "Kituwah spirit." Although some "early-day Cherokees called themselves *Ani Kitu hwagi,* or 'people of Kituwah,' alluding to their ancient settlement of *Kitu wha*" (Campbell and Sam, "Primal Fire Lingers," 467), that geographic self-designation was not necessarily universal, as noted by Richard Allen: "I argue that Kituwah was just one town—the northern most of our ancient towns—and not all Cherokee people would agree with you on the use of Kituwah" (personal e-mail correspondence, 13 May 2004). Most Cherokee language authorities hold that the more widely used self-designation of aboriginal (and many contemporary) Cherokees was Ani-Yunwiya, for "the Real People" or "Real Human Beings." Most Cherokees today use either the English derivation of the Choctaw trade-jargon word, "Cherokee" (for "people who live in caves") or its corollary in the Cherokee language, "Tsalagi."

15. Holm, Pearson, and Chavis, "Peoplehood," 12. Although the interdependence of the elements of peoplehood points to an inherent fragility of the concept, it should be pointed out that peoplehood is also quite adaptive. Thus, when Cherokees were driven from their traditional homelands in what is now the southeastern United States to the Indian Territory, they were able to reestablish themselves in what was to many of them an alien landscape. As the principles of relationship were already embedded within broader cultural values, they were applied to the new land and its spirits. As a result, the Cherokees were by and large able to develop relational roots to their new home, and their Indigenousness and nationhood remained intact.

16. Thomas, "Redbird Smith Movement," 163.

17. Hudson, *Southeastern Indians,* 126.

18. Strickland, *Fire and the Spirits,* 189. One of Redbird Smith's sons expands on this description: "The sacred ritualism of the original Kee-Too-Wah is performed only with the sacred ceremonial fire. When the council of the Kee-Too-Wah is to go in session, the fire keepers start the fire at the council grounds before the sun appears in the east. This fire must not be started with a match but through the old custom" (qtd. in Perdue, *Nations Remembered,* 99).

19. Weaver, *That the People Might Live*, viii.

20. Thomas, "Redbird Smith Movement," 161.

21. The Keetoowah traditionalist movement under the guidance of Redbird Smith was an explicitly tribal nationalist movement, yet it drew inspiration from the related wisdom traditions of Natchez and Creek traditionalists as well, especially in its early years. Smith learned from the Creeks' recent renewals of the fire: "John Smith, Redbird's son, told [Robert K.] Thomas that the Creeks had kept a ceremonial ground going and after the Civil War brought the fire to Notchee Town, but when the dancing died out and the people fell away the Fire had gone down. When stomp dancing began to be revived the Fire came up" (Hendrix, "Redbird Smith and the Nighthawk Keetoowahs," 76).

22. Thomas, "Redbird Smith Movement," 165.

23. Hudson, *Southeastern Indians*, 156.

24. Ibid., 136.

25. Churchill, "Walking the 'White Path,'" 161. Although Churchill's work examines similar issues and proposes a somewhat similar analytical structure, such as the dynamic interaction between dualistic concepts and social structures, she limits her analysis to what she calls the white path—peace and harmony, as opposed to war and conflict—a term related to the Beloved Path of this study. (I've chosen "Beloved" instead of "white" in this study to highlight the particular social principles and structures of the late eighteenth century, as well as to avoid possible conflation of Cherokee color symbolism with racialized associations of White vs. Indian.) The white path without the red provides an incomplete understanding of these concepts of dualism and balance; as a result, Churchill's analysis is illuminating but limited.

26. Ibid., 191.

27. Some scholars have questioned whether this division functioned as such in pre-republic Cherokee politics, most notably John Philip Reid in *A Law of Blood*. (See also Duane Champagne's concurring opinion in "Symbolic Structure and Political Change in Cherokee Society," 88.) While most evidence indicates that this division was not as well-defined or as encompassing as that of the Creeks, a number of scholars—including Strickland, Thomas, Fogelson, Minges, and Perdue—seem to agree that the red/white political system did operate in varying degrees among Cherokee towns before their consolidation in the nineteenth century. Perdue follows Fogelson's suggestion that the "'red' and 'white' designations were based in part on age," a much more dynamic and less institutional concept of social structure than the rigid moiety system proposed by Fred O. Gearing's *Priests and Warriors: Social Structures for Cherokee Politics in the Eighteenth Century* (1962) (see Perdue, *Cherokee Women*, 217n22).

28. Strickland, *Fire and the Spirits*, 24.

29. Holm, "Politics Came First," 45–46.

30. According to Holm, Thomas believed that Tsiyu Gansini and the Chicka-mauga resistance "marked the true beginnings of Cherokee divisiveness and the subsequent disruption of the Cherokee social order" during the U.S. Revolutionary War, primarily because the Chickamauga secession in effect "pulled apart the two balancing and distinct governing bodies of the Cherokee Nation . . . and marginalized their distinct ceremonial functions" (Holm, "Politics Came First," 49). I would argue instead that it was the U.S. citizenry and leaders who forced the division, as their coercive insistence on unreasonable land cessions compelled the white leadership to usurp the authority of the war chiefs and abandon the tradition of consensus. Part of that tradition is the right of dissenting participants to withdraw from negotiations without recrimination.

31. The spelling of some historical Cherokee names will differ in this text from many standard historical studies of the periods discussed. I am here drawing on Robert Conley's rationale: "Dragging Canoe was certainly on target when he predicted that there was a danger that some day nothing would be left of Native People but their 'names imperfectly recorded.' The evidence of his startling foresight is in the historical records, where history has left us with such names as Moytoy, Amouskossittee, Attacullaculla, Cotetoy, Cunecote, Totaiahoi, and many others, equally un-Cherokee in appearance and unpronounceable to a Cherokee speaker. Where close examination of these names, or research, or the help of fluent speakers of the Cherokee language has allowed me to arrive at the probable original from which these atrocities were arrived, I have used that probable original name in my text. For example, I have used 'Ma'dohi rather than Moytoy, Ada-gal'kala rather than Attacullaculla, and so on. Explanations are provided in the glossary following the text. Where I have been unable to untangle an incorrectly recorded name, I have used the corrupt form and made a note of it in the glossary" (*Cherokee Dragon,* viii). As Conley's work is both well researched and informed by Cherokee linguistic and cultural authorities such as historian Brent Cox, traditional stomp dancer and teacher Tommy Wildcat, and Cherokee Nation Principal Chiefs Wilma Mankiller and Chad Smith, among others, I am quite comfortable in following his example here.

32. Chota (Echota) was, according to James Mooney, "the Cherokee town of refuge, commonly designated as the 'white town' or 'peace town'" (*Myths of the Cherokee,* 207n20). These peace towns were sacred sites wherein anyone seeking sanctuary was protected from harm, even from the code of blood vengeance that was the primary law of the indigenous Cherokees. Reid sharply disagrees with this thesis; he dismisses accounts brought through oral tradition to the present, finding little evidence in the largely Eurowestern historical record of such an institution. That Nanye'hi, longtime advocate of peace, was often referred to even in those same sources as the Woman of Chota reflects both her own dedication to resolving conflicts without bloodshed and the town's importance as a site where

"the Cherokee . . . still observed the law so strictly in this regard that even a wilful murderer who might succeed in making his escape to that town was safe so long as he remained there" (ibid., 207n20). Whatever the original nature of Chota, it is clear that Nanye'hi's presence and role there contributed to its reputation as a site of security and peace, and certainly contemporary Cherokees identify it as a peace city of central importance to the People during its time (and even today). Eurowestern troops never hesitated, however, to demonstrate their scorn for these traditions, as Chota was repeatedly devastated by their attacks.

33. Kassee, "Nancy Ward," 447.

34. War Women were those who had demonstrated their bravery and skill in battle; as such, they were extensions of and participants in the red/war sphere. Beloved Women, on the other hand, while most often War Women in their youth, were generally older women who had moved into the white/peace sphere—as was the case with many of the older male warriors—and were thus charged with maintaining peace within the community and, when necessary, beyond it. In this way they were distinct from their male counterparts, as they were free to extend their influence and move outside of the white sphere in ways that were generally unacceptable for Beloved Men. Both War Woman and Beloved Women were anomalies: "Women were not supposed to engage directly in warfare; only men who had carefully prepared themselves for war through fasting and purification could expect to meet with success. How then could they explain a woman who killed enemy warriors and led Cherokee warriors to victory? Such a woman was obviously an anomaly: she was no longer merely a woman nor, of course, was she a warrior. As an anomaly, she possessed extraordinary power: through war and menstruation she had male and female contact with blood. Each experience singly was a source of power and danger; when the two came together, the power was phenomenal and permitted these women to move between the worlds of men and women" (Perdue, *Cherokee Women,* 39).

35. Reid, *Law of Blood,* 63.

36. Conley, *Cherokee Dragon,* vii.

37. Cox, *Heart of the Eagle,* 44.

38. E. Raymond Evans (Cherokee) gives the following account of the origin of Tsiyu Gansini's name: "Some time around the middle of the eighteenth century Attacullaculla prepared to lead a war band from Chota against the Shawnee towns. His young son longed to go with his father, but was flatly refused permission. The boy slipped away, however, ahead of the warriors to a portage which he knew they would use, and hid in a dug-out canoe. The warriors found him there, and his father told him he could come along—if he was able to carry the canoe over the portage. The boy was unable to lift the heavy vessel, but, determined to go, he took it by one end and began dragging it. Much impressed, the Cherokee warriors began to shout encouragement. 'Tsi.yu Gansi.ni' cried one, 'Tsi.yu Gansi.ni'

which means 'He is Dragging the Canoe.' Others took up the cry, and from that time on the boy was known as 'Tsi.yu Gansi.ni,' or 'Dragging Canoe'" ("Dragging Canoe," 176). There are two points of particular interest in this account. The first is the mention of the war party of Chota, which would hint that, if the city itself was a site of peace, it was also a location where some war parties originated, thus reflecting the red/white distinctions of most Cherokee communities quite clearly. Though Ada-gal'kala was known, later in life, as a staunch Beloved Man who advocated peace for Chota alongside his niece, in his youth he was also famed as a skilled warrior. The other curious point of this account connects to the relationship between Ada-gal'kala and his son; as they were father and son rather than uncle and nephew, it is unlikely they had the close bond portrayed in this brief passage, although their familial ties and strong political positions within the Chota community may well have brought them closer together than most fathers and sons of the time. Whatever their earlier relationship, it is certain that it was strained beyond repair by the time of the Treaty of Sycamore Shoals.

39. Evans, "Dragging Canoe," 179.

40. Alderman, *Nancy Ward and Dragging Canoe,* 40.

41. Evans, "Dragging Canoe," 186–87.

42. Cox, *Heart of the Eagle,* ix–x. Seneca scholar Barbara Alice Mann commented on this episode in a recent e-mail: "The settlers' fears that he might 'resurrect' from bones shows a fair amount of Cherokee traditional knowledge on their part. According to old Cherokee thought, death was never a natural, but always a caused event. When it occurred before its time, and a person's bones were together, that person might resuscitate and, of course, be very angry with whomever or whatever dispatched him before his time" (personal e-mail correspondence, 24 May 2004).

43. Evans, "Dragging Canoe," 187.

44. Ibid., 180.

45. Carney, "Testament to Tenacity," 31.

46. There are numerous texts about Nanye'hi that ignore her devotion to the People and place her firmly in the "Cherokee Princess" mold, starting with the memorial monument over her grave, which reads: "Princess and Prophetess / of the Cherokee Nation / The Pocahontas of Tennessee / The Constant Friend / of the American Pioneer" (Carney, "Testament to Tenacity," 31). Any number of overimaginative non-Natives have expanded on these concepts in works of dubious historical or literary merit, but perhaps none more offensively than E. Sterling King, whose 1895 pseudo-biography, *The Wild Rose of Cherokee . . . or, Nancy Ward, the Pocahontas of the West,* is perhaps the most remarkable example of this misrepresentation in action. After a brief liaison with an Englishman named Francis, Nancy (Wild Rose) leads her people, sent by her fictional brother Raven to find her, away from Francis: "she turned and ran toward her pursuers.

"The first one she saw was Raven, her brother, with his face distorted with rage, looking all the more hideous on account of his war paint. His hard features relaxed when he saw his sister coming toward him with outstretched hands. He smiled and gave a howl of delight as he took her in his arms and held her to his breast.

"'Ug! Ug! did the ugly pale face think he steal my pet, my "Wild Rose"? Where is he? Me hack him to pieces—me tie him to a stake, and roast him like venison.'

"'He's gone on,' she gasped, almost out of breath, and waved her soft, pretty hand in the direction she had come" (3).

"Wild Rose," due to her innate virtue and intelligence, speaks in complete and complex sentences: earlier in the novel, she tells Francis to run quickly, as "I could but follow you to see you hacked to pieces by savages. Fly! Fly! down this mountain—across the river—and for your life gain the far off settlements in Virginia" (2). The wicked Raven, who has no known counterpart in Nanye'hi's life (unless this is a nasty swipe at her cousin Tsiyu Gansini), is nothing more than a vicious brute who barely grunts above monosyllables. Everything about the characters reflects demeaning stereotypes, and Nanye'hi is lost again in the Indian Princess role of what Rayna Green (Cherokee) calls "the Pocahontas Perplex," an antagonistic colonialist dualism that recognizes only two options for Indian womanhood: the lovely, nubile Indian Princess, who is the epitome of sylph-like beauty and virtue (and who generally sacrifices everything for her White lover); and the savage, treacherous Squaw, a promiscuous and thoroughly degraded creature who betrays her people for the sensual addiction of the world of Whites. European class consciousness is transferred onto American Indians with the naming of the so-called "Princess," and it should perhaps not be surprising that to bolster King's offensive representation, he claims to have heard the story from an ancient woman who "belonged to the old Cherokee royalty" (vi), and that his greatest hope is to "revive the memory of 'The Princess of Chota'—'The Prophetess of Cherokee'—'The Beloved and Pretty Woman of the Tribe'" (viii). The historical Nanye'hi—Beloved Woman, diplomat, and speaker to the spirit world—is thus erased, and the whitewashed Cherokee Princess takes her place.

47. Perdue, "Nancy Ward," 96.

48. Carney, "Testament to Tenacity," 57.

49. Kassee, "Nancy Ward," 448.

50. Carney, "Testament to Tenacity," 50–51.

51. Ibid., 53–54.

52. Ibid., 56.

53. Mooney, *Myths of the Cherokee,* 53.

54. Thornton, *Cherokees: A Population History,* 38.

PART II. GEOGRAPHIES OF REMOVAL

1. King, *Truth About Stories,* 2.

2. Teuton, "Writing Home," 116.

3. In "Yellow Bird: An Imaginary Autobiography," Robert Conley includes a brief section on some of these, "The Migrations of the Cherokees," in which he includes "The Migration of Legend" from "times to history lost" (19), the migration of Chief Bowl and his followers in 1794 and the 1809 journey of Tahlonteskee, that of John Jolly in 1818, and the emigration of the Treaty Party. The section ends with the horrors of the Trail of Tears (19–25).

4. Most standard academic histories of North American Indigenous peoples cite this origin account as the authoritative account, even when they deign to acknowledge variant tribal accounts. Métis historian Olive Dickason's *Canada's First Nations* notes that the "most generally held anthropological theory, based on observable data, [is] that *Homo sapiens sapiens* came from Asia via the Bering Strait" (4), while also proposing the possibility that humans immigrated via ocean travel; she provides four times the commentary on these theories than she provides for the Indigenous peopling accounts. *Major Problems in American Indian History,* edited by Albert L. Hurtado and Peter Iverson, similarly acknowledges Indigenous accounts while simultaneously stripping them of authority through a privileged discussion of the Bering Strait story (see 18–19). Roger L. Nichols's *Indians in the United States and Canada* begins with the following sentence: "Their ancestors migrated east from Siberia into Alaska and then south into the rest of North America some twelve thousand to fourteen thousand or more years before any Europeans 'discovered' the continent at the end of the fifteenth century" (1). He fails to even mention alternative accounts of the peopling of the Americas, erasing almost entirely any complex sense of Indigenous cultural vitality before the onset of European Invasion.

Not all historical analyses of this issue are so dismissive of Indigenous accounts, however. Vine Deloria Jr. (Standing Rock Sioux) has challenged both the philosophical and scientific foundations of the Bering land bridge theory in *Red Earth, White Lies,* and Elaine Dewar's *Bones* deftly chronicles the debates and controversies about the origins of Indigenous peoples in the Americas.

5. Mankiller and Wallis, *Mankiller,* 18.

6. Womack, *Red on Red,* 191. It is useful here to distinguish between Womack's sense of imagination and the loose colloquial use of the word, which often means "fanciful" or even "false." The visionary imagination is a generative force of creation, the expression of the power of stories to transform the world around us; there is nothing false about it: "I grew up with grandparents who told stories about sharecropping for white people in eastern Oklahoma, and they created that landscape for me in my imagination, supplementing the tellings with physical journeys across I-40 and home to the 'real' place, but the 'real' locale was no more or less 'real' than their verbal creation of it" (191).

7. Ibid., 95.

8. Alexander Longe, "How They Came on This Maine," quoted in Hill, *Weaving New Worlds,* 62–64.

9. Longe in ibid., 62.

10. Longe in ibid., 62–63.

11. This civil war could be related to the overthrow of the *Ani-Kutani,* the ancient priesthood that dominated the ancient Cherokee people in some old stories. In most versions of the story, the *Ani-Kutani* became proud and abusive, and in their arrogance drove the People to shatter the priesthood and turn away from a single hierarchical government to the communal and autonomous town system. Such a story may have been of particular interest to conservative Cherokees of the late eighteenth century, who saw increasing political centralization as a threat to the autonomy and authority of the old town and clan system. Robert Conley's Real People series, especially *The Way of the Priests* (1992), provides a fictional exploration of these events.

12. Longe in Hill, *Weaving New Worlds,* 63.

13. Longe in ibid., 63. This account is linked to the controversial book by Traveler Bird, *Tell Them They Lie* (1971). Largely dismissed by scholars as a questionable anecdotal history, Bird's account maintains that Sequoyah—George Guess—was not the mixedblood, illiterate, and lame silversmith portrayed by the historical establishment. Instead, Bird presents Sequoyah as a conservative Chickamauga war leader and fullblood traditionalist. Rather than being the creator of the syllabary, Sequoyah in this account is a protector of the ancient wisdom system that was used by traditionalists to maintain ceremonial knowledge during times of great chaos as well as a method of exchanging information between resistance fighters. More recent scholarship is reexamining Bird's text with a more sympathetic perspective; see Susan Kalter's "'American Histories' Revisited."

14. Hill, *Weaving New Worlds,* 63.

15. Ibid., 64.

16. Meredith and Sobral, *Cherokee Vision of Elohi,* 33.

17. Ibid., 38. The "stone of truth" is likely the *uluhnsadi,* a crystal used for medicine-making and divination, which is said to come from the forehead of the fearsome *Uk'ten',* an anomalous creature that straddled the Upper, Middle, and Lower worlds: it was a giant snake with deer antlers, in some accounts with panther claws and owl wings; although extremely dangerous, with poisonous blood and a taste for human flesh, the *Uk'ten'* was also a creature of powerful medicine. The *uluhnsadi* possessed great healing and divinatory power and was much sought after by aboriginal priests and later medicine-makers.

18. Ibid., 35–37.

19. Ibid., 37.

20. This concern with language preservation and reunification could be a repudiation of my own claims in the previous chapter about the Indigenousness of Cherokee English; indeed, I would read it so. There's no doubt that the introduction of the English language—along with British mercantilism and gender mores—contributed to the instability of Cherokee society during the eighteenth

century, with reverberations following through to the present day. Yet, like most things introduced by colonialism, the language became a tool that many Cherokees used to maintain their culture while fending off other assaults of colonialism.

21. Mankiller and Wallis, *Mankiller,* 18. The ancient wampum belts that are today maintained by Keetoowah ceremonialists were given by Delaware emissaries to the Cherokees to seal a peace treaty between the two peoples in the late eighteenth century.

22. Starr, *History of the Cherokee Indians,* 22–23.

2. THE TRAIL WHERE WE CRIED

1. The reflections of Sidner Larson (Gros Ventre) on this issue are of particular note here: "A way to start this story is by acknowledging that American Indian people have recently experienced the end of the world. . . . They are postapocalypse people who, as such, have tremendous experience to offer all other people who must, in their own time, experience their own cultural death as part of the natural cycle. The ways in which American Indian people have suffered, survived, and managed to go on, communicated through storytelling, have tremendous potential to affect the future of all mankind" (*Captured in the Middle,* 18). Although the assumption that the invasion and colonization of the Americas by Europeans as a "part of the natural cycle" is problematic in the extreme, Larson's comment about "going on" being more than simply survival is helpful for understanding Cherokee continuity beyond the tragedies of Removal.

2. It's not certain that these three brothers—Archibald, James, and Joseph Spear—are my ancestors of the same names (my maternal grandmother's family name is Spears, not Spear), but it seems probable, especially given the time frame and relationships (Starr, *History of the Cherokee Indians,* 364–65). If not the men in question, they're most likely cousins to the Spears line. For the brief mention of the Spear men and their part in the execution of John Ridge, see Wilkins's *Cherokee Tragedy,* 322–23.

3. For an overview of the Removal period, see the following: Anderson, *Cherokee Removal*; Perdue and Green, *Cherokee Removal*; and Thornton, *Cherokees: A Population History.*

4. Quoted in Woodward, *Cherokees,* 160.

5. Trollope, *Domestic Manners of the Americans,* 11–13.

6. Jackson, *Century of Dishonor,* 270.

7. Ibid., 31.

8. For an incisive analysis of the tense and tangled relationships between rhetoric, writing, and Indigenous sovereignty, see Ojibwe/Mdewakanton Dakota theorist Scott Richard Lyons's "Rhetorical Sovereignty," 447–68.

9. Not all White opponents of the Indian Removal Act were blind to the suf-

fering of the Cherokees. Noah Webster was among the most eloquent crusaders. Yet it was Theodore Frelinghuysen, a senator from New Jersey, who "led the attack in the upper house with a six-hour speech that extended over three days. The thrust of his argument was to uphold the sovereignty of the Cherokee Nation, condemn Georgia's extension of jurisdiction and Jackson's refusal to protect the Cherokees from Georgia law, charge that the entire scheme was a transparent attempt to force the Cherokees and other tribes out of their lands, and predict terrible suffering for the Indian victims of the policy" (Perdue and Green, *Cherokee Removal,* 114). Davy Crockett's own adamant opposition to the Act ended his political career. Ironically, the former Tennessee congressman followed his vigorous defense of the Cherokees by joining a group of White Texas settlers and soldiers who advocated U.S. expansionism into Mexico—a cause not unlike that of the state of Georgia in its claims against the Cherokee Nation. Crockett died at the Alamo in 1836, two years before the Trail of Tears.

10. Konkle, *Writing Indian Nations,* 43.

11. Prucha, *Documents,* 52.

12. Ibid., 53, emphasis original.

13. See chapter 3 for an extended discussion of Starr's position.

14. Prucha, *Documents,* 53.

15. Ibid.

16. Ibid., 52–53, emphasis mine.

17. Ibid., 53, latter emphasis mine.

18. Mankiller and Wallis, *Mankiller,* 23–24.

19. Nichols, *Indians in the United States and Canada,* 55.

20. Williams, *Linking Arms Together,* 9.

21. Mankiller and Wallis, *Mankiller,* 26.

22. Randall, *Thomas Jefferson,* 17. Even if we read Jefferson's perspective of Indians as generally benign in comparison with other White thinkers of his time, he certainly didn't extend much philosophical generosity to Africans and African Americans, whom he considered subhuman at best, and certainly not as culturally significant as Native peoples. Historian Scott Michaelsen notes in his study of Jefferson's *Notes on the State of Virginia* that "Africans and Indians are figured differently. They are measured in terms of their relationship to white civilization by separate criteria. . . . [H]e argues that Indian difference is situational, not natural—a product of living conditions, not biology." For Africans, however, "Jefferson goes to great lengths to discount any understanding of African difference, including intellect, as a product of 'situation,' of slavery." Instead, Jefferson focused on "the significance, the primacy, of color" (Michaelsen, *Limits of Multiculturalism,* 66–67).

23. Quoted in Wallace, "Jefferson and the Native Americans," 30.

24. Prucha, *Great Father,* 50.

25. Wallace, "Jefferson and the Native Americans," 30.

26. For more on Jefferson's duplicitous dealings with Indians, see Drinnon, *Facing West*, particularly chapters 8 through 10.

27. Perdue and Green, *Cherokee Removal*, 58.

28. E. Raymond Evans notes that "[i]t was no accident that Major John Walker, Major Ridge, and virtually every notable Cherokee leader of this period came from Dragging Canoe's Chickamauga faction," with John Ross "perhaps the best known of all Cherokee political leaders" from this group. "Dragging Canoe," 187.

29. See Ross, *Papers*.

30. Prucha, *Great Father*, xxviii.

31. Ross, *Papers*, 1:38–40.

32. Ibid., 1:42–43.

33. Ibid., 1:44.

34. Ibid., 1:44–45.

35. Ibid., 1:45.

36. Ibid., 1:59–60.

37. Ibid., 1:104–5.

38. Boudinot was at this time a staunch defender of Cherokee land tenure and defiance of Georgia, in the years before signing the 1835 Treaty of New Echota. His reversal on the issue, as that of John Ridge, came in the aftermath of the pro-Cherokee decision of *Worcester v. Georgia* (1832), when President Jackson refused to enforce the court's judgment in restraining Georgia from persecuting the Cherokees on their own lands. This position, which conflicted with that of most of the Cherokees, including Chief Ross, led Boudinot to resign as the editor of the *Cherokee Phoenix* that same year. For a detailed analysis of this turbulent period, see Wilkins's *Cherokee Tragedy*, 229–33.

39. Williams, *Linking Arms Together*, 18.

40. Ibid., 18.

41. Perdue and Green, *Cherokee Removal*, 59.

42. Konkle, *Writing Indian Nations*, 44.

43. McLoughlin, *Cherokees and Christianity*, 19.

44. Ross, *Papers*, 1:142.

45. Everett, *Texas Cherokees*, 9.

46. U.S. Congress, *American State Papers*, 11:655.

47. Wilkins, *Cherokee Tragedy*, 275.

48. Perdue and Green, *Cherokee Removal*, 20.

49. Twist, "Dispossession," 11.

50. See Prucha's *Documents* for extended discussion of these cases. In *Cherokee Nation v. Georgia* (58–60), the Cherokees argued that, because the Nation was an independent, foreign government within the boundaries of the United States, Georgia had no authority to impose its laws upon the Nation and its people. The

Court found that, rather than being a foreign government, the Cherokees (and all Native governments) were "domestic dependent nations," but left open the case of state authority. The Cherokees took advantage of this opening shortly thereafter in *Worcester v. Georgia* (60–62), when the Georgia militia arrested two White missionaries to the Cherokees, Samuel Austin Worcester and Elizur Butler, for refusing to swear allegiance to the State of Georgia. In this case, in support of a White defendant's claim of immunity from state authority in Cherokee territory, the Court maintained that "the Cherokees were a nation free from the jurisdiction of the state" (60)—but not, of course, of the jurisdiction of the U.S. government.

51. Quoted in Chamberlin, *If This Is Your Land, Where Are Your Stories?* 57.

52. Scherer, "'Now Let Him Enforce It,'" 17. In this largely sympathetic treatment of Jackson, Scherer claims that Jackson was in the highly uncomfortable situation of choosing between Indian Removal and possible civil war on the part of Georgia and other southern states. Scherer largely ignores Jackson's pro-Removal enthusiasm and consistent treachery toward the tribes during his long military and political career, and he treats the very real human devastation Removal caused among Indian nations with only cursory interest.

53. Ross, *Papers,* 1:171.

54. Ibid., 1:172.

55. Perdue and Green, *Cherokee Removal,* 145.

56. Quoted in Washburn, *American Indian,* 4:2462.

57. Ibid.

58. Ibid., 4:2463, emphasis in original.

59. Ibid.

60. Ibid., 4:2466.

61. Ibid., 4:2467.

62. Ibid.

63. Ibid., 4:2468.

64. Konkle, *Writing Indian Nations,* 79.

65. Perdue and Green, *Cherokee Removal,* 19–20.

66. Washburn, *American Indian,* 4:2470.

67. Wilkins, *Cherokee Tragedy,* 278.

68. Ross, *Papers,* 1:218.

69. Ibid., 1:634.

3. Unruly Cherokees in the Indian Territory

1. Conley, *Medicine War,* 2.

2. Washburn, *Assault on Indian Tribalism,* 3.

3. Jaimes, "Federal Indian Identification Policy," 126.

4. Ibid.

5. Redbird Smith was the great-grandfather of the current Principal Chief of the Cherokee Nation, Chad "Corntassel" Smith.

6. Starr, *History of the Cherokee Indians,* 480.

7. Womack, *Red on Red,* 146.

8. Braunlich, *Haunted by Home,* 72.

9. Loughery, *Other Side of Silence,* 81.

10. Womack, *Red on Red,* 276.

11. See "Lynn Riggs as Code Talker: Toward a Queer Oklahomo Theory and the Radicalization of Native American Studies," the final chapter of Womack, *Red on Red,* and Jace Weaver's foreword to *The Cherokee Night and Other Plays.* Aside from published work by Womack and Weaver, there is surprisingly little critical analysis of Riggs's work, aside from Phyllis Braunlich's rich but flawed biography, *Haunted by Home.* Womack notes that although the biography is a strong documentary history, its principal weaknesses are "no analysis whatsoever of what Riggs and many others considered to be his most important play, *The Cherokee Night,* or its relation to Riggs's Cherokee identity; nor any discussion of the meaning of Riggs's homosexuality in terms of its impact on his life and work" (*Red on Red,* 271). Thanks to Womack and Weaver, there is growing scholarly interest in Riggs as both a Native and gay Native literary artist.

12. Womack, *Red on Red,* 286.

13. The General Allotment Act of 8 February 1887; the creation of the Commission to the Five Civilized Tribes on 3 March 1893; the Curtis Act of 28 June 1898; and the final Act to Allot the Lands of the Cherokee Nation, passed by the U.S. Congress on 1 July 1902.

14. Braunlich, Riggs's biographer, writes that Rosie Riggs had received an allotment of 160 acres (*Haunted by Home,* 22), the standard acreage under the Dawes Act according to most sources. However, Francis Paul Prucha writes that the Curtis Act, which broadened the Dawes Act, provided different allotment sizes according to tribe: "Choctaws and Chickasaws received 320 acres each, Cherokees 110 acres, Creeks 160 acres, and Seminoles 120 acres. . . . Some part of each allotment was designated a homestead and made inalienable for a period of years" (Prucha, *Great Father,* 754).

15. Braunlich, *Haunted by Home,* 24.

16. Ibid. Given the many martyred birth mothers and sadistic stepmothers in his plays, and the deep significance that the landscape of Claremore has within his work—being the named or implied site of most of his plays, including the one most explicitly about Indians, *The Cherokee Night* (1930)—it's reasonable to assume that the final sale of the land, which Riggs had released from mortgage *three* different times and waited to sell until he was at least in his forties, was deeply painful, in many ways the truest removal from his mother and everything she represented. After the sale of the allotment Riggs's visits to Claremore were rare,

eventually drying up so completely that he didn't even attend his own father's funeral in 1951.

17. Quoted in Braunlich, *Haunted by Home,* 143.

18. Weaver's reading of Riggs's most famous play is a particularly tantalizing challenge to this statement. He suggests that, rather than being "devoid of Indian characters at all," *Green Grow the Lilacs* is, "in some sense, a play *about* them." See *That the People Might Live,* especially 99–100.

19. Quoted in Braunlich, *Haunted by Home,* 80.

20. Weaver, *That the People Might Live,* 101. For a Cherokee historian's perspective on the heritage of Claremore Mound, see Rachel Caroline Eaton's "Legend of the Battle of Claremore Mound."

21. Lynn Riggs, *Cherokee Night,* 112.

22. Womack, *Red on Red,* 288–89.

23. The presumption of Indigenous blood purity was itself fundamentally flawed, as historian Theda Perdue points out: "Most southern tribes had many members who had not been born to them, although the Cherokees apparently carried adoption to the extreme. When a Mohawk, Major John Norton, toured the Cherokee Nation in the early nineteenth century, he discovered a number of his own people as well as Europeans and Natives of other nations living there as adopted Cherokees. Because of their 'universal custom of adopting in their own Nation the captive females and youths they had taken from hostile tribes,' the Cherokees, he observed, had 'less regularity' in their appearance than other Indians" (*"Mixed Blood" Indians,* 8). Cherokee speculative fiction writer William Sanders adds a humorous aside to blood quantum and its complicated applicability to Cherokees in his postapocalyptic America story, "Elvis Bearpaw's Luck": "'Clear back in Yuasa [U.S.A.] times, there were lots of mixed-bloods. Toward the end they outnumbered the full-bloods in a lot of tribes. Cherokees damn near screwed ourselves white, in fact, before it was over. How do you think your Grandmother Badwater got that red hair?'

"'What about you, *eduda*?' I asked.

"'Oh, I'm full-blood Cherokee,' he said immediately. 'And so were both my parents. But my grandmother on my father's side, now, she was part white'" (97).

Here, as among many Cherokees, it is dedication to the particular attributes of nationhood—traditions, language, proper behavior, etc.—that determine where one stands on the mixedblood/fullblood spectrum, not necessarily degree of Cherokee "blood."

24. For further discussion of the link between blood quantum and competency policy, see "The General Allotment Act 'Eligibility' Hoax" (esp. pp. 259–60), John P. LaVelle's scathing indictment of Jaimes's reading of the General Allotment Act and its purported blood quantum qualifications.

25. By the early years of the twentieth century, Cherokee land loss was facilitated by the U.S. Indian Office largely due to blood quantum policies. Boards of competency were established for those of half-Indian blood or more who wanted to manage their own affairs; if they were deemed incompetent, they were typically appointed a trustee by the board who had complete authority over the allotment, its use, and its revenues, a system that also worked to the detriment of Indian people when land-hungry Whites had themselves named as trustees and then dispossessed their "wards" of the land and resources. See LaVelle's "General Allotment Act 'Eligibility' Hoax," Zissu's *Blood Matters,* and Fixico's *Invasion of Indian Country in the Twentieth Century.*

26. Sturm, *Blood Politics,* 80. Although blood quantum guidelines were relaxed to some degree with the Five Tribes, they still had a catastrophic effect on many Indians' conceptions of themselves and their communities, as access to resources was increasingly limited by the U.S. government to those who were enrolled as Indians by blood and thus of identifiable blood quantum. It worked fully to the advantage of predatory Whites and their assimilated and privileged Indian allies, and to the devastating disadvantage of the vast majority of tribal peoples.

27. Weaver, "Foreword," xiii–xiv.

28. Riggs, *Cherokee Night,* 151.

29. Womack, *Red on Red,* 295.

30. Riggs, *Cherokee Night,* 151.

31. Ibid.

32. Ibid., 154.

33. Ibid.

34. Weaver, *That the People Might Live,* 103.

35. In the short story "Tookh Steh's Mistake," Oskison notes that "political ambition is the birthright of a Cherokee" (62); and see Holm's "Politics Came First," in which the author elaborates on Thomas's claim that "'With Cherokees . . . politics came first'" (45).

36. Riggs, *Cherokee Night,* 180.

37. Ibid., 209.

38. Womack, *Red on Red,* 293.

39. Riggs, *Cherokee Night,* 152.

40. It's important to point out, however, that not all Indians who favored allotment were assimilated or supported the policy out of base self-interest. In fact, some Indians saw allotment as the best way to preserve their land base and traditions, especially given the brutality and corruption of many White Indian agents who often terrorized the communities under their authority and sold tribal commodities, resource rights, and even manual labor to other opportunistic Whites. Malea Powell explores this complex issue in the case of Paiute intellectual and

activist Sarah Winnemucca: "[O]ne of the primary focuses of Indian reform at this time was the destruction of tribalism and the instantiation of individualism, a shift best signified in reformers' minds through the holding of private property, a concept that [Winnemucca's book] *Life [Among the Piutes]* argues for both in Winnemucca's critique of corrupt Indian agents and in the solution she posits: that the Paiutes 'can enjoy lands in severalty without losing their tribal relations, so essential to their happiness and good character, and . . . citizenship, implied in this distribution of land, will defend them from the encroachments of the white settlers, so detrimental to their interests and virtues.' . . . Further, Winnemucca's writing carefully balances reform beliefs about individualism and the need to be heard by reformers as a part of a tribal community in order to authenticate herself as a representative for the Paiute peoples as a whole" (Powell, "Rhetorics of Survivance," 407–8). Allotment, then, is one among a limited number of problematic options that the Paiutes can use to insure their own survival in the face of entrenched U.S. greed and corruption.

41. Washburn, *Assault on Indian Tribalism,* 17.

42. Ibid., 18.

43. One of the most vociferous opponents of the protribal and anti-individualist reparations in the Wheeler-Howard Bill was, in fact, a Cherokee: W. W. Hastings, an assimilated "progressive" for whom tribalism was little more than a quaint throwback to primitivism.

44. Riggs, *Cherokee Night,* 128.

45. Womack, *Red on Red,* 289–90.

46. Ibid., 289.

47. Riggs, *Cherokee Night,* 162.

48. Ibid., 164.

49. Ibid., 164–65.

50. Womack, *Red on Red,* 303.

51. Oskison, *Tecumseh and His Times,* 237.

52. Ibid., v.

53. Ibid., vii.

54. Ibid., 231.

55. Ibid.

56. Oskison, *Tale of the Old I.T.,* I.1. Much of the autobiography is paginated by chapter and page, but this pagination shifts in the latter portion of the text. I've chosen here to follow Oskison's typed pagination.

57. Ibid., II.3.

58. Ibid., II.8.

59. Ibid., II.14.

60. Ibid., III.9.

61. Oskison, *Singing Bird,* 28.

62. Oskison's autobiography suggests a degree of uncertainty and discomfort about African Americans (and, to some degree, Mexicans), and references to Black slavery in *The Singing Bird* provide an interesting commentary on these attitudes. In an early scene where Dan and Paul are choosing supplies for the mission, Paul makes the suggestion that they "buy a black woman for the kitchen." Having just mentioned that their mission "must be a welcome port of call for all, red, white, or black," Dan is shocked, and he responds strongly: "'Paul!' Dan's sharp word was a rebuke. Then he explained, 'It is not politic for us to condemn slavery openly among people, Indians or whites, who take it for granted, but we won't countenance it in our own establishment. If we require a black, we will purchase her freedom, but we must never forget that we are under obligation to labor as diligently in the fields and kitchen as any hired man or woman'" (35). Paul, as narrator, mentions a few more times that their most significant concern relating to Black slavery is the public relation interests of the mission, not the brutal institution of slavery itself. While perhaps a coldly pragmatic response to a highly charged issue, it's also a striking example of moral cowardice, myopia, and naked self-interest, and one that Paul refuses to interrogate further. Racism against Indians is thus a dehumanizing stain, but racism against African Americans is treated as an inevitable state of affairs. Oskison has room through Paul's interior reflections to challenge this state, but Paul is more concerned with a drunken traveler's profane tirade against Dan than he is the cruelty of slavery.

63. Oskison, *Singing Bird,* 45–46.

64. Oskison, "Friends of the Indian," 333.

65. Oskison asserts here that the Indian capitalist—freed from the yoke of U.S. trusteeship and given the funds held by the U.S. government for the sale of Indian lands and resource rights—would be in the best position to become independent of that colonialist authority. His own ethnocentrism and higher class status are painfully obvious in this piece, especially in his commentary about the personal hygiene of traditionalist "tepee" Indians. Yet for Oskison, the survival of the People is due precisely to their ability to use White education and capitalism to *their own ends,* individualistic in action but out of a concern for community continuity, rather than continuing to be victimized by the system as it is used by Whites. He critiques anti-Indian racism and advocates integrated schooling for Indian students as a way to correct the "ignorance" that has left them unprepared for the sudden onslaught of White culture. He notes that allotment was roundly attacked by the tribes and radically changed their lifestyles, but also contends that, with those communal land holdings now erased and the old ways unable to fully meet these new social and economic challenges, Indians will be at a distinct disadvantage without access to capitalist education and their U.S.-held

trust funds. Thus, a generous reading of the essay would seem to indicate that it's not exactly their erasure as Indian peoples that he's advocating, but rather their transformation into self-sustaining peoples who can stand on their own without debilitating support or obstruction from the U.S. government, the ideal vision of a "shrewd Indian who wishes to preserve his race as industrial competitors" ("Remaining Causes of Indian Discontent," 493). Still, the piece is surprisingly more strident in its assimilative emphasis than much of his other work, and far more forgiving of the negative results of that process.

66. Oskison, "Friends of the Indian," 333.

67. Ketchum, *Will Rogers,* 390–91.

68. Rogers, *Autobiography,* 5. Following the lead of Rogers's biographer, Ben Yagoda, I've chosen not to correct or indicate spelling errors, as any attempt at containing Rogers's idiosyncratic writing style seems both intrusive and contrary to the deliberate spirit of the work. Rogers was a thoughtful and attentive writer; rather than try to adjust his style to conventional spelling and syntactic expectations, I'll just let him speak for himself with as little varnish as possible. Unlike figures like Muskogee writer Alex Posey who drew on what Craig Womack calls "Red English," a particular literary device "characterized by dropped articles, elimination of 'to be' verbs, no use of nominative personal pronouns as reflexives or possessives, and the use of 'maybe so' to indicate a conditional action or possibility" (Womack, *Red on Red,* 155–56), Rogers's dialect writing is that of the unschooled rural sage, marked by casual anecdotal familiarity and Oklahoma colloquialisms but still firmly within the frame of English as a first language. Both Red English and Rogers's ruralisms should be understood, however, as literary devices of defiance, for both enabled their writers to express subversive ideas in ways that might be underestimated by a mainstream audience.

69. Day, *Will Rogers,* 1.

70. Yagoda, *Will Rogers,* xii–xiii.

71. Ketchum, *Will Rogers,* 58.

72. It seems that Rogers's most direct and scarring experiences with racism involved his relationships with women, especially in his youth. Yagoda notes that when a teenaged Will was sent by his father to Scarritt College in Missouri, he "was nicknamed 'Wild Indian,' and for months his only friends were the three other Cherokees.... He once invited a town girl named Maggie May to a party... and Maggie refused him, she later said, because '[her] mother would not let [her] go out with this wild Indian boy from the territory who drank wine'" (Yagoda, *Will Rogers,* 25). In 1905, while performing in a Wild West show in New York City, Rogers flirted with some young women in the audience, only to overhear one of them remark upon discovering that he was an Indian that "she could stand being entertained by the darkest inhabitants of Africa, but an Indian went against

her nature" (quoted in ibid., 85). Even his future wife, Betty Blake, seemed for a while to be influenced by this stigma, as "marriage to an Indian, even a wealthy and presentable quarter-blood Cherokee, couldn't be seen as anything other than a social step down" (ibid., 79).

73. Yagoda, *Will Rogers*, xii.

74. Baird, "Are There 'Real' Indians in Oklahoma?" 5–6.

75. Will and his father had a contentious relationship throughout Clem's life, and given Will's strong criticism of Oklahoma statehood and its impact on Indian Territory, it is easy to assume that Clem's participation in the allotment process and the drafting of the Oklahoma constitution would have sat poorly with Will. Clem predicted the impact that allotment would have on the Nation (and his own finances) and worked diligently to head off any difficulty and to enrich himself in the process through ranching, becoming known as "Clem Rogers, the Oologah wheat king" (Ketchum, *Will Rogers*, 51). In the end, the break-up of community-held land holdings devastated the Rogers ranch, and Clem moved into town to pursue other business ventures. A detailed study of the history surrounding the Rogers ranch can be found in Collings, *Old Home Ranch*.

76. Throughout his life, Rogers was deeply concerned about U.S. legislation regarding Indians, having seen and experienced its effects on Indian Territory. He was a strong supporter of John Collier's proposals for U.S. Indian policy reform, noting in 1934 that "[i]f that Wheeler-Howard Indian bill don't pass there is no justice. I think we got a real Indian agent in this man Collier. The Indian has just lost 100 years in his civilization, and Collier is trying to get him back" (Rogers, *Daily Telegrams*, 4:182).

77. Kilpatrick and Kilpatrick, *Friends of Thunder*, 123.

78. Ibid.

79. Rogers, *Letters of a Self-Made Diplomat to His President*, 11–12.

80. Rogers, *Will Rogers: His Wife's Story*, 33.

81. Rogers, *Weekly Articles*, 1:27.

82. Ben Yagoda states that Rogers's "skepticism about the efficacy of the League of Nations, the World Court, and the succession of international conferences held in the twenties and thirties qualified him as an isolationist, although unlike many people traditionally designated as such he was consistent, opposing U.S. military intervention in such places as Nicaragua, Mexico, and the Philippines, as well as Europe" (Yagoda, *Will Rogers*, 286). An apt but limited reading, as the explicit anti-imperialist criticism in many of Rogers's political commentaries adds another dimension to this principled isolationist perspective. Sadly, as Yagoda reveals throughout his biography of Rogers, Will's sensitive understanding of colonized people in the Americas and Pacific didn't extend to African Americans, about whom he made some shockingly racist remarks. See in particular ibid., pp. 200 and 309.

83. Rogers, *Daily Telegrams,* 4:347.

84. Quoted in Ketchum, *Will Rogers,* 354–55.

85. Quoted in ibid., 355. Rogers's opinion of religion—indeed, of most dog-matic philosophies—was rather bleak. Ben Yagoda points to a grim cynicism at the core of Rogers's humor: "His commonsense cosmology was a wonderful humor-producing engine, as it punctured all pretension, cut through all the ver-biage that cluttered the cultural ether. It also tended to disassemble the structures of language and belief that gave comfort to others. Will was too respectful to publicly doubt the existence or beneficence of God. But he didn't belong to any church. He was inaccurately dubbed 'The Philosopher with a Lariat' by an un-inspired headline writer . . . but to the extent that he had a general view of the world it was nihilistic, stark, and rather cold" (Yagoda, *Will Rogers,* 281).

86. Rogers, *Weekly Articles,* 4:67.

87. Ibid., 5:218.

88. Rogers, *"How to Be Funny" and Other Writings,* 24.

89. Rogers, *Weekly Articles,* 3:128.

90. Ibid., 3:128–29.

91. Rogers, *"How to Be Funny" and Other Writings,* 88.

92. Yagoda, *Will Rogers,* 281.

93. Rogers, *Weekly Articles,* 4:125.

94. Rogers, *More Letters,* 13.

95. Rogers, *Daily Telegrams,* 3:10.

96. Rogers, *Weekly Articles,* 5:90.

97. Ibid., 4:143.

98. Rogers, *More Letters,* 91.

99. Ibid., 223–24.

100. Rogers, *Radio Broadcasts,* 20. The removal of Whites from America was a theme that Rogers returned to from time to time, even when commenting on po-litical issues that did not, on the surface, have anything to do with Indians, such as in his 1935 commentary on international politics: "It would be interesting if they would allow every country to do like they did yesterday with this Saar—vote on whether they wanted to go back with who they come from or go with someone else, or go with the League of Nations, or go it alone? Australia, India, Canada, Philippines, Manchuria and Louisiana. . . . In fact, I make this in the nature of a motion. I think you would see a lot of changes. In fact, I think you would see our own country given back to the Indians" (*Daily Telegrams,* 4:264).

101. Rogers, *Radio Broadcasts,* 164.

102. Ibid., 18.

103. Rogers, *Weekly Articles,* 6:126.

104. Rogers, *Radio Broadcasts,* 119.

105. Ibid., 119–20.

106. Rogers, *Will Rogers: His Wife's Story,* 310.

107. Cox, *Heart of the Eagle,* xiv.

108. Strickland and Gregory, "Emmet Starr," 106.

109. Ibid., 111.

110. Ibid., 108.

111. Ibid., 109. There is certainly a degree of irony in this fact, as Starr was a firm opponent of allotment and a sympathizer with the Keetoowah defiance. His purpose in compiling the information wasn't to aid the Dawes Commission; rather, it was to provide Cherokees with a firm sense of national identity through community and kinship ties. The documents in the book largely speak for themselves, and they all remark upon a sophisticated and complex people with a rich cultural legacy under siege by the U.S. assimilationist directive.

112. Starr, *History of the Cherokee Indians,* 9.

113. The images do not actually come from Echota/Chota, which stood in what is present-day Tennessee. Rather, they are sketches of reconstructed Mississippian artifacts unearthed from the Funeral Mound at the Etowah Mounds site near what is now Cartersville, Georgia.

114. Strickland and Gregory, "Emmet Starr," 108. Starr shared this distinction with White historian Angie Debo, whose histories of the Five Tribes, while weakened by "vanishing Indian" stereotypes, were scathing critiques of the greedy and manipulative Eurowestern families who dominated the politics and economy of Oklahoma. These families' money and power came as a direct result of the disenfranchisement—largely through allotment—of the Native peoples of that land. Starr's criticisms of Grant Foreman were many, but none so much as those in reference to Foreman's "preconceived pro-statehood and allotment-of-Indian-land attributes"; in fact, Starr wrote, "I have long ago judged Mr. Foreman . . . over opinionated and vacuous" (Strickland and Gregory, "Emmet Starr," 108).

115. Starr certainly wasn't the only Cherokee to subscribe to this theory. In fact, John Ross was among those who found a defiant strength in the idea: after all, if Christians believed that the Israelites were truly their God's chosen people, and if the Cherokees were truly a long-lost tribe of Israel, then they, too, would be among the elect. In that case, the Whites who oppressed the Cherokees weren't just going against the principles of U.S. justice, they were also going against the will of the Judeo-Christian God. For a detailed and fascinating analysis of the contesting claims about Cherokee origins, see McLoughlin and Conser, "'First Man Was Red.'"

116. Starr, *History of the Cherokee Indians,* 24.

117. For Mooney, see the *Nineteenth Annual Report of the Bureau of American Ethnology to the Secretary of the Smithsonian Institution, 1897–1898: in Two Parts,* now most commonly known today as *Myths of the Cherokee.* For Jack and Anna

Kilpatrick, see in particular *Friends of Thunder, Walk in Your Soul,* and *Run Toward the Nightland*. For Alan Kilpatrick, see *Night Has a Naked Soul*.

118. Starr, *History of the Cherokee Indians,* 479–80.

119. Ibid., 480.

120. Quoted in Strickland and Gregory, "Emmet Starr," 110.

121. Ibid., 105.

122. Ibid., 111.

123. Smith, "Latter Days of Dr. Emmet Starr," 339.

124. Starr, *History of the Cherokee Indians,* 482.

125. Starr, letter to Thoburn, 23 September 1928.

126. Strickland and Gregory, "Emmet Starr," 111.

127. This is particularly the case in his letters dating from 4 May 1919 onward. The bitterness of these letters occasionally bleeds through in unpleasant ways, as in the anti-Semitic tone of one letter: "Am now working for a Jew. Thirteen hours for five days and fifteen on Saturdays, but expect to quit him and commence for myself by the first of the year" (letter to Thoburn, 10 October 1927). In spite of his belief that he was being overworked by his employer, a Mr. Keane, Starr never left his position at The Book World, nor did he ever realize his dream of owning his own bookstore (Smith, "Latter Days of Emmet Starr," 339).

128. Starr, letter to Thoburn, 3 June 1929. This letter, the last in the Thoburn file, demonstrates Starr's continued dedication to accurate history: after a rant against various people who misrepresent the history of Oklahoma, and a note of praise for Thoburn's own work—"I am especially glad as you are the one person that accurately knows more of Oklahoma history than any and always dares to tell the truth"—Starr follows with a response to a query about a medal of honor given to Sequoyah by John Ross in 1825. Just eight months before his death, Starr was still concerning himself with his most abiding love: the accurate representation of Cherokee history.

129. Rogers, *Will Rogers: His Wife's Story,* 35.

130. Cherokee miners haven't been unusual in the Pikes Peak region; in fact, Cherokees and gold mining have had a not infrequent intimacy since the early nineteenth century. The first Cherokee novelist, John Rollin Ridge, fled from the Cherokee Nation after killing a man in an argument and followed a number of his kinsmen to the California gold country with the hopes of striking it rich. In both 1850 and 1858 groups of Cherokees from Georgia and the Indian Territory prospected along the Colorado Front Range; the Cherokee Trail that passes beside Pikes Peak is named for them. The most experienced members of the later group, John Beck and William Green Russell, gained most of their mining knowledge from their work in the gold fields of Georgia—the very gold strike that drove White Georgians into a land-hungry frenzy for Cherokee lands. A Delaware prospector and guide, Fall Leaf, had a certain degree of fame among prospectors in

the Pikes Peak region. For brief accounts of the Cherokee gold mining movements, see Parins, *John Rollin Ridge,* especially 61–75; Brown, *Great Pikes Peak Gold Rush,* especially 12–20; and West, *Contested Plains,* especially 98–105.

Part III. Regeneration

1. Smith, "Introduction," 12.

2. Conley, *Sequoyah,* 180.

3. I've noted elsewhere that *"Poachers* is a term coined by James Cox to describe those non-Indians who come into Native studies to nab a few of our resources, pick up a publication or two, tell the Indian folks who we are and how we think, and then head back to tenure land, leaving us with the bloody gut pile and, yet again, nothing to help our communities, either intellectually or physically." See Justice, "We're Not There Yet, Kemo Sabe," 268. In a recent conversation, Jace Weaver extended this concept further, noting that in addition to poachers, we also have a category of *squatters* in the field who, as with the Georgia lottery of Cherokee land, lay claim to the field and remain to exploit it and the People. The one positive attribute of the poachers is that they leave; the squatters lay claim to place and actively work to displace Indians from the field and its discourses.

4. Readings in Contemporary Cherokee Literature

1. See chapter 1, note 7, for current citizen populations of the three U.S.-recognized Cherokee communities. Engagement with the processes of nationhood includes participation in the political, ceremonial, and/or cultural lives of each respective community, which takes place in many ways. Although the details are beyond the scope of this project, one good example would be voting in tribal elections. In the Cherokee Nation election for Principal Chief in 2003, 12,760 votes were cast—just a few thousand short of the number of the entire Cherokee Nation at the time of the Trail of Tears (though considerably shorter than the 202,114 eligible voters) (Agent, "Reflections on the Elections," 13). This is just one example of national engagement, which can be multiplied exponentially if you add voting patterns in the other communities, subscribers to tribal newspapers, participants in ceremonies at stomp grounds or Cherokee Baptist churches, student groups, warrior and women's societies, etc. For a compelling discussion of some of these issues, see Sturm's *Blood Politics.*

2. See, for example, Slotkin, *Regeneration through Violence,* and Drinnon, *Facing West.*

3. Strickland, "In Search of Cherokee History," xiv.

4. Awiakta, *Selu,* 9.

5. For example, in an unflinching reflection on the suicide of his friend,

Choctaw-Cherokee literary theorist and writer Louis Owens, King writes: "we were both hopeful pessimists. That is, we wrote knowing that none of the stories we told would change the world. We wrote in the hope that they would" (*Truth About Stories,* 92).

6. Owens, *Mixedblood Messages,* 227.

7. Awiakta, *Selu,* 66.

8. Awiakta, telephone interview, 16 February 1999.

9. Awiakta, *Selu,* 72.

10. Awiakta, personal correspondence, 4.

11. Awiakta, personal correspondence, 4. She notes in *Selu* that "Within the quark, scientists now perceive matter refining beyond space-time into a kind of mathematic operation, as nebulous and real as an unspoken thought" (69). This intriguing link between thought, quantum physics, and creation brings to mind what Jack and Anna Kilpatrick call one of the "fundamental truths" of Cherokee magic: "in any magical ritual all generative power resides in thought, and the *i:gawé:sdi* [the thought or spoken component of the ritual], which focuses and directs that thought, alone is inviolate" (*Run Toward the Nightland,* 6). That Eurowestern science is recognizing the links between cosmic creation and the complexity of human thought is compelling, but it seems that Cherokee medicine people have been a bit ahead of physicists on this one for quite some time.

12. Awiakta, *Selu,* 32.

13. Brant, *Writing as Witness,* 14.

14. Crowe, "Marilou Awiakta," 47.

15. Awiakta, *Selu,* 6.

16. Ibid., 266.

17. *Eloh'* means, "at one and the same time, land, history, law, and culture" as well as religion (Weaver, *That the People Might Live,* viii). Cherokee artist Jimmie Durham elaborates on this definition: "We cannot separate our place on earth from our lives on the earth nor from our vision nor our meaning as a people. . . . So when we speak of land, we are not speaking of property, territory, or even a piece of ground upon which our houses sit and our crops are grown, we are speaking of something truly sacred" (qtd. in Brown's *Religion, Law, and the Land,* 38).

18. Hernández-Ávila, "Relocations upon Relocations," 492.

19. On 29 November 1979, the sluice gates of the Tellico Dam in Tennessee closed, and the waters that rose behind them destroyed the remnants of Chota, the sacred city and capital of the pre-Removal Cherokee Nation. Few beyond the immediate region understood the significance of this act, knowing of the dam only through ecological sound bites on the evening news about the destruction of snail darter habitat. The Tennessee Valley Authority's (TVA) Tellico Dam project had long been criticized—from as early as 1936, when it was first proposed—within the U.S. federal government and from without, by environmentalists, the

U.S. General Accounting Office, land rights activists, and others, exposing the project to be economically unjustified and unnecessary for an area with an energy surplus. In spite of such opposition, the representatives of the TVA (who stood to gain over 11,000 acres of prime lakefront property for development, as well as votes based on a platform of job creation) attached the Tellico project to an appropriations bill, which was signed into law (the Baker-Duncan Amendment) by President Carter on 25 September 1979, thus exempting it from every federal law that would have prevented its completion.

In addition to *Selu*, for further reading on the Tellico controversy, see the following: Matthiessen, *Indian Country*; Stambor, "Manifest Destiny and American Indian Religious Freedom"; and Brown's abovementioned *Religion, Law, and the Land*, especially chapter 1, "*Sequoyah v. Tennessee Valley Authority*: The Tellico Dam and the Submersion of Cherokee Sacred Homeland," 9–38.

20. Awiakta, *Selu*, 60.

21. Ibid., 61.

22. Ibid., 63.

23. Ibid., 92.

24. Ibid.

25. Ibid., 95.

26. Ibid., 97.

27. Ibid., 99.

28. Ibid., 42.

29. Crowe, "Marilou Awiakta," 42.

30. Ibid., 52.

31. See Weaver, *That the People Might Live*, 151–54.

32. Quoted in ibid., 151.

33. Sioui, *Huron-Wendat*, xi.

34. King, *Truth and Bright Water*, 14.

35. Ibid., 107–8.

36. In the original edition of *Indian Removal* (1932), Foreman included a photograph of Neugin (between pp. 242 and 243), along with a short interview (302–3). The interview was cited again in his subsequent monograph, *Five Civilized Tribes*, 283.

37. King, *Truth and Bright Water*, 108.

38. See, for example, King's *Truth About Stories*, which features ducks in both an earth-diver story and a Coyote story.

39. For the Dayunisi story, see Mooney, *Myths of the Cherokee*, 239. Other Indian communities—including those of the Iroquois confederacy and Blackfoot peoples—share the earth-diver story in their ceremonial histories. Here the links King makes between the earth-diver and the particularities of Cherokee history

seem to me a significant act of naming that goes beyond the invocation of pan-Indian story traditions.

40. Late in the novel, Tecumseh has a dream connecting ducks to the Falling Woman stories that appear elsewhere in King's work.

41. Foreman, *Five Civilized Tribes,* 283. My thanks to Thomas King for pointing out this connection in a conversation during his visit to the University of Toronto in April 2002.

42. Ridington, "Happy Trails to You," 95.

43. King, *Truth and Bright Water,* 108–9.

44. Ibid., 208.

45. Ibid.

46. Ibid., 232.

47. King, *Truth About Stories,* 2.

48. King, *Truth and Bright Water,* 265.

49. Ibid., 280.

50. My identification of Chickamauga features in Hobson's work in no way presumes an erasure of his other tribal affiliations (Quapaw/Chickasaw) and their influence. As I have attempted to demonstrate throughout this study, the presence of one set of principles doesn't necessitate the exclusion of others; all can inhabit the same space and, indeed, enrich one another within that space. It's useful to point out here that the original Chickamauga communities weren't comprised of Cherokees alone; they included Creeks, Shawnees, Whites, and other people resisting the westward expansion of the United States. Rather than see Chickamauga consciousness as being inevitably racial, I understand it fundamentally as a defiant political exercise of Cherokee nationhood that can encompass other communities under the peoplehood principles put forward by Robert Thomas and others cited in chapter 1. Here, though Darko is an Ofo character, Hobson informs him with a Chickamauga consciousness, one that respects Darko's Ofoness while drawing on the red principles of resistance and—as Womack reminded me—Hobson's respectful familiarity with the Louisiana Delta region of his upbringing and later life that mark this Chickamauga orientation.

51. Mankiller and Wallis, *Mankiller,* 62. Wallis, a "biographer and historian of the American West" (293), is listed as coauthor, but the more florid prose of his other works—such as his biographies of Charles Arthur "Pretty Boy" Floyd and oil tycoon Frank Phillips—is significantly minimized in this text, indicating Mankiller's own direct style as the primary structural voice in fact as well as in advertisement.

52. Mankiller and Wallis, *Mankiller,* xiii.

53. Ibid., 14.

54. Hobson, *Last of the Ofos,* 4.

55. Ibid., 17–18.

56. Ibid., 19.

57. Mankiller and Wallis, *Mankiller,* 68. For a brief but thoughtful analysis of the termination policy, of which relocation was a feature, see Part Nine of Prucha's *Great Father;* for relocation in particular, see 1079–84.

58. Mankiller and Wallis, *Mankiller,* 69.

59. Ibid., 72.

60. Ibid., 73.

61. Hobson, *Last of the Ofos,* 60.

62. Ibid., 12.

63. Ibid., 64.

64. Ibid., 91.

65. Ibid., 92.

66. Ibid., 24.

67. See, for example, Dumont (Klamath), "Politics of Scientific Objections to Repatriation," for a compelling and deeply disturbing examination of the sort of defense that scholars in the Smight school of thought might use in defense of their work. The essay is also noteworthy for its suggested responses that embed the discourse in respectful regard for Indian people. It's not an attack on anthropology itself, but rather a criticism of the dehumanizing excesses of the field.

68. Hobson, *Last of the Ofos,* 90.

69. Ibid., 110.

70. Ibid., 18.

71. Ibid., 111.

72. Ibid., 114.

73. Mankiller and Wallis, *Mankiller,* 226.

74. Mankiller, "Keeping Pace," 209.

75. Ibid., 211.

76. Ibid., 212.

77. Ibid., 216.

78. Mankiller and Wallis, *Mankiller,* 241.

79. Ibid., 242.

80. Perdue, *Cherokee Women,* 55.

81. Mankiller and Wallis, *Mankiller,* 257.

82. Hobson, "Indian Academics Must Speak for Themselves," 279–80.

83. King, *Truth About Stories,* 115.

84. Glancy, *West Pole,* 12.

85. Glancy, *Cold-and-Hunger Dance,* 101.

86. There are fascinating parallels between the primary narrative thread of Conley's text and that of the fake Cherokee autobiography, *The Education of Little Tree,* by Asa "Forrest" Carter, starting with the youthful male narrator who

learns of Cherokee traditions from his traditional and somewhat mischievous grandparents in the Appalachian mountains. Like Little Tree, Sonny learns the names and stories of many animals and plants, but in *Mountain Windsong* the lessons are intimately connected with realities of Cherokee life and tradition, not the imaginary and generic animals named in *Little Tree*. Like Little Tree, the education Sonny receives from his loving grandparents is foundational to his future understandings of himself as a Cherokee, but in *Little Tree* the education is generalized and pan-Indian, with none of the cultural or geographic specificity of *Windsong*. It seems unlikely that these similarities are accidental; rather, the structural narrative of *Mountain Windsong* engages in a sort of conversation with *Little Tree* to expose the absence of anything truly Cherokee in the latter. *Windsong* isn't a romantic excursion into feel-good Indian erasure: while Little Tree ends his story as the last of his kind, the only survivor of all the Indians in the novel, young Sonny ends his narrative with the full richness of his embrace of his living community.

87. Glancy, *Pushing the Bear*, 88.

88. Ibid., 237.

89. Ibid., 166.

90. Ibid., 37.

91. Ibid., 75.

92. Conley, *Mountain Windsong*, 150.

93. Ibid., 156.

94. Ibid.

95. Ibid., 157.

96. Ibid., 158.

97. Glancy, *Pushing the Bear*, 186.

98. Womack, *Red on Red*, 42.

99. Awiakta, *Selu*, 108.

Afterword

1. Mankiller, *Mankiller*, 255.

2. Ms. Chambers requested that Mom come to school for a parent-teacher conference and asked if our family life was okay. Mom replied that it was, prompting the follow-up question, "Does your son get along with his father?" As my mother was the disciplinarian of the household and Dad let me get away with pretty much anything I wanted, Mom replied dryly, "Yes. If he wanted anyone to drink poison water, it would probably be me." While she was certainly overstating our degree of conflict for dramatic effect (she's no slouch as a storyteller herself), I'm happy to report that our relationship has warmed considerably since I was five.

3. See, for example, Cook-Lynn, "Intellectualism and the New Indian Story," 111–38, and her collection, *Why I Can't Read Wallace Stegner and Other Essays.*

4. The deep meaning-making function of the codices was, naturally, a threat to the authority of the Spanish Invaders, and they targeted it with the same fury they brought to other facets of their imperial campaign: through fire, bloodshed, and terror. Weaver quotes a grief-filled Mayan response to the burning: "We could not stop the fires. We could only cling desperately to our memories and weep. They took generations of our hearts and minds, the books, and they threw them into the fires. And we could not stop them" (*That the People Might Live,* 48).

5. Womack, *Red on Red,* 14.

6. Christopher Teuton, personal e-mail correspondence, 30 July 2004.

7. Teuton has developed a sophisticated model of this genealogy, identifying three primary critical modes of interpretation: "The three modes may be differentiated by the central questions they ask, and the progression of the modes marks a gradual shift from non-Native centered to Native-centered epistemologies employed in the analysis of Native literature. Mode one criticism is ethnographically focused and asks questions such as, 'Who and what is an Indian?' Mode two criticism attempts to correct the misrepresentation of Native people and cultures, and asks questions such as, 'Who can say who and what is an Indian but an Indian?' Mode three criticism bypasses questions of representation to theorize how academic work can be made accountable and in dialogue with the needs of Native people and communities. Mode three criticism asks questions such as, 'How are we Native people and nations to become who we want to become?' Although each mode asks different types of questions, they often exist side by side; the borders between each mode are potentially fluid" (personal correspondence, 30 July 2004). Teuton expands at length on this model of criticism in a forthcoming essay, "Theorizing American Indian Literature: Applying Oral Concepts to Written Traditions."

8. For Elvira Pulitano, see *Toward a Native American Critical Theory,* especially chapter 2, "Intellectual Sovereignty and Red Stick Theory: The Nativist Approach of Robert Allen Warrior and Craig S. Womack." For Louis Owens, see *Mixedblood Messages,* especially "'This Song Is Very Short': Native American Literature and Literary Theory." For Arnold Krupat, see *Red Matters,* particularly chapter 1, "Nationalism, Indigenism, Cosmopolitanism: Three Perspectives on Native American Literatures."

9. Garroutte, *Real Indians,* 9.

10. Ibid., 126.

11. Pulitano, *Toward a Native American Critical Theory,* 81.

12. Quoted in Teuton, "Writing Home," 119.

13. Thomas, "Some Thoughts on the Indian Scene," 11.

14. See Justice, "We're Not There Yet, Kemo Sabe," 265.

15. Hogan, *Woman Who Watches Over the World,* 15.

16. Smith, "Introduction," 13.

17. Thomas, "Some Thoughts on the Indian Scene," 11.

Bibliography

Agent, Dan. "Reflections on the Elections." *Cherokee Phoenix* 28, no. 7 (2004): 13.

Alderman, Pat. *Nancy Ward: Cherokee Chieftainess and Dragging Canoe: Cherokee-Chickamauga War Chief.* Johnson City, TN: Overmountain Press, 1978.

Alfred, Gerald. *Heeding the Voices of Our Ancestors: Kahnawake Mohawk Politics and Rise of Native Nationalism.* Toronto: Oxford University Press, 1995.

——— (as Taiaiake Alfred). *Peace, Power, Righteousness: An Indigenous Manifesto.* Toronto: Oxford University Press, 1999.

Allen, Richard. "A White Paper on Cherokee Community." Unpublished paper. Author's files.

Anderson, William L., ed. *Cherokee Removal: Before and After.* Athens: University of Georgia Press, 1991.

Awiakta, Marilou. *Selu: Seeking the Corn-Mother's Wisdom.* Golden, CO: Fulcrum Publishing, 1993.

Baird, W. David. "Are There 'Real' Indians in Oklahoma? Historical Perceptions of the Five Civilized Tribes." *Chronicles of Oklahoma* 68, no. 1 (1990): 4–23.

Bird, Traveler. *Tell Them They Lie: The Sequoyah Myth.* Los Angeles: Westernlore, 1971.

Brant, Beth. *Writing as Witness: Essay and Talk.* Toronto: Women's Press, 1994.

Braunlich, Phyllis Cole. *Haunted by Home: The Life and Letters of Lynn Riggs.* Norman: University of Oklahoma Press, 1988.

Brown, Brian Edward. *Religion, Law, and the Land: Native Americans and the Judicial Interpretations of Sacred Land.* Westport, CT: Greenwood Press, 1999.

Brown, Robert L. *The Great Pikes Peak Gold Rush.* Caldwell, ID: Caxton Printers, 1985.

Bureau of Indian Affairs. *Labor Force Report 2001.* brc.arch.uiuc.edu/ihbg/negreg/ July/response34_bia.pdf.

Burton, Jeffrey. *Indian Territory and the United States, 1866–1906: Courts, Government, and the Movement for Oklahoma Statehood.* Norman: University of Oklahoma Press, 1995.

Campbell, Janet, and Archie Sam. "The Primal Fire Lingers." *Chronicles of Oklahoma* 53, no. 4 (1975–76): 463–75.

Carney, Virginia Moore. "A Testament to Tenacity: Cultural Persistence in the Letters and Speeches of Eastern Band Cherokee Women." PhD diss., University of Kentucky, 2000.

Carter, Forrest (Asa). *The Education of Little Tree.* 1976. Reprint, Albuquerque: University of New Mexico Press, 1986.

Chamberlin, J. Edward. *If This Is Your Land, Where Are Your Stories? Finding Common Ground.* Toronto: Alfred A. Knopf Canada, 2003.

Champagne, Duane. "Symbolic Structure and Political Change in Cherokee Society." *Journal of Cherokee Studies* 8, no. 2 (1983): 87–96.

Chavez, Will. "Tribal Powers Pitted against Each Other in Controversy." *Cherokee Advocate,* March–April 1997, 1 and 6.

Cherokee Advocate. "Boycotts Lead to Employee Layoffs, Angry Cherokees." May–June 1998, 1 and 8.

———. "Four Vie for Top Seats in Runoff." June 1999, 1 and 10.

———. "Smith Sworn in as Chief." August 1999, 1 and 4.

Churchill, Mary C. "Walking the 'White Path': Toward a Cherokee-Centric Hermeneutic for Interpreting Cherokee Literatures." PhD diss., UC Santa Barbara, 1997.

Cobb, Amanda J. *Listening to Our Grandmothers' Stories: The Bloomfield Academy for Chickasaw Females, 1852–1949.* Lincoln: University of Nebraska Press, 2000.

Collings, Ellsworth. *The Old Home Ranch: The Will Rogers Range in the Indian Territory.* Stillwater, OK: Redlands, 1964.

Conley, Robert J. *Cherokee Dragon.* New York: St. Martin's Press, 2000.

———. *Medicine War.* New York: Signet, 2001.

———. *Mountain Windsong: A Novel of the Trail of Tears.* Norman: University of Oklahoma Press, 1992.

———. *Ned Christie's War.* New York: St. Martin's Press, 1990.

———. *Sequoyah.* New York: St. Martin's Press, 2002.

———. *The Way of the Priests.* 1992. Reprint, Norman: University of Oklahoma Press, 2000.

———. "Yellow Bird: An Imaginary Autobiography." In *The Witch of Goingsnake and Other Stories,* 3–37. Norman: University of Oklahoma Press, 1988.

Conley, Robert J. (text), and David G. Fitzgerald (photographs). *Cherokee.* Portland, OR: Graphic Arts Center Publishing, 2002.

Cook-Lynn, Elizabeth. "Intellectualism and the New Indian Story." In *Natives and Academics: Researching and Writing about American Indians,* ed. Devon A. Mihesuah, 111–38. Lincoln: University of Nebraska Press, 1998.

———. *Why I Can't Read Wallace Stegner and Other Essays.* Madison: University of Wisconsin Press, 1996.

Cox, Brent Alan Yanusdi. *Heart of the Eagle: Dragging Canoe and the Emergence of the Chickamauga Confederacy.* Milan, TN: Chenanee Publishing, 1999.

Crowe, Thomas Rain. "Marilou Awiakta: Reweaving the Future." *Appalachian Journal* 18, no. 1 (1990): 40–54.

Cunningham, Hugh T. "A History of the Cherokee Indians." *Chronicles of Oklahoma* 8, no. 4 (1930): 407–40.

Day, Donald. *Will Rogers: A Biography.* New York: David McKay, 1962.

Debo, Angie. *And Still the Waters Run: The Betrayal of the Five Civilized Tribes.* Princeton: Princeton University Press, 1940.

Deloria, Vine, Jr. *Red Earth, White Lies: Native Americans and the Myth of Scientific Fact.* Golden, CO: Fulcrum Publishing, 1997.

Dewar, Elaine. *Bones: Discovering the First Americans.* Toronto: Vintage Canada, 2001.

Dickason, Olive Patricia. *Canada's First Nations: A History of Founding Peoples from Earliest Times.* 3rd ed. Don Mills, ON: Oxford University Press, 2002.

Drinnon, Richard. *Facing West: The Metaphysics of Indian-Hating and Empire Building.* Minneapolis: University of Minnesota Press, 1980.

Dumont, Clayton W., Jr. "The Politics of Scientific Objections to Repatriation." *Wicazo Sa Review* 18, no. 1 (2003): 109–28.

Duncan, DeWitt Clinton (Too-qua-stee). "A Momentous Occasion." In *Native American Writing in the Southeast: An Anthology, 1875–1935,* ed. Daniel F. Littlefield Jr. and James W. Parins, 31–37. Jackson: University of Mississippi Press, 1995.

Eaton, Rachel Caroline. "The Legend of the Battle of Claremore Mound." In *Native American Writing in the Southeast: An Anthology, 1875–1935,* ed. Daniel F. Littlefield Jr. and James W. Parins, 236–42. Jackson: University of Mississippi Press, 1995.

Evans, E. Raymond. "Notable Persons in Cherokee History: Dragging Canoe." *Journal of Cherokee Studies* 2, no. 1 (1977): 176–89.

Everett, Dianna. *The Texas Cherokees: A People between Two Fires, 1819–1840.* Norman: University of Oklahoma Press, 1990.

Finley, Lisa. "Cherokee Controversy . . . the Facts behind the Crisis." *Cherokee Advocate,* March–April 1997, 1.

Fixico, Donald. *The Invasion of Indian Country in the Twentieth Century: American Capitalism and Tribal Natural Resources.* Niwot: University Press of Colorado, 1998.

Foreman, Grant. *The Five Civilized Tribes.* Norman: University of Oklahoma Press, 1934.

———. *Indian Removal: The Emigration of the Five Civilized Tribes of Indians.* Norman: University of Oklahoma Press, 1932.

Garroutte, Eva Marie. *Real Indians: Identity and the Survival of Native America.* Berkeley: University of California Press, 2003.

Giago, Tim. "Integrity Fuels Newspapers." *Indian Country Today,* 22–29 September 1997, A4.

———. "A New Form of Royalty Rises in Indian Country." *Omaha World-Herald,* 6 March 2000, 9.

Glancy, Diane. *The Cold-and-Hunger Dance.* Lincoln: University of Nebraska Press, 1998.

———. *Pushing the Bear: A Novel of the Trail of Tears.* San Diego: Harcourt Brace, 1996.

———. *The West Pole.* Minneapolis: University of Minnesota Press, 1997.

Harjo, Joy, and Gloria Bird. "Introduction." In *Reinventing the Enemy's Language: Contemporary Native Women's Writings of North America,* ed. Joy Harjo and Gloria Bird, 19–31. New York: W. W. Norton, 1997.

Hendrix, Janey B. "Redbird Smith and the Nighthawk Keetoowahs." *Journal of Cherokee Studies* 8, no. 2 (1983): 73–85.

Hernández-Ávila, Inés. "Relocations upon Relocations: Home, Language, and Native American Women's Writings." *American Indian Quarterly* 19, no. 4 (1995): 491–507.

Hill, Sarah H. *Weaving New Worlds: Southeastern Cherokee Women and Their Basketry.* Chapel Hill: University of North Carolina Press, 1997.

Hobson, Geary. "Indian Academics Must Speak for Themselves." In Kimberly Roppolo, "Wisdom of the Elders: Geary Hobson, P. Jane Hafen, Jeane Breinig, Clifford E. Trafzer, Carol Miller, Louis Owens and Vine Deloria." *Paradoxa* 15 (2001): 279–80.

———. *The Last of the Ofos.* Tucson: University of Arizona Press, 2000.

Hogan, Linda. *The Woman Who Watches Over the World: A Native Memoir.* New York: W. W. Norton, 2001.

Holm, Tom. "Politics Came First: A Reflection on Robert K. Thomas and Cherokee History." In *A Good Cherokee, a Good Anthropologist: Papers in Honor of Robert K. Thomas,* ed. Steve Pavlik, 41–55. Los Angeles: UCLA American Indian Studies Center, 1998.

Holm, Tom, J. Diane Pearson, and Ben Chavis. "Peoplehood: A Model for the

Extension of Sovereignty in American Indian Studies." *Wicazo Sa Review* 18, no. 1 (2003): 7–24.

Hudson, Charles. *The Southeastern Indians.* Knoxville: University of Tennessee Press, 1976.

Hurtado, Albert L., and Peter Iverson, eds. *Major Problems in American Indian History.* 2nd ed. Houghton Mifflin Major Problems in American History Series. Boston: Houghton Mifflin, 2001.

Indian Country Today. "Cherokee Leaders Trying to Bring Order to Unrest." 1–8 September 1997, A2.

———. "Cherokee Nation Rehires Former Cherokee Marshals." 15–22 September 1997, A2.

———. "Former Leader Addresses Tribe's Internal Problems." 11–18 August 1997, A3.

Jackson, Helen Hunt. *A Century of Dishonor: A Sketch of the United States Government's Dealings with Some of the Indian Tribes.* New York: Harper and Bros., 1881.

Jaimes, M. Annette. "Federal Indian Identification Policy: A Usurpation of Indigenous Sovereignty in North America." In *The State of Native America: Genocide, Colonization, and Resistance,* ed. M. Annette Jaimes, 123–38. Boston: South End Press, 1992.

Justice, Daniel Heath. "We're Not There Yet, Kemo Sabe: Positing a Future for American Indian Literary Studies." *American Indian Quarterly* 25, no. 2 (2001): 256–69.

Kalter, Susan. "'American Histories' Revisited: The Case of *Tell Them They Lie.*" *American Indian Quarterly* 25, no. 3 (2001): 329–51.

Kassee, Cynthia R. "Nancy Ward." In *Notable Native Americans,* ed. Sharon Malinowski, 447–48. Detroit: Gail Research, 1995.

Ketchum, Richard M. *Will Rogers: The Man and His Times.* New York: American Heritage, 1973.

Kilpatrick, Alan. *The Night Has a Naked Soul: Witchcraft and Sorcery among the Western Cherokee.* Syracuse: Syracuse University Press, 1997.

Kilpatrick, Jack Frederick, and Anna Gritts Kilpatrick. *Friends of Thunder: Folktales of the Oklahoma Cherokees.* 1964. Reprint, Norman: University of Oklahoma Press, 1995.

———. *Run Toward the Nightland: Magic of the Oklahoma Cherokees.* Dallas: Southern Methodist University Press, 1967.

———. *Walk in Your Soul: Love Incantations of the Oklahoma Cherokees.* Dallas: Southern Methodist University Press, 1965.

King, E. Sterling. *The Wild Rose of Cherokee . . . or, Nancy Ward, the Pocahontas of the West.* Kingsport, TN: Kingsport Press, 1895.

King, Thomas. *The Truth About Stories: A Native Narrative.* Toronto: House of Anansi Press, 2003.

——. *Truth and Bright Water.* Toronto: HarperCollins Canada, 1999.

Konkle, Maureen. *Writing Indian Nations: Native Intellectuals and the Politics of Historiography, 1827–1863.* Chapel Hill: University of North Carolina Press, 2004.

Krupat, Arnold. *Red Matters: Native American Studies.* Philadelphia: University of Pennsylvania Press, 2002.

Larson, Sidner. *Captured in the Middle: Tradition and Experience in Contemporary Native American Writing.* Seattle: University of Washington Press, 2000.

LaVelle, John P. "The General Allotment Act 'Eligibility' Hoax: Distortions of Law, Policy, and History in Derogation of Indian Tribes." *Wicazo Sa Review* 14, no. 1 (1999): 251–302.

Leeds, Georgia Rae. *The United Keetoowah Band of Cherokee Indians in Oklahoma.* New York: Peter Lang, 1996.

Loughery, John. *The Other Side of Silence: Men's Lives and Gay Identities: A Twentieth-Century History.* New York: Henry Holt, 1998.

Lyons, Scott Richard. "Rhetorical Sovereignty: What Do American Indians Want from Writing?" *CCC* 51, no. 3 (2000): 447–68.

Mankiller, Wilma. "Keeping Pace with the Rest of the World." In *Aniyunwiya/Real Human Beings: An Anthology of Contemporary Cherokee Prose,* ed. Joseph Bruchac, 208–16. Greenfield Center, NY: Greenfield Review Press, 1995.

Mankiller, Wilma, and Michael Wallis. *Mankiller: A Chief and Her People.* New York: St. Martin's Press, 1993.

Matthiessen, Peter. *Indian Country.* New York: Viking, 1984.

McConnell, Janet. *The Dispossession of the American Indian, 1887–1934.* Bloomington: Indiana University Press, 1991.

McLoughlin, William G. *After the Trail of Tears: The Cherokees' Struggle for Sovereignty, 1839–1880.* Chapel Hill: University of North Carolina Press, 1993.

——. *The Cherokees and Christianity, 1794–1870: Essays on Acculturation and Cultural Persistence.* Athens: University of Georgia Press, 1994.

McLoughlin, William G., and Walter H. Conser Jr. "'The First Man Was Red'—Cherokee Responses to the Debate over Indian Origins, 1760–1860." *American Quarterly* 41, no. 2 (1989): 243–64.

Meredith, Howard, and Virginia Milam Sobral, eds. *Cherokee Vision of Elohi.* Trans. Wesley Proctor. Oklahoma City: Noksi Press, 1997.

Meredith, Mary Ellen, and Howard Meredith. *Reflections on Cherokee Literary Expression.* Native American Studies Series 12. Lewiston, NY: Edwin Mellen, 2003.

Michaelsen, Scott. *The Limits of Multiculturalism: Interrogating the Origins of American Anthropology.* Minneapolis: University of Minnesota Press, 1999.

Minges, Patrick N. *Slavery in the Cherokee Nation: The Keetoowah Society and the Defining of a People 1855–1867.* New York: Routledge, 2003.

Mooney, James. *Myths of the Cherokee.* 1900. Reprint, Mineola, NY: Dover, 1995.

Nichols, Roger L. *Indians in the United States and Canada: A Comparative History.* Lincoln: University of Nebraska Press, 1998.

Oskison, John M[ilton]. "Friends of the Indian." *New York Evening Post,* 1905, 332–33.

———. "Remaining Causes of Indian Discontent." *North American Review* 184 (1 March 1907): 486–93.

———. *The Singing Bird.* Unpublished manuscript. Western History Collection. University of Oklahoma.

———. *A Tale of the Old I.T.* Unpublished manuscript. Oklahoma Historical Society.

———. *Tecumseh and His Times: The Story of a Great Indian.* New York: G. P. Putnam's Sons, 1938.

———. "Tookh Steh's Mistake." In *Native American Writing in the Southeast: An Anthology, 1875–1935,* ed. Daniel F. Littlefield Jr. and James W. Parins, 61–65. Jackson: University of Mississippi Press, 1995.

Owens, Louis. *Mixedblood Messages: Literature, Film, Family, Place.* Norman: University of Oklahoma Press, 1998.

Parins, James W. *John Rollin Ridge: His Life and Works.* Lincoln: University of Nebraska Press, 1991.

Perdue, Theda. *Cherokee Women: Gender and Culture Change, 1700–1835.* Lincoln: University of Nebraska Press, 1998.

———. *"Mixed Blood" Indians: Racial Construction in the Early South.* Athens: University of Georgia Press, 2003.

———. "Nancy Ward." In *Portraits of American Women: From Settlement to the Present,* ed. G. J. Barker-Benfield and Catherine Clinton, 83–100. New York: St. Martin's Press, 1991.

———. *Nations Remembered: An Oral History of the Cherokees, Chickasaws, Choctaws, Creeks, and Seminoles in Oklahoma, 1865–1907.* Norman: University of Oklahoma Press, 1993.

Perdue, Theda, and Michael D. Green, eds. *The Cherokee Removal: A Brief History with Documents.* Boston: Bedford Books of St. Martin's Press, 1995.

Powell, Malea. "Rhetorics of Survivance: How American Indians *Use* Writing." *CCC* 53, no. 3 (2002): 396–434.

Prucha, Francis Paul. *Documents of United States Indian Policy.* 2nd ed. Lincoln: University of Nebraska Press, 1990.

———. *The Great Father: The United States Government and the American Indians.* Unabridged. Lincoln: University of Nebraska Press, 1984.

Pulitano, Elvira. *Toward a Native American Critical Theory.* Lincoln: University of Nebraska Press, 2003.

Randall, Willard Sterne. *Thomas Jefferson: A Life.* New York: HarperCollins, 1993.

Reid, John Philip. *A Law of Blood: The Primitive Law of the Cherokee Nation.* New York: New York University Press, 1970.

Ridington, Robin. "Happy Trails to You: Contexted Discourse and Indian Removals in Thomas King's *Truth and Bright Water*." *Canadian Literature* 167 (Winter 2000): 89–107.

Riggs, Lynn. *The Cherokee Night and Other Plays.* Norman: University of Oklahoma Press, 2003.

Rogers, Betty. *Will Rogers: His Wife's Story.* Indianapolis: Bobbs-Merrill, 1941.

Rogers, Will. *The Autobiography of Will Rogers.* Ed. Donald Day. Boston: Houghton Mifflin, 1949.

———. *"How to Be Funny" and Other Writings of Will Rogers.* Ed. Steven K. Gragert. Stillwater: Oklahoma State University Press, 1983.

———. *Letters of a Self-Made Diplomat to His President.* Ed. Joseph A. Stout Jr. Stillwater: Oklahoma State University Press, 1977.

———. *More Letters of a Self-Made Diplomat.* Ed. Steven K. Gragert. Stillwater: Oklahoma State University Press, 1982.

———. *Radio Broadcasts of Will Rogers.* Ed. Steven K. Gragert. Stillwater: Oklahoma State University Press, 1983.

———. *Will Rogers' Daily Telegrams.* Vol. 3: *The Hoover Years: 1931–1933.* Ed. James M. Smallwood. Stillwater: Oklahoma State University Press, 1979.

———. *Will Rogers' Daily Telegrams.* Vol. 4: *The Roosevelt Years: 1933–1935.* Ed. James M. Smallwood. Stillwater: Oklahoma State University Press, 1979.

———. *Will Rogers' Weekly Articles.* Vol. 1: *The Harding/Coolidge Years: 1922–1925.* Ed. James M. Smallwood. Stillwater: Oklahoma State University Press, 1980.

———. *Will Rogers' Weekly Articles.* Vol. 3: *The Coolidge Years: 1927–1929.* Ed. James M. Smallwood. Stillwater: Oklahoma State University Press, 1981.

———. *Will Rogers' Weekly Articles.* Vol. 4: *The Hoover Years: 1929–1931.* Ed. Steven K. Gragert. Stillwater: Oklahoma State University Press, 1981.

———. *Will Rogers' Weekly Articles.* Vol. 5: *The Hoover Years: 1931–1933.* Ed. Steven K. Gragert. Stillwater: Oklahoma State University Press, 1982.

———. *Will Rogers' Weekly Articles.* Vol. 6: *The Roosevelt Years: 1933–1935.* Ed. Steven K. Gragert. Stillwater: Oklahoma State University Press, 1982.

Ross, John. *The Papers of Chief John Ross.* Ed. Gary E. Moulton. 2 vols. Norman: University of Oklahoma Press, 1985.

Sanders, William. "Elvis Bearpaw's Luck." In *Are We Having Fun Yet? American Indian Fantasy Stories by William Sanders,* 94–114. Holicong, PA: Wildside Press, 2002.

Scherer, Mark R. "'Now Let Him Enforce It': Exploring the Myth of Andrew Jackson's Response to *Worcester v. Georgia* (1832)." *Chronicles of Oklahoma* 74, no. 1 (1996): 16–29.

Sioui, Georges E. *Huron-Wendat: The Heritage of the Circle.* Rev. ed. Trans. Jane Brierley. Vancouver: University of British Columbia Press, 1999.

Slotkin, Richard. *Regeneration through Violence: The Mythology of the American Frontier, 1600–1860.* Middletown, CT: Wesleyan University Press, 1973.

Smith, Chadwick. "Introduction." In *Cherokee,* text by Robert J. Conley, photography by David G. Fitzgerald, 12–13. Portland, OR: Graphic Arts Center Publishing, 2002.

Smith, Micah Pearce. "The Latter Days of Dr. Emmet Starr." *Chronicles of Oklahoma* 8, no. 3 (1930): 339–42.

Stambor, Howard. "Manifest Destiny and American Indian Religious Freedom: Sequoyah, Badoni, and the Drowned Gods." In *Native Americans and the Law: Contemporary and Historical Perspectives on American Indian Rights, Freedoms, and Sovereignty,* ed. John R. Wunder, 193–223. New York: Garland, 1996.

Starr, Emmet. *History of the Cherokee Indians and Their Legends and Folk Lore.* 1921. Reprint, Millwood, NY: Klaus Reprint, 1977.

———. Letter to Joseph B. Thoburn. 10 October 1927. Box 29, File 25. Thoburn Collection. Oklahoma Historical Society.

———. Letter to Joseph B. Thoburn. 23 September 1928. Box 29, File 25. Thoburn Collection. Oklahoma Historical Society.

———. Letter to Joseph B. Thoburn. 3 June 1929. Box 29, File 25. Thoburn Collection. Oklahoma Historical Society.

Strickland, Rennard. *Fire and the Spirits: Cherokee Law from Clan to Court.* Norman: University of Oklahoma Press, 1975.

———. "In Search of Cherokee History: A Bibliographical Foreword to the Second Printing." In Morris L. Wardell, *A Political History of the Cherokee Nation, 1838–1907,* i–xxxviii. Norman: University of Oklahoma Press, 1977.

Strickland, Rennard, and Jack Gregory. "Emmet Starr: Heroic Historian." In *American Indian Intellectuals,* ed. Margot Liberty, 104–14. St. Paul, MN: West Publishing, 1976.

Sturm, Circe. *Blood Politics: Race, Culture, and Identity in the Cherokee Nation of Oklahoma.* Berkeley: University of California Press, 2002.

Teuton, Christopher. "Theorizing American Indian Literature: Applying Oral Concepts to Written Traditions." Forthcoming.

Teuton, Sean. "Writing Home: An Interview with Robert J. Conley." *Wicazo Sa Review* 16, no. 2 (2001): 115–28.

Thomas, Robert K. "The Redbird Smith Movement." In *Symposium on Cherokee and Iroquois Culture,* ed. William N. Fenton and John Gulick, Smithsonian

Institution Bureau of American Ethnology Bulletin 180, 159–66. Washington, DC: U.S. Government Printing Office, 1961.

———. "Some Thoughts on the Indian Scene." In *Getting to the Heart of the Matter: Collected Letters and Papers,* 7–11. Vancouver: Native Ministries Consortium, 1990.

Thornton, Russell. *The Cherokees: A Population History.* Lincoln: University of Nebraska Press, 1990.

Trollope, Frances. *Domestic Manners of the Americans.* New York: Dodd, Mead, 1901.

Turnbull-Lewis, Linda, and Dan Agent. "Chronology of Events in the Cherokee Nation Crisis." *Cherokee Observer,* 17 September 1997, 1–9.

Twist, Glenn J. "The Dispossession." In *Boston Mountain Tales: Stories from a Cherokee Family,* 8–28. Greenfield Center, NY: Greenfield Review Press, 1997.

United States Congress. *American State Papers: Documents, Legislative and Executive, of the Congress of the United States.* Vol. 11. Washington, DC: Gales and Seaton.

Wallace, Anthony F. C. "Jefferson and the Native Americans." In *Thomas Jefferson and the Changing West,* ed. James P. Ronda, 25–41. Albuquerque: University of New Mexico Press, 1997.

Warrior, Robert Allen. *Tribal Secrets: Recovering American Indian Intellectual Traditions.* Minneapolis: University of Minnesota Press, 1995.

Washburn, Wilcomb E., ed. *The American Indian and the United States: A Documentary History.* Vol. 4. New York: Random House, 1973.

———. *The Assault on Indian Tribalism: The General Allotment Law (Dawes Act) of 1887.* Ed. Harold M. Hyman. Philadelphia: J. B. Lippincott, 1975.

Weaver, Jace. "Foreword." In Lynn Riggs, *The Cherokee Night and Other Plays,* ix–xv. Norman: University of Oklahoma Press, 2003.

———. *That the People Might Live: Native American Literatures and Native American Community.* New York: Oxford University Press, 1997.

West, Elliott. *The Contested Plains: Indians, Goldseekers, and the Rush to Colorado.* Lawrence: University Press of Kansas, 1998.

Wilkins, Thurman. *Cherokee Tragedy: The Story of the Ridge Family and the Decimation of a People.* New York: Macmillan, 1970.

Williams, Roger A., Jr. *Linking Arms Together: American Indian Treaty Visions of Law and Peace, 1600–1800.* New York: Oxford University Press, 1997.

Womack, Craig S. *Red on Red: Native American Literary Separatism.* Minneapolis: University of Minnesota Press, 1999.

Woodward, Grace Steele. *The Cherokees.* Norman: University of Oklahoma Press, 1963.

Yagoda, Ben. *Will Rogers: A Biography.* New York: Alfred A. Knopf, 1993.

Zissu, Erik M. *Blood Matters: The Five Civilized Tribes and the Search for Unity in the Twentieth Century.* New York: Routledge, 2001.

Index

Ada-gal'kala, 31–32, 35, 167; relationship with Tsiyu Gansini, 229–30n38

Adams, John Quincy, 73–74

Agent, Dan: on Cherokee Nation constitutional crisis, 224n6

Alfred, Gerald/Taiaiake, 24, 215

Allen, Richard: on Cherokee community, 224–25n8; on Kituwah town and name, 226n14

allotment policy, 21, 89–92, 96, 99–100, 138, 238n13; competency regulations, 99, 239n24, 240n25; Indian support for, 240–41n40. *See also* Curtis Act; General Allotment (Dawes) Act

Ani-Kutani, 137, 233n11

assimilation: distinction from acculturation, xvi; Eurowestern policies, 46. *See also* U.S. civilization policy

Awiakta, Marilou, v, 151, 158–70, 179, 219; balance, 164–69; on Cherokee spirituality and Eurowestern science, 249n11; on gender and

gender relations, 163, 165–66; on poetry, 169; photograph, 159; on the sacred fire, 203. *See also* Beloved Path reading: Awiakta and King; *Selu: Seeking the Corn-Mother's Wisdom*

Awi Usdi (Little Deer), 105, 158, 163–64

Baird, W. David: on Oklahoma Indians, 122

Beloved and Chickamauga reading: Glancy and Conley, 194–203.

Beloved Path, 16, 30–32, 37–39, 41–42, 79, 84–85, 93–96, 101, 151–52, 155–57, 219–20. *See also* Beloved Path reading; Beloved and Chickamauga reading; Nanye'hi

Beloved Path reading: Awiakta and King, 158–79

Beloved Women, 29–33, 168; distinction from War Women, 38–39, 229n34. *See also* Nanye'hi

Bird, Gloria: on English use by Indians, 12

267

Bird, Traveler: *Tell Them They Lie*
controversy, 233n13
blood quantum: in *The Cherokee
Night,* 98–103; competency policy
and, 240n25; General Allotment
(Dawes) Act and, 239n24; impact
on Five Tribes, 240n26; Oklahoma
Indians and, 122
Boudinot, Elias, 80; contributions to
Treaty of New Echota, 81; reversal
of Removal position, 236n38;
scholarly representation, 56
Brant, Beth, 15, 163
Braunlich, Phyllis: biography of Lynn
Riggs, 238n11
Byrd, Joe, 21–22, 179. *See also* Chero-
kee Nation, Oklahoma: constitu-
tional crisis

Calhoun, John C., 71–72
Carney, Virginia, 38–39, 41, 219
Carroll, General William, 80–81,
83–85. *See also* Removal; Treaty of
New Echota
Carter, Asa "Forrest," 192, 252–53n86.
See also Education of Little Tree, The
Chavis, Ben, 25
Cherokee Constitution of 1827, 68, 75,
209. *See also* Removal; Georgia:
campaign against Cherokees
Cherokee Nation v. Georgia (1831), 79,
236–37n50
Cherokee Nation, Oklahoma, 23;
constitutional crisis, 21–22, 224n6;
history of, 20; judiciary, 21
Cherokee Night, The (Riggs), 92,
94–108, 212; Beloved Path reading,
107–8; blood quantum and sexuality, 105–7; blood quantum, land,
and Cherokee identity, 98–103,
105–8; Cherokee traditions and,

105; representations of African
Americans, 106–7. *See also* Riggs,
Rollie Lynn
Cherokee Phoenix (Cherokee national
newspaper), 22, 78, 80
Cherokee Princess, 3–4, 13, 222n11;
queen, 279
Cherokee society: attitudes toward
war, 29–30; balance, 27–28, 37–38,
79, 155, 157; being "good" Cherokees, 14, 92, 216; "civilized" status,
41, 71, 77, 90; complementary
dualism, 27–28, 30, 136, 155–56;
conflicts with other Indigenous
nations, 52–53; cultural change,
nineteenth century, 65, 68;
gender relations, 39–40, 229n34;
"good life" 25; history, general,
223–24n3; humor, 123; interaction
with Europe and United States,
early, 63–64; kinship, 225n10;
language, 11–12; literature and social history, 7, 31; literature before
syllabary, 50; literature in English,
11–12; mixedbloods, impact of,
65–68, 99–100; parental roles, 70;
peace towns, 228–29n32; peopling
stories, 49–53; political authority, 33, 39; politics, importance of,
102, 240n35; U.S. Revolutionary
War and, 41; war/peace political spheres, 16, 20, 28–31, 42,
151, 155–56, 217, 227n25, 227n27,
229n34
Cherokee Vision of Elohi, 50–52
Cherokees, Oklahoma. *See* Oklahoma
Cherokees; Cherokee Nation, Oklahoma; Nighthawk Keetoowahs;
United Keetoowah Band of Cherokee Indians
Cherokees: blood quantum and

Muskogee Creeks: resistance to allotment, 92. *See also* Harjo, Chitto

NAGPRA (Native American Graves
  Protection and Repatriation Act),
  166
Nanye'hi, 15, 47, 136, 215, 217; Awiakta
  and, 161, 167–68; Beloved Woman
  of Chota, 228–29n32; duties as
  Beloved Woman, 31–36, 38–42;
  stereotypes, 230–31n46. *See also*
  Beloved Path; King, E. Sterling
nationalism: Indigenous/tribal, 8,
  23–24; nation-state, 8, 23–24
nationhood, 7, 15–16, 20, 22–23, 27,
  41–42, 47–48, 75–76, 85, 93, 98,
  149–51, 153, 155, 205–6, 213–15,
  217–19, 226n15, 251n50; allotment
  era, 92, 102, 135, 139; blood and,
  216–17, 239n23; practice of, 248n1
Neugin, Rebecca, 250n36; in *Truth
  and Bright Water* (King), 173–75.
  See also Foreman, Grant: Rebecca
  Neugin and
Nichols, Roger L.: on colonialist cultures of Europe, 64
Nighthawk Keetoowahs, 21, 91–92;
  sacred fire and, 226n18; Emmet
  Starr on, 134, 136–37, 140–41;
  tribal nationalist movement,
  227n21. *See also* Oklahoma Cherokees; United Keetoowah Band of
  Cherokee Indians

Oklahoma Cherokees, 11, 20, 122;
  Cherokee Executive Council, 20;
  resistance to allotment, 91–92. *See
  also* Cherokee Nation, Oklahoma;
  Five Tribes; Oklahoma Indians;
  United Keetoowah Band of Cherokee Indians

Oklahoma Historical Society, 138, 142
Oklahoma Indians: stereotypes, 122.
  See also blood quantum; *Cherokee
  Night, The*; Five Tribes
Oklahoma: constitutional convention,
  123; statehood, 21, 89, 93–94, 138,
  140
Old Settlers, 55, 68, 84; migration due
  to Removal, 77; Osages and, 55,
  84; Treaty of New Echota and, 84
Oskison, John Milton, 93, 108–19,
  218; African Americans, attitude
  toward, 110, 115, 242n62; assimilationist leanings, 118, 242–43n65;
  Beloved Path and, 112, 114–15,
  118; Cherokee nationhood and,
  110, 112; cynicism toward Whites,
  117–19; photograph, 109; Will
  Rogers and, 111; U.S. civilization
  policy, 113–14; writing, 112–13,
  118. *See also Tale of the Old I.T., A*;
  Singing Bird, The
Owens, Louis, 45, 211; ecosystemic
  vs. egosystemic, 160–61; on
  mixedbloodedness, 212, 214; on
  movement and migration, 48–49;
  Thomas King on, 248–49n5

Pearson, J. Diane, 25
peoplehood matrix, 25
peoplehood, 24, 27, 207; as central principle of Indigenous literatures, 214
Perdue, Theda: on Beloved and War
  Women, 229n34; on Cherokee
  war/peace division, 227n27
Perdue, Theda and Michael Green, 74
Phoenix (Cherokee creature of legend),
  8, 26
Powell, Malea, 240–41n40
progressivism. *See* Eurowestern society: progressivism

*D*aniel Heath Justice (Cherokee Nation) grew up in the mining town of Victor, Colorado, in the traditional lands of the Ute Nation. He is assistant professor of Aboriginal literatures at the University of Toronto.